Miss Kobayashi's
Dragon maid
Kanna's Daily Life

story & art by
Mitsuhiro Kimura

original story by
coolkyousinnjya

Miss Kobayashi's
Dragon maid
Kanna's Daily Life

GOOD DAY, SUNSHINE!

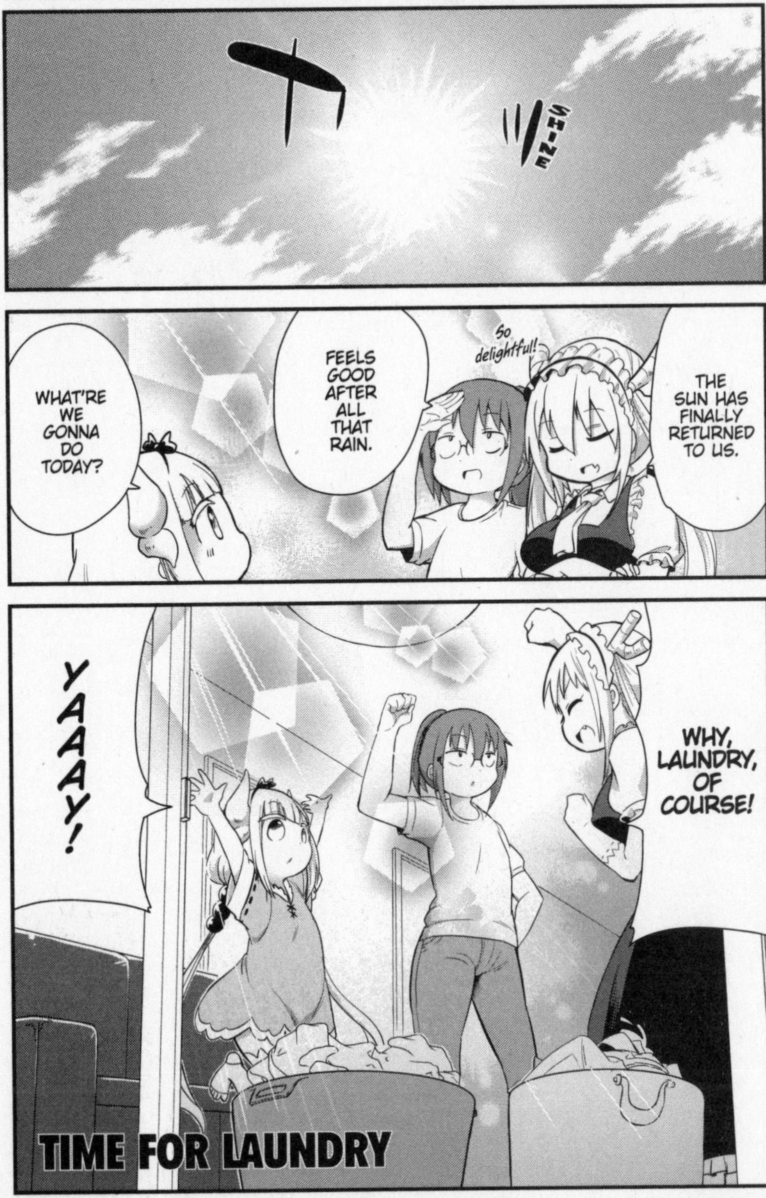
SHINE
THE SUN HAS FINALLY RETURNED TO US.
So delightful!
FEELS GOOD AFTER ALL THAT RAIN.
WHAT'RE WE GONNA DO TODAY?
WHY, LAUNDRY, OF COURSE!
YAAAAY!
TIME FOR LAUNDRY

THE PEACEFUL KOBAYASHI HOUSEHOLD

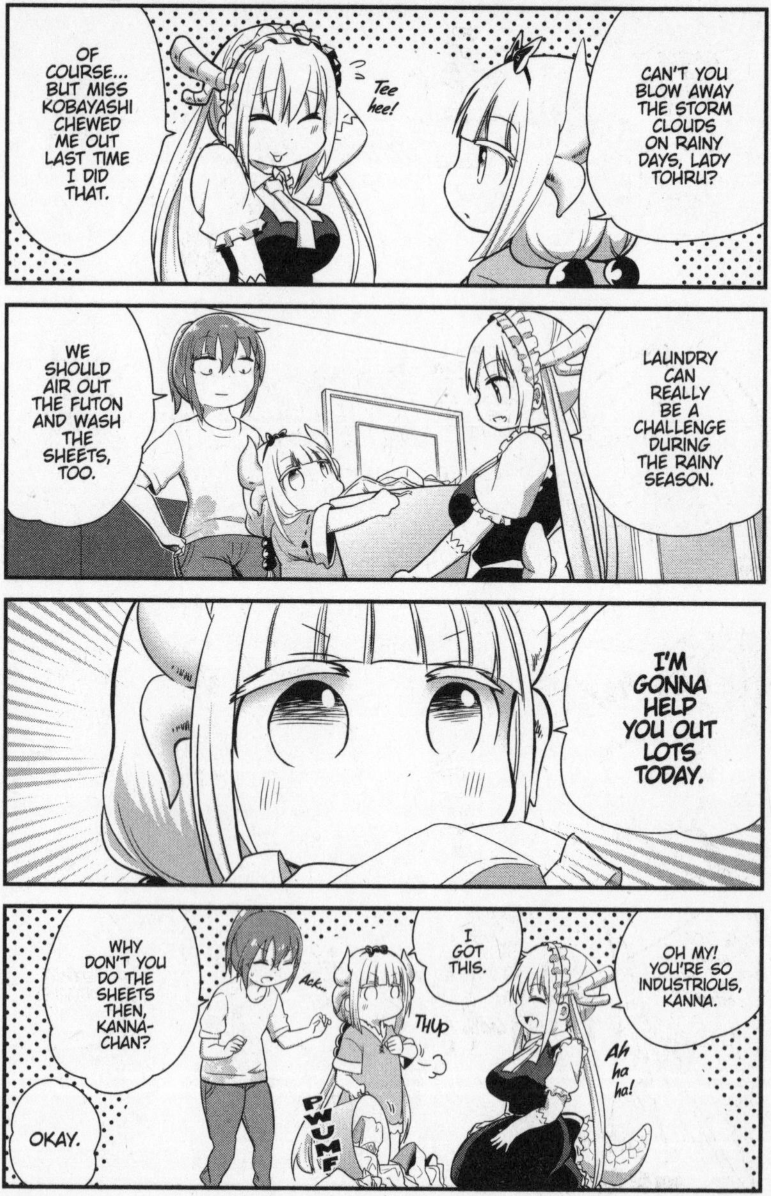

CAN'T YOU BLOW AWAY THE STORM CLOUDS ON RAINY DAYS, LADY TOHRU?
Tee hee!
OF COURSE... BUT MISS KOBAYASHI CHEWED ME OUT LAST TIME I DID THAT.
LAUNDRY CAN REALLY BE A CHALLENGE DURING THE RAINY SEASON.
WE SHOULD AIR OUT THE FUTON AND WASH THE SHEETS, TOO.
I'M GONNA HELP YOU OUT LOTS TODAY.
OH MY! YOU'RE SO INDUSTRIOUS, KANNA.
Ah ha ha!
I GOT THIS.
THUp
Ack...
WHY DON'T YOU DO THE SHEETS THEN, KANNA-CHAN?
PWUMF
OKAY.

TRAGEDY

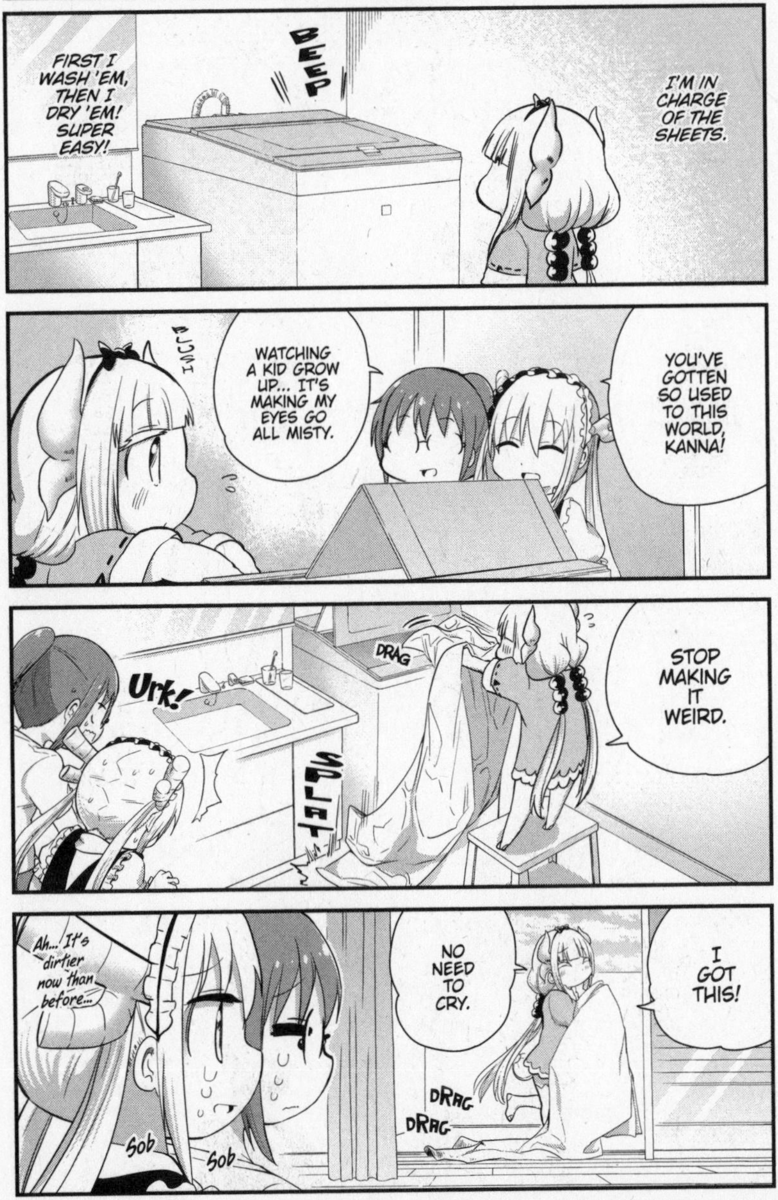
I'M IN CHARGE OF THE SHEETS.
BEEP
FIRST I WASH 'EM, THEN I DRY 'EM! SUPER EASY!
YOU'VE GOTTEN SO USED TO THIS WORLD, KANNA!
WATCHING A KID GROW UP... IT'S MAKING MY EYES GO ALL MISTY.
BLUSH
STOP MAKING IT WEIRD.
DRAG
SPLAT
Urk!
I GOT THIS!
NO NEED TO CRY.
DRAG
DRAG
Ah... It's dirtier now than before...
Sob
Sob

STILL TOO COMPLICATED

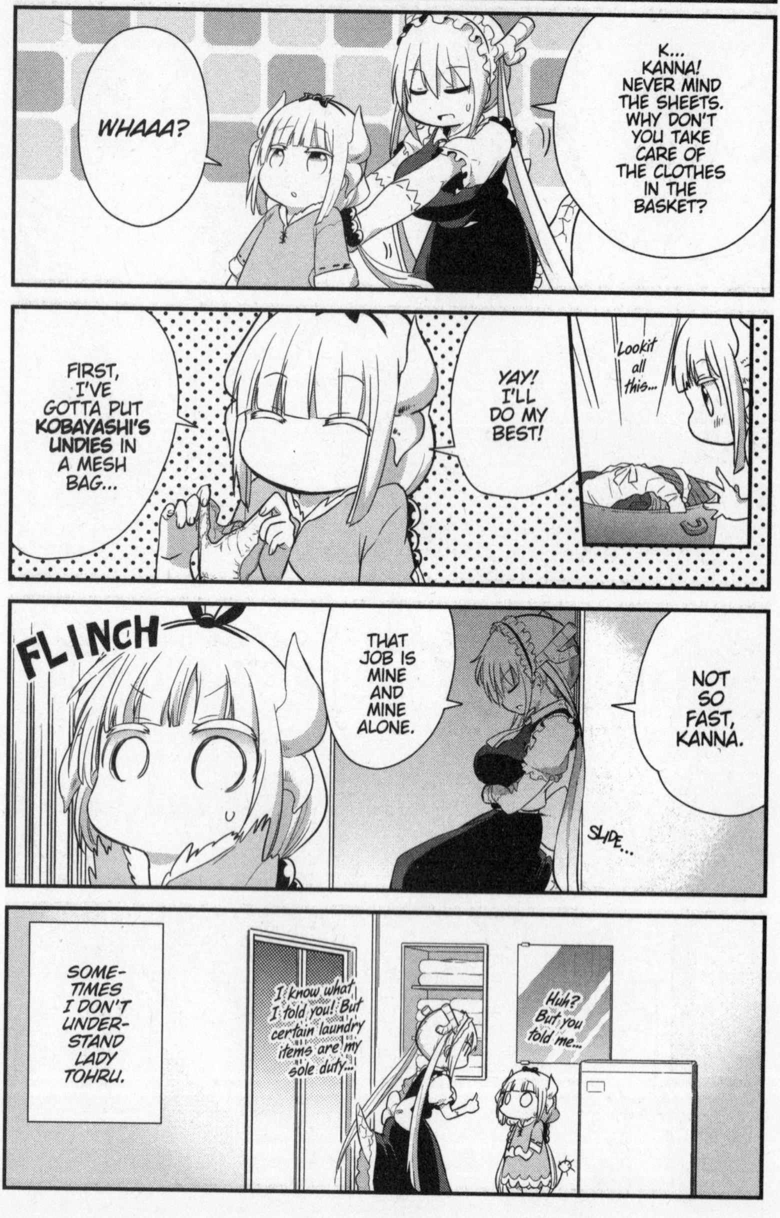
K... KANNA! NEVER MIND THE SHEETS. WHY DON'T YOU TAKE CARE OF THE CLOTHES IN THE BASKET?
WHAAA?
Lookit all this...
YAY! I'LL DO MY BEST!
FIRST, I'VE GOTTA PUT KOBAYASHI'S UNDIES IN A MESH BAG...
NOT SO FAST, KANNA.
SLIDE...
THAT JOB IS MINE AND MINE ALONE.
FLINCH
Huh? But you told me...
I know what I told you! But certain laundry items are my sole duty...
SOMETIMES I DON'T UNDERSTAND LADY TOHRU.

LEAVE MISS KOBAYASHI'S TO ME!

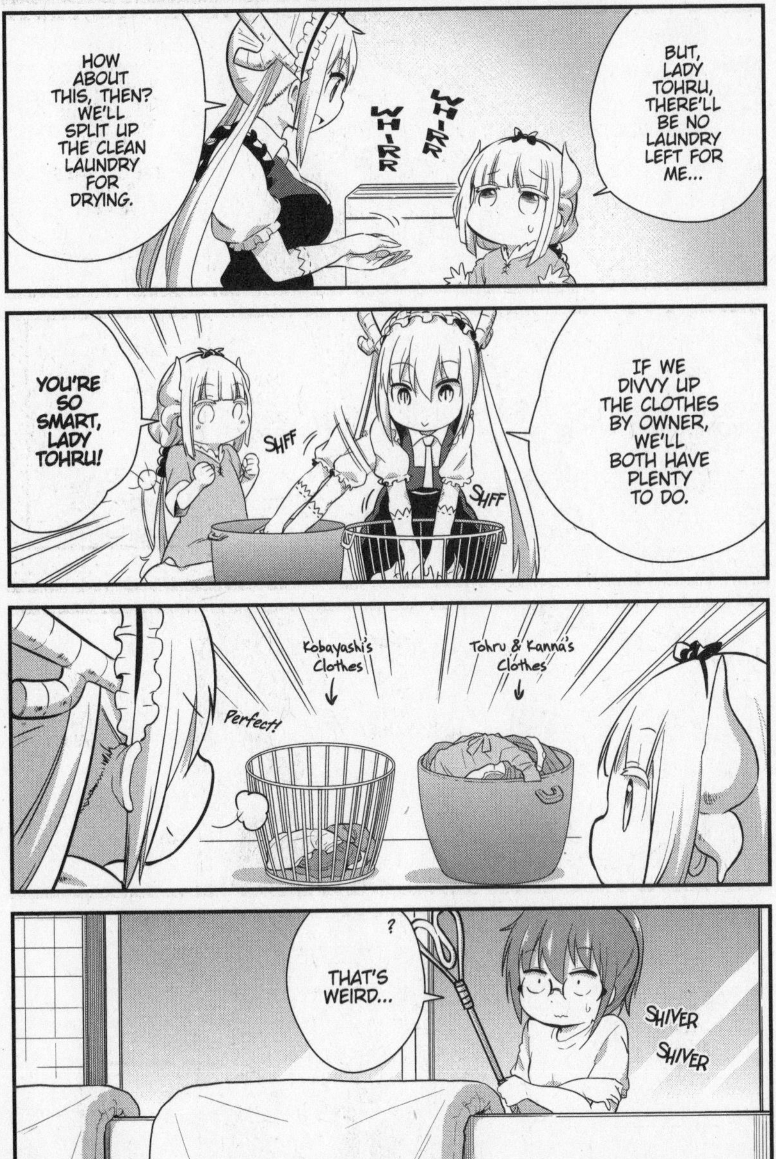
BUT, LADY TOHRU, THERE'LL BE NO LAUNDRY LEFT FOR ME...
WHIRR
WHIRR
HOW ABOUT THIS, THEN? WE'LL SPLIT UP THE CLEAN LAUNDRY FOR DRYING.
IF WE DIVVY UP THE CLOTHES BY OWNER, WE'LL BOTH HAVE PLENTY TO DO.
SHFF
SHFF
YOU'RE SO SMART, LADY TOHRU!
Tohru & Kanna's Clothes
Kobayashi's Clothes
Perfect!
SHIVER
SHIVER
?
THAT'S WEIRD...

EYE OF THE BEHOLDER

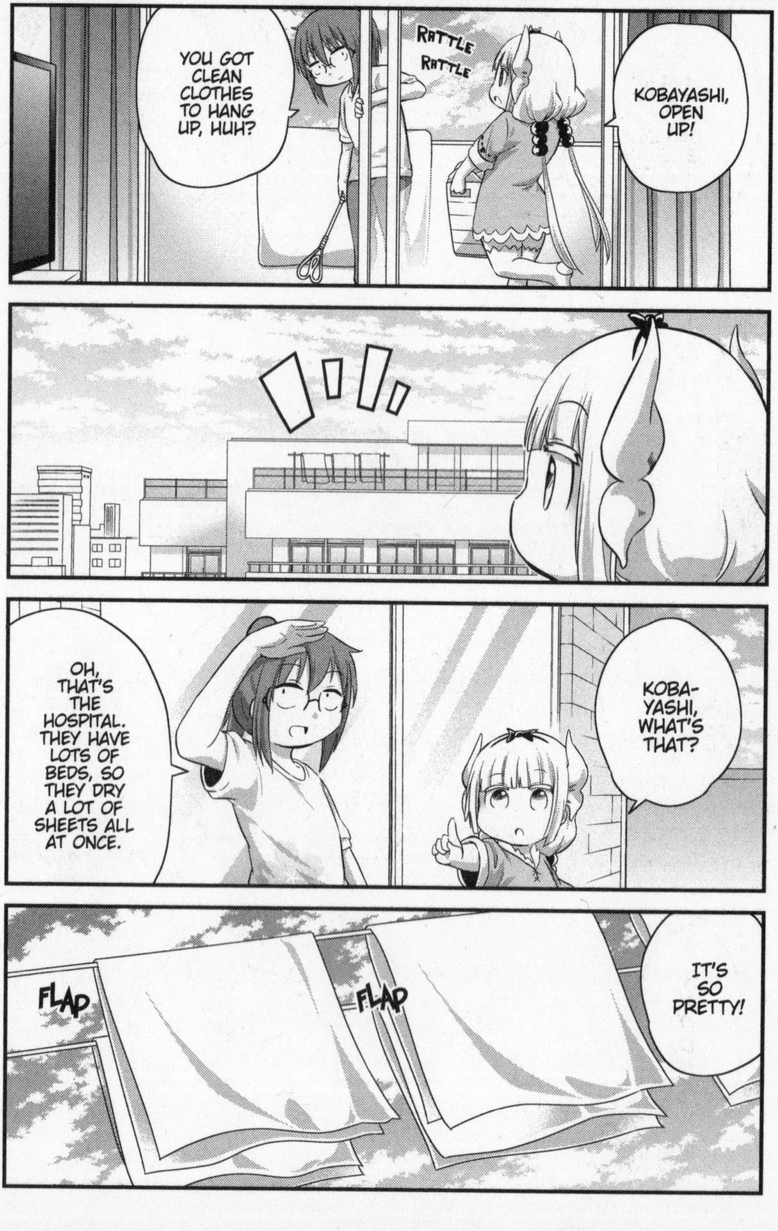
KOBAYASHI, OPEN UP!
RATTLE RATTLE
YOU GOT CLEAN CLOTHES TO HANG UP, HUH?
KOBA-YASHI, WHAT'S THAT?
OH, THAT'S THE HOSPITAL. THEY HAVE LOTS OF BEDS, SO THEY DRY A LOT OF SHEETS ALL AT ONCE.
IT'S SO PRETTY!
FLAP
FLAP

A CUNNING PLAN!

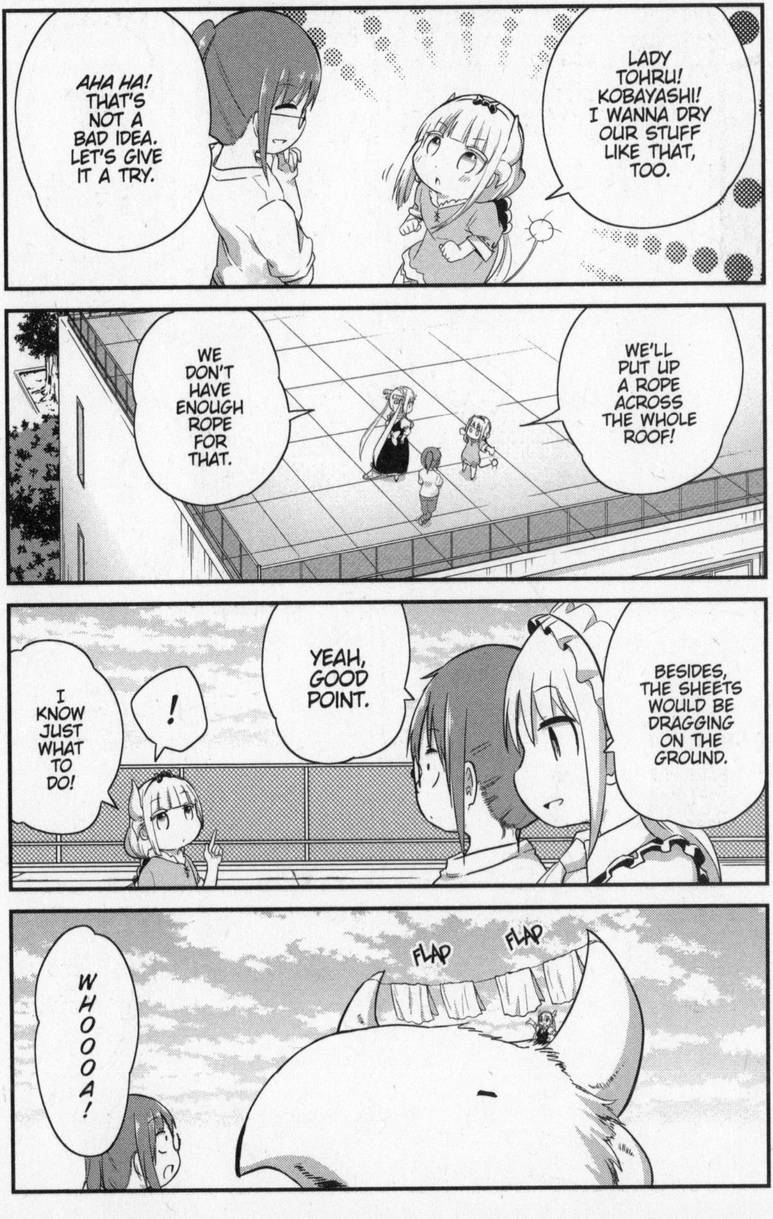
LADY TOHRU! KOBAYASHI! I WANNA DRY OUR STUFF LIKE THAT, TOO.
AHA HA! THAT'S NOT A BAD IDEA. LET'S GIVE IT A TRY.
WE'LL PUT UP A ROPE ACROSS THE WHOLE ROOF!
WE DON'T HAVE ENOUGH ROPE FOR THAT.
BESIDES, THE SHEETS WOULD BE DRAGGING ON THE GROUND.
YEAH, GOOD POINT.
!
I KNOW JUST WHAT TO DO!
FLAP
FLAP
WHOOOOA!

NOT APPROPRIATE!

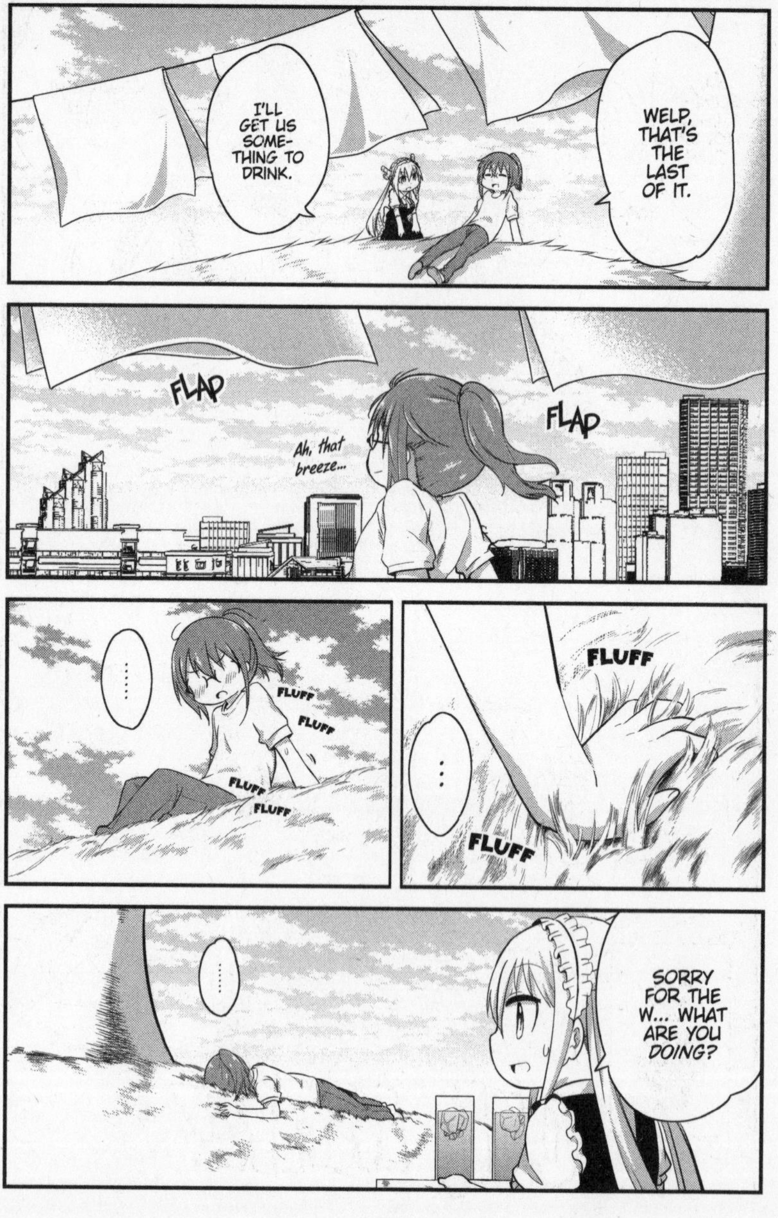
WELP, THAT'S THE LAST OF IT.
I'LL GET US SOME-THING TO DRINK.
FLAP
FLAP
Ah, that breeze...
FLUFF
...
FLUFF
......
FLUFF
FLUFF
FLUFF
FLUFF
SORRY FOR THE W... WHAT ARE YOU DOING?
......

A LOSS FOR WORDS

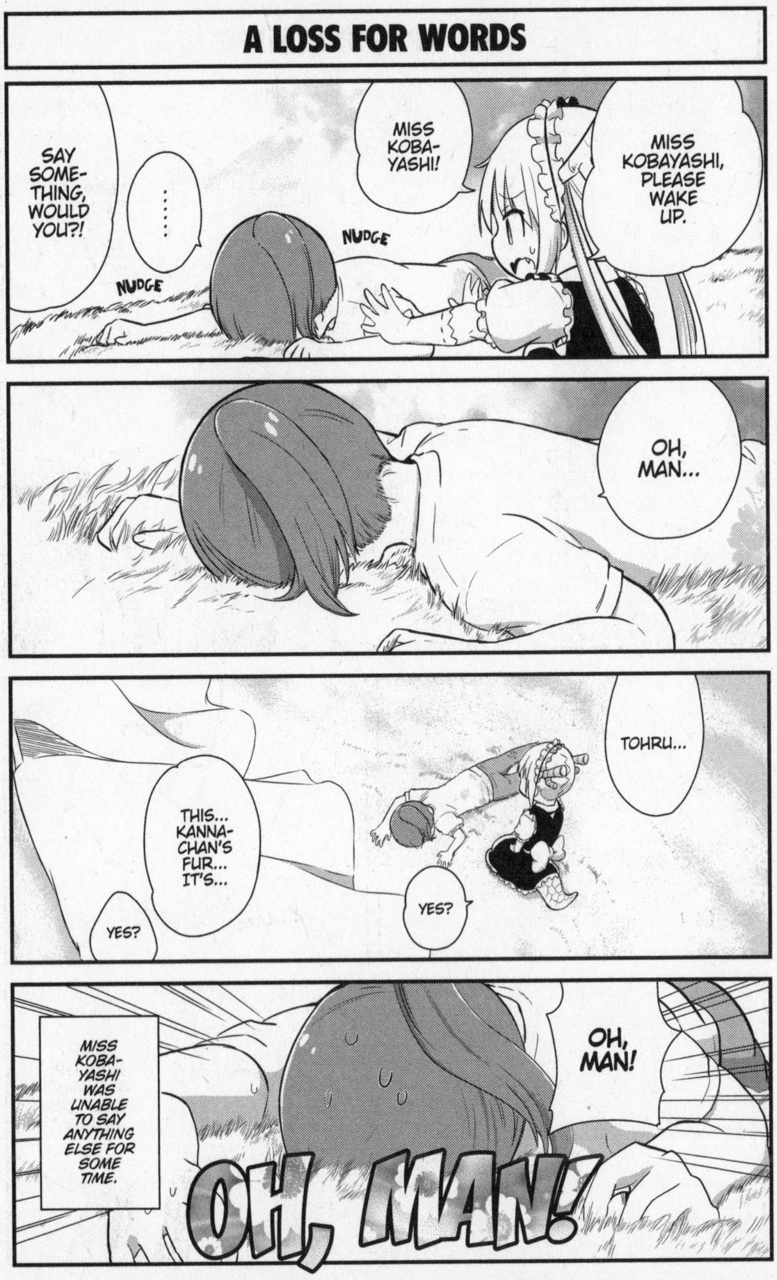
MISS KOBAYASHI, PLEASE WAKE UP.
MISS KOBA-YASHI!
NUDGE
……
SAY SOME-THING, WOULD YOU?!
NUDGE
OH, MAN...
TOHRU...
YES?
THIS... KANNA-CHAN'S FUR... IT'S...
YES?
OH, MAN!
OH, MAN!
MISS KOBA-YASHI WAS UNABLE TO SAY ANYTHING ELSE FOR SOME TIME.

ANOTHER HARD DAY'S WORK

LADY TOHRU? KOBAYASHI? WHAT ARE YOU DOING? IT TICKLES.

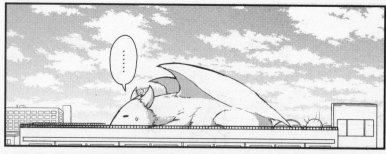

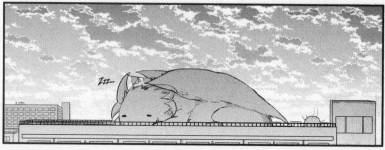

PHRASING

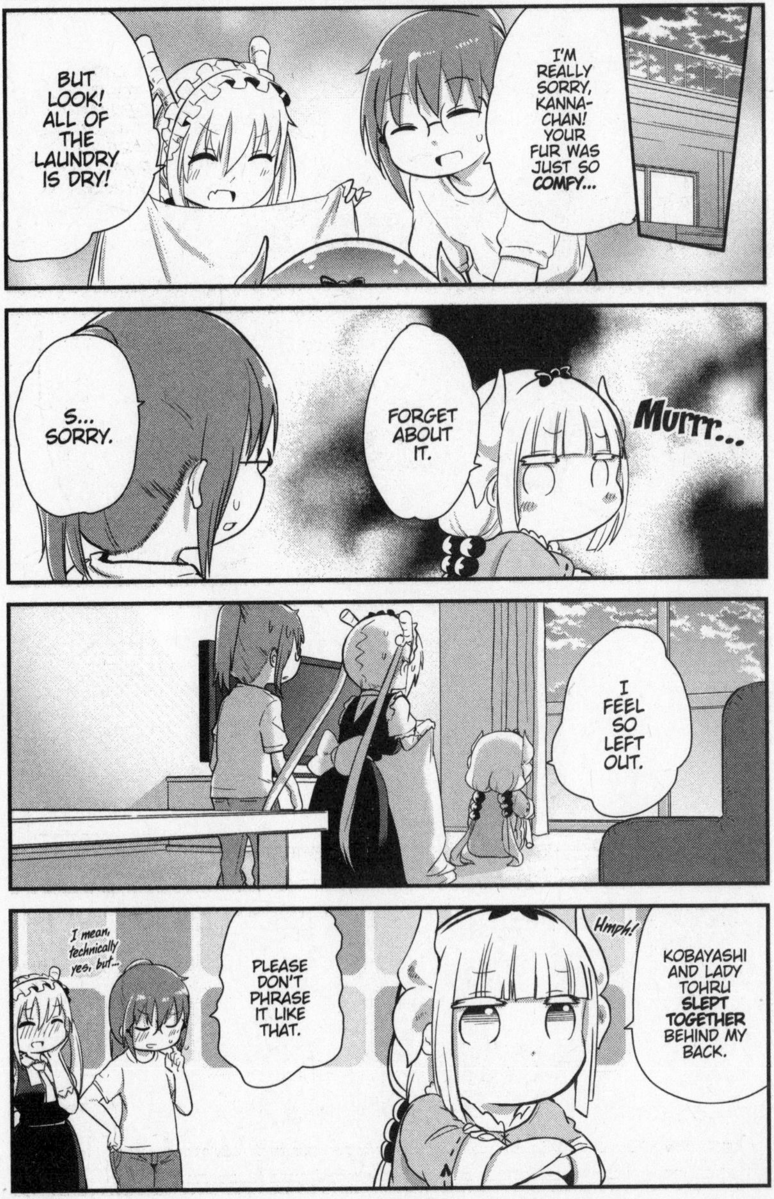

I'M REALLY SORRY, KANNA-CHAN! YOUR FUR WAS JUST SO **COMFY**...
BUT LOOK! ALL OF THE LAUNDRY IS DRY!
Murrr...
FORGET ABOUT IT.
S... SORRY.
I FEEL SO LEFT OUT.
Hmph!
KOBAYASHI AND LADY TOHRU **SLEPT TOGETHER** BEHIND MY BACK.
PLEASE DON'T PHRASE IT LIKE THAT.
I mean, technically yes, but...

DOWN FOR THE COUNT

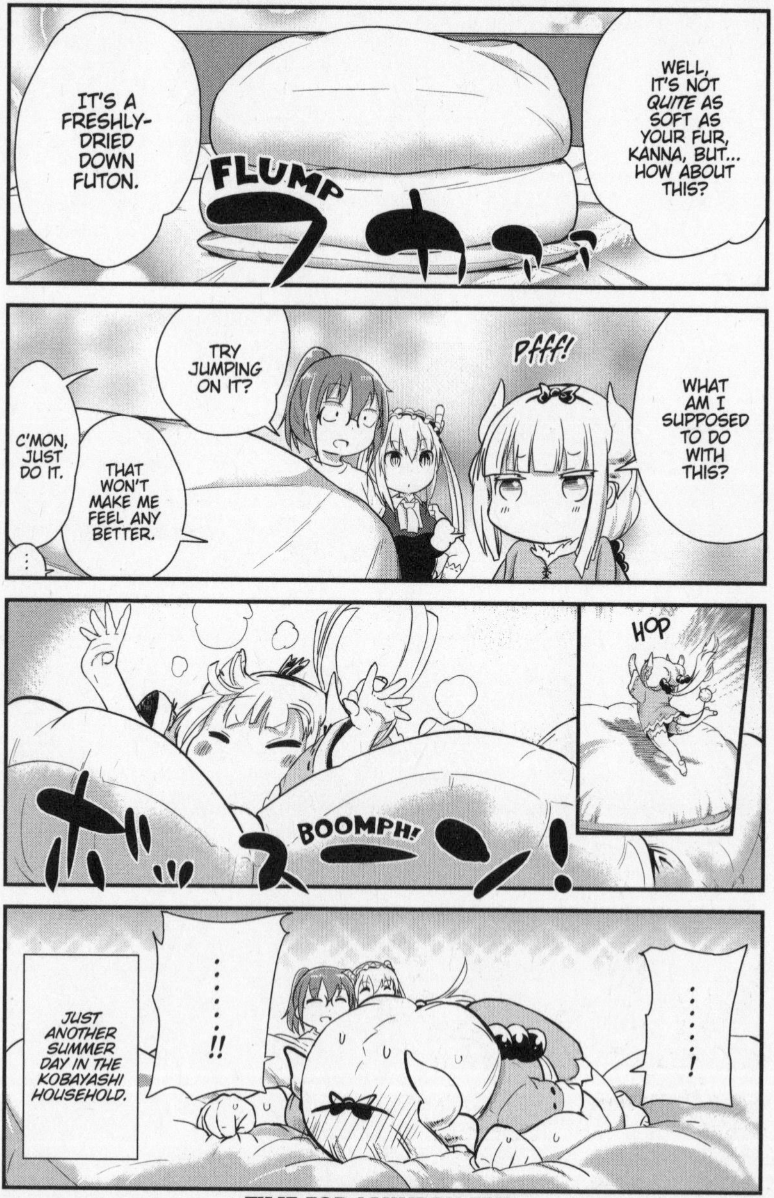
WELL, IT'S NOT *QUITE* AS SOFT AS YOUR FUR, KANNA, BUT... HOW ABOUT THIS?
IT'S A FRESHLY-DRIED DOWN FUTON.
FLUMP
WHAT AM I SUPPOSED TO DO WITH THIS?
Pfff!
TRY JUMPING ON IT?
THAT WON'T MAKE ME FEEL ANY BETTER.
C'MON, JUST DO IT.
...
HOP
BOOMPH!
......!
......!!
JUST ANOTHER SUMMER DAY IN THE KOBAYASHI HOUSEHOLD.

TIME FOR LAUNDRY/END

I'm a laundry expert now, so I'll do Kobayashi's for her.

Clean Clothes.

Miss Kobayashi's Dragon Maid
Kanna's Daily Life

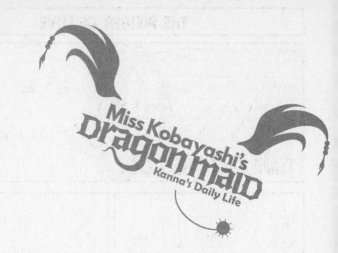

THE WEIGHT OF LOVE

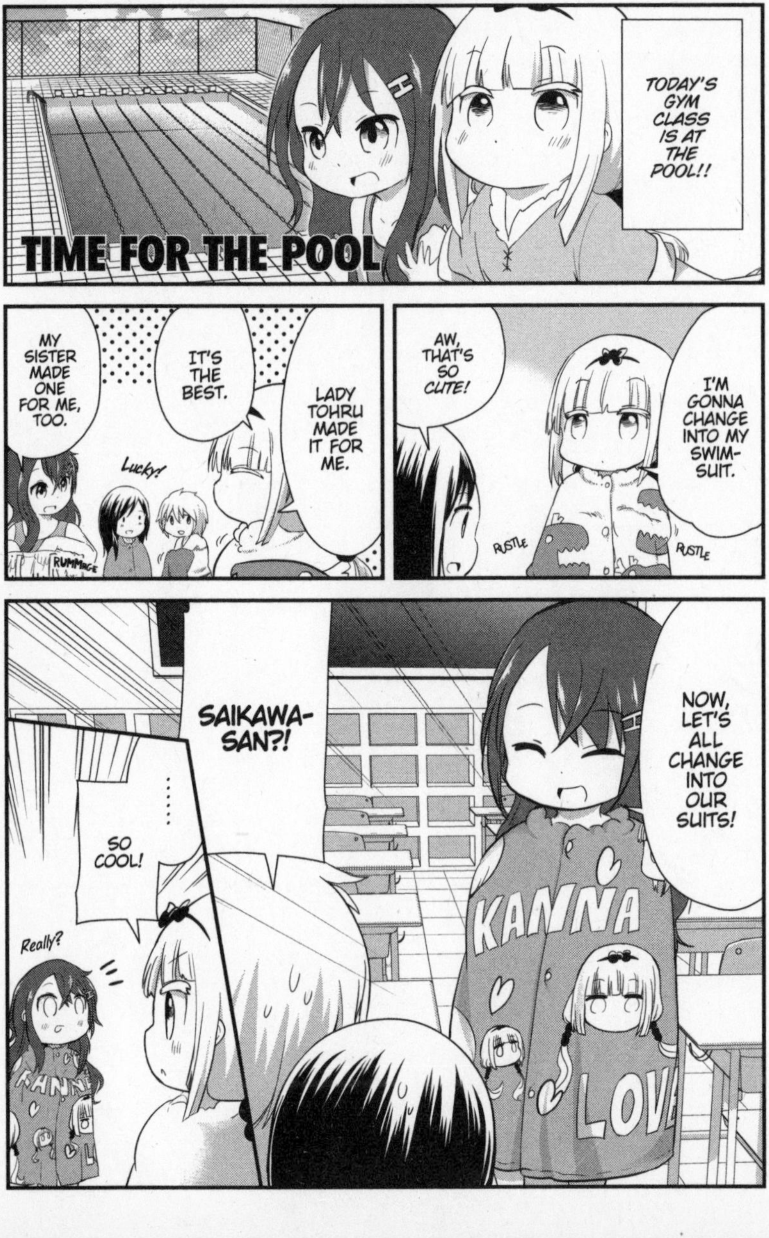
TIME FOR THE POOL
TODAY'S GYM CLASS IS AT THE POOL!!
I'M GONNA CHANGE INTO MY SWIM-SUIT.
RUSTLE
RUSTLE
AW, THAT'S SO CUTE!
LADY TOHRU MADE IT FOR ME.
IT'S THE BEST.
MY SISTER MADE ONE FOR ME, TOO.
Lucky!
RUMMAGE
NOW, LET'S ALL CHANGE INTO OUR SUITS!
SAIKAWA-SAN?!
......
SO COOL!
Really?
KANNA
LOVE

GOTTA GET IT RIGHT

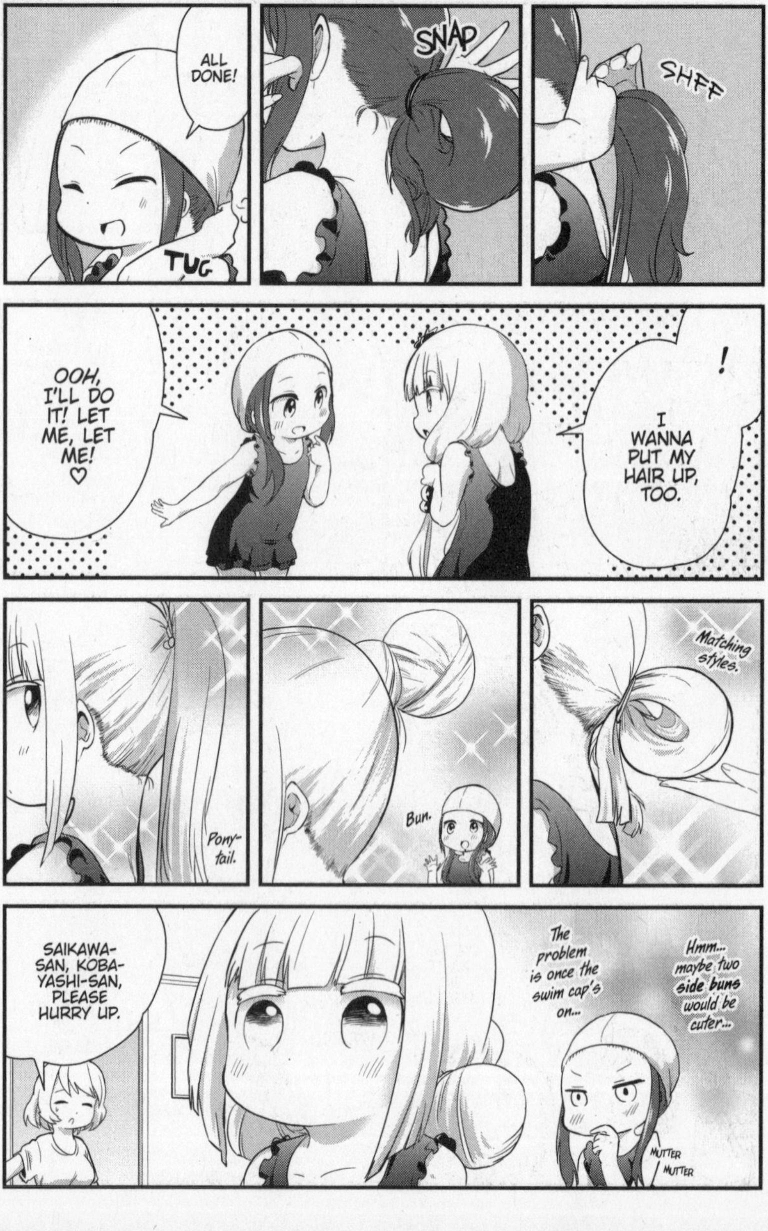
SHFF
SNAP
ALL DONE!
TUG
!
I WANNA PUT MY HAIR UP, TOO.
OOH, I'LL DO IT! LET ME, LET ME! ♡
Matching styles.
Bun.
Pony-tail.
Hmm... maybe two side buns would be cuter...
The problem is once the swim cap's on...
MUTTER MUTTER
SAIKAWA-SAN, KOBA-YASHI-SAN, PLEASE HURRY UP.

WHEN KINDNESS BACKFIRES

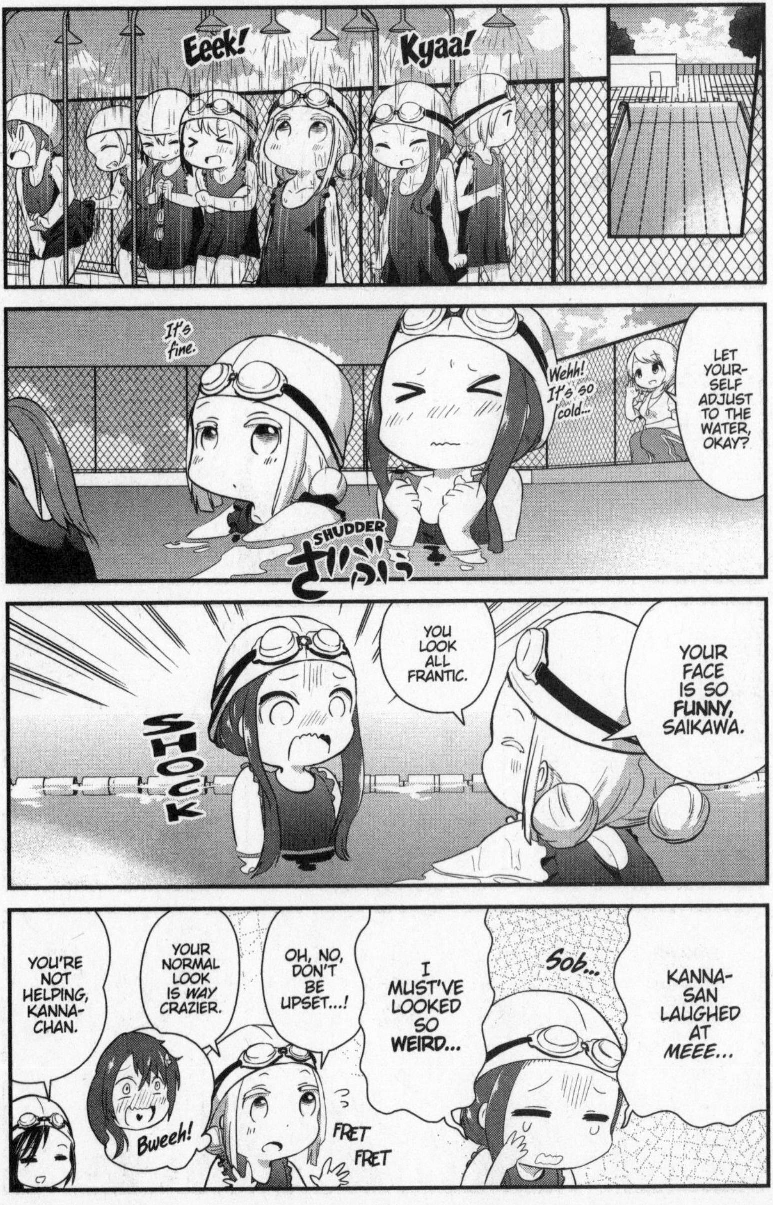
Kyaa!
Eeek!
LET YOURSELF ADJUST TO THE WATER, OKAY?
Wehh! It's so cold...
It's fine.
SHUDDER
YOUR FACE IS SO FUNNY, SAIKAWA.
YOU LOOK ALL FRANTIC.
SHOCK
KANNA-SAN LAUGHED AT MEEE...
Sob...
I MUST'VE LOOKED SO WEIRD...
OH, NO, DON'T BE UPSET...!
FRET
FRET
YOUR NORMAL LOOK IS WAY CRAZIER.
Bweeh!
YOU'RE NOT HELPING, KANNA-CHAN.

SAIKAWA-SAN'S SECRET!

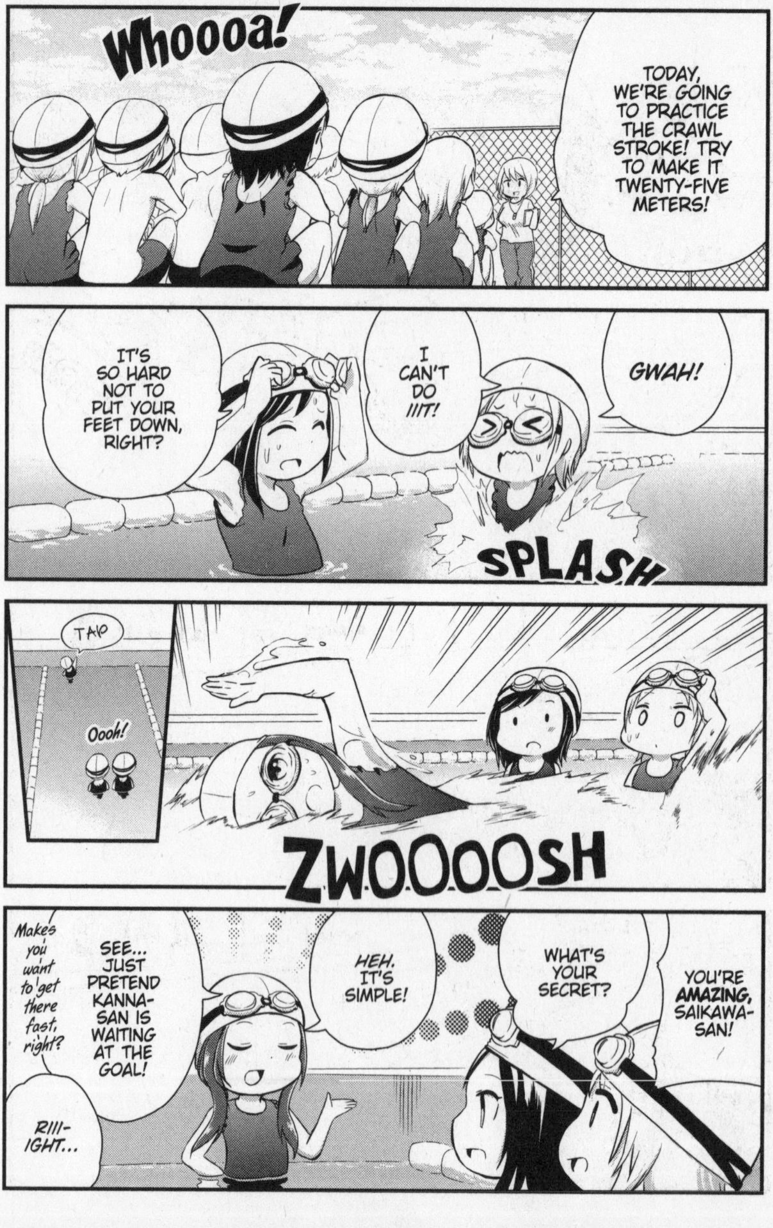
TODAY, WE'RE GOING TO PRACTICE THE CRAWL STROKE! TRY TO MAKE IT TWENTY-FIVE METERS!
Whoooa!
GWAH!
I CAN'T DO IIIT!
IT'S SO HARD NOT TO PUT YOUR FEET DOWN, RIGHT?
SPLASH
ZWOOOOSH
TAP
Oooh!
YOU'RE AMAZING, SAIKAWA-SAN!
WHAT'S YOUR SECRET?
HEH. IT'S SIMPLE!
SEE... JUST PRETEND KANNA-SAN IS WAITING AT THE GOAL!
Makes you want to get there fast, right?
RIII-IGHT...

IT'S TRUE!

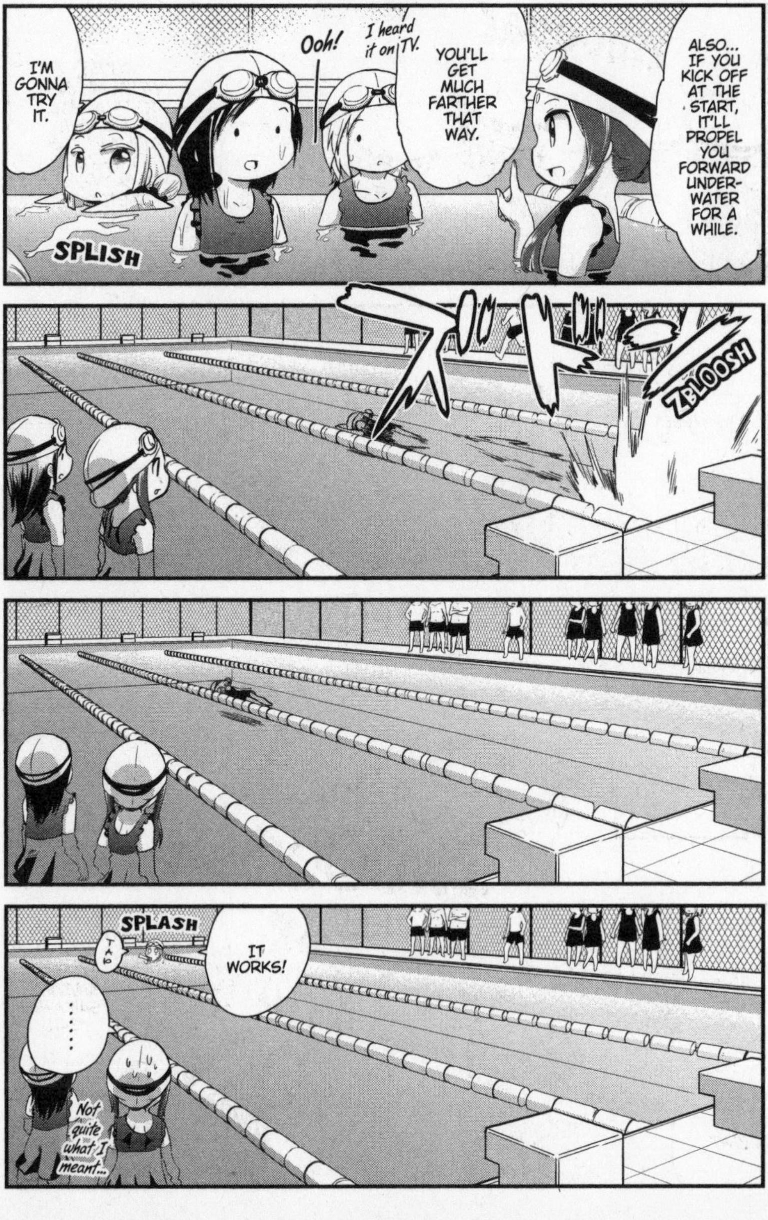
ALSO... IF YOU KICK OFF AT THE START, IT'LL PROPEL YOU FORWARD UNDERWATER FOR A WHILE.
YOU'LL GET MUCH FARTHER THAT WAY.
I heard it on TV.
Ooh!
I'M GONNA TRY IT.
SPLISH
ZBLOOSH
IT WORKS!
SPLASH
......
Not quite what I meant...

I HATE YOU, KICKBOARD

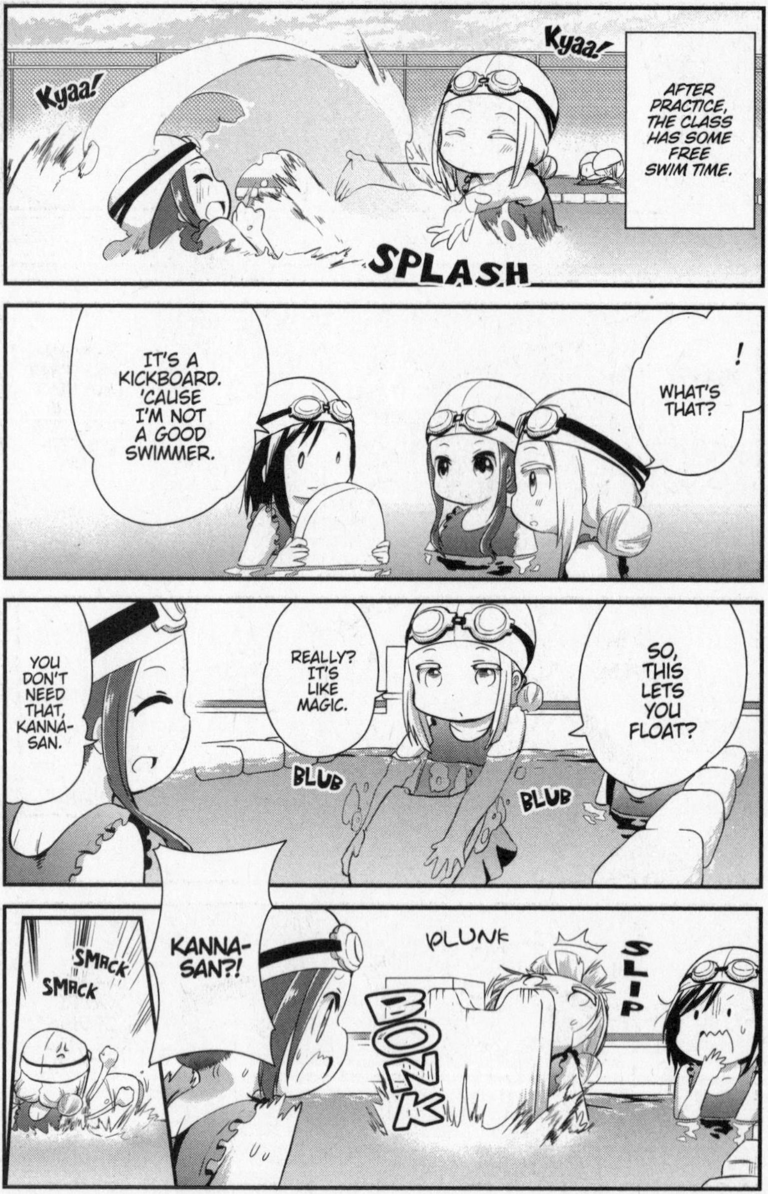
AFTER PRACTICE, THE CLASS HAS SOME FREE SWIM TIME.
Kyaa!
Kyaa!
SPLASH
!
WHAT'S THAT?
IT'S A KICKBOARD. 'CAUSE I'M NOT A GOOD SWIMMER.
SO, THIS LETS YOU FLOAT?
REALLY? IT'S LIKE MAGIC.
YOU DON'T NEED THAT, KANNA-SAN.
BLUB
BLUB
SLIP
PLUNK
BONK
KANNA-SAN?!
SMACK
SMACK

TOO CLOSE FOR COMFORT

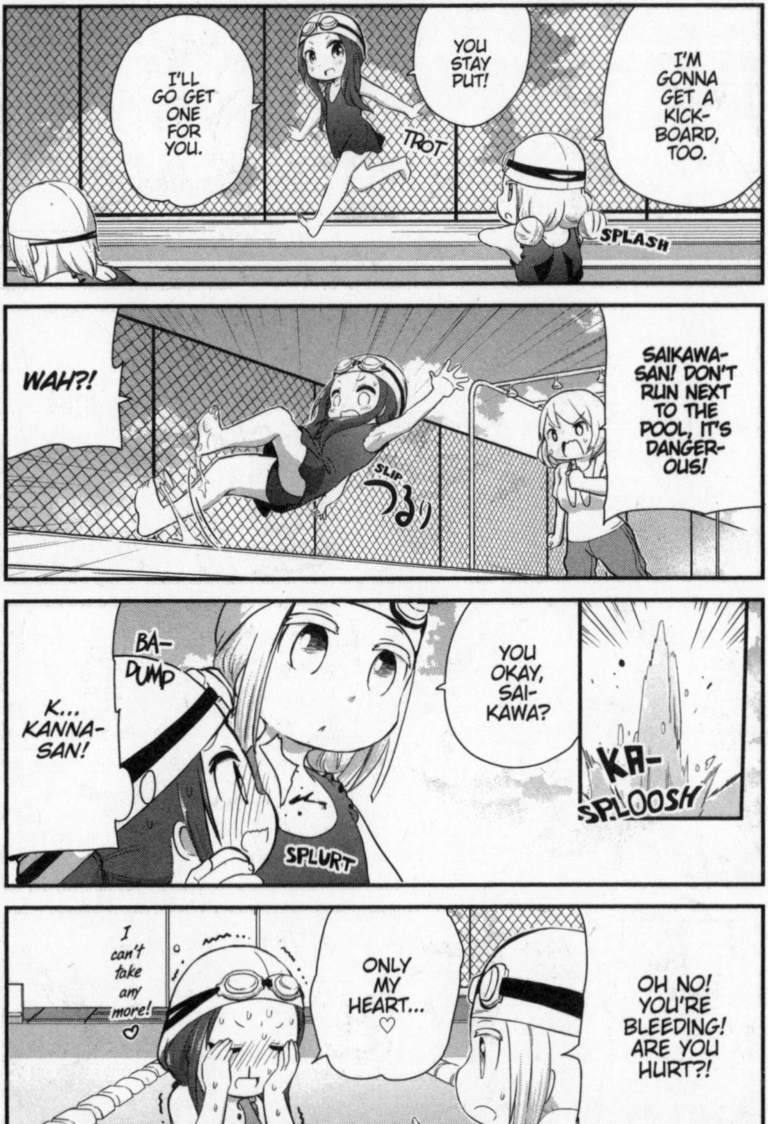
I'M GONNA GET A KICK-BOARD, TOO.
SPLASH
YOU STAY PUT!
TROT
I'LL GO GET ONE FOR YOU.
SAIKAWA-SAN! DON'T RUN NEXT TO THE POOL, IT'S DANGEROUS!
SLIP
つるり
WAH?!
KA-SPLOOSH
YOU OKAY, SAI-KAWA?
BA-DUMP
K... KANNA-SAN!
SPLURT
OH NO! YOU'RE BLEEDING! ARE YOU HURT?!
ONLY MY HEART... ♡
I can't take any more! ♡

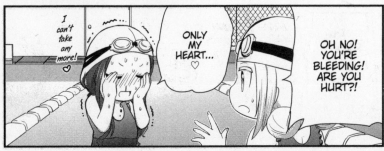

THE HITS KEEP COMING!

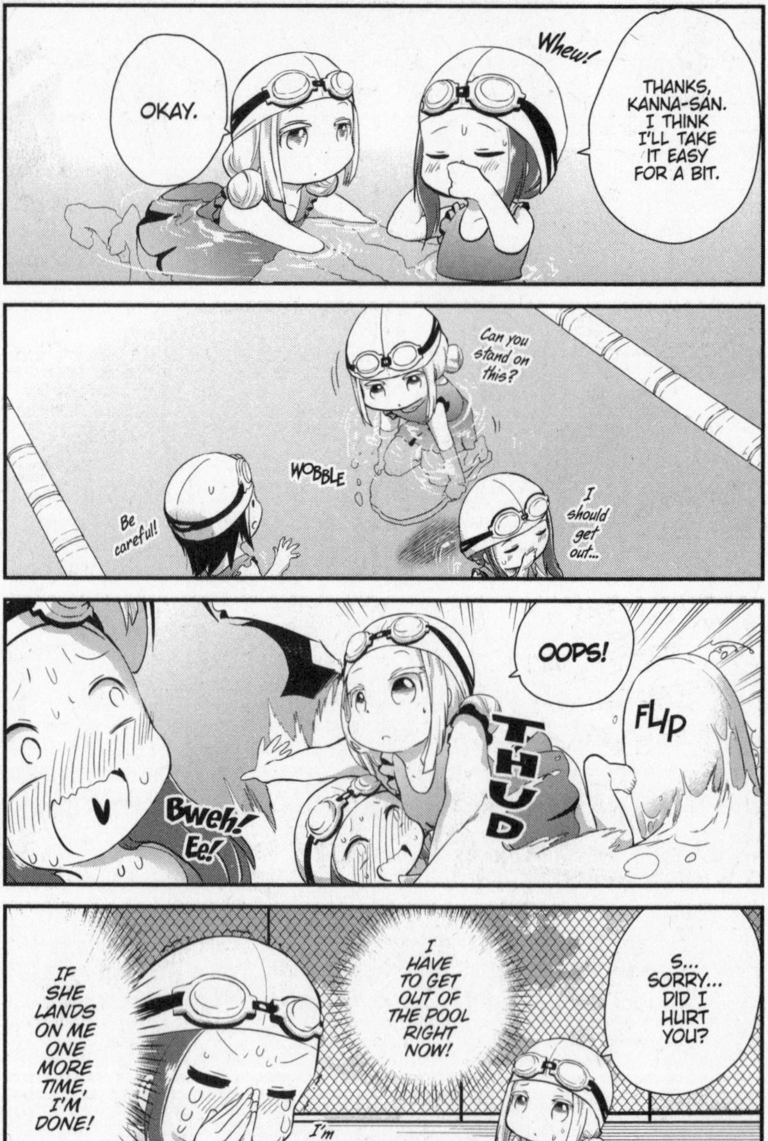
Whew!
THANKS, KANNA-SAN. I THINK I'LL TAKE IT EASY FOR A BIT.
OKAY.
Can you stand on this?
I should get out...
WOBBLE
Be careful!
OOPS!
FLIP
THUD
Bweh! Ee!
S... SORRY... DID I HURT YOU?
I HAVE TO GET OUT OF THE POOL RIGHT NOW!
IF SHE LANDS ON ME ONE MORE TIME, I'M DONE!
I'm gonna die...

FORCEFUL MOVES

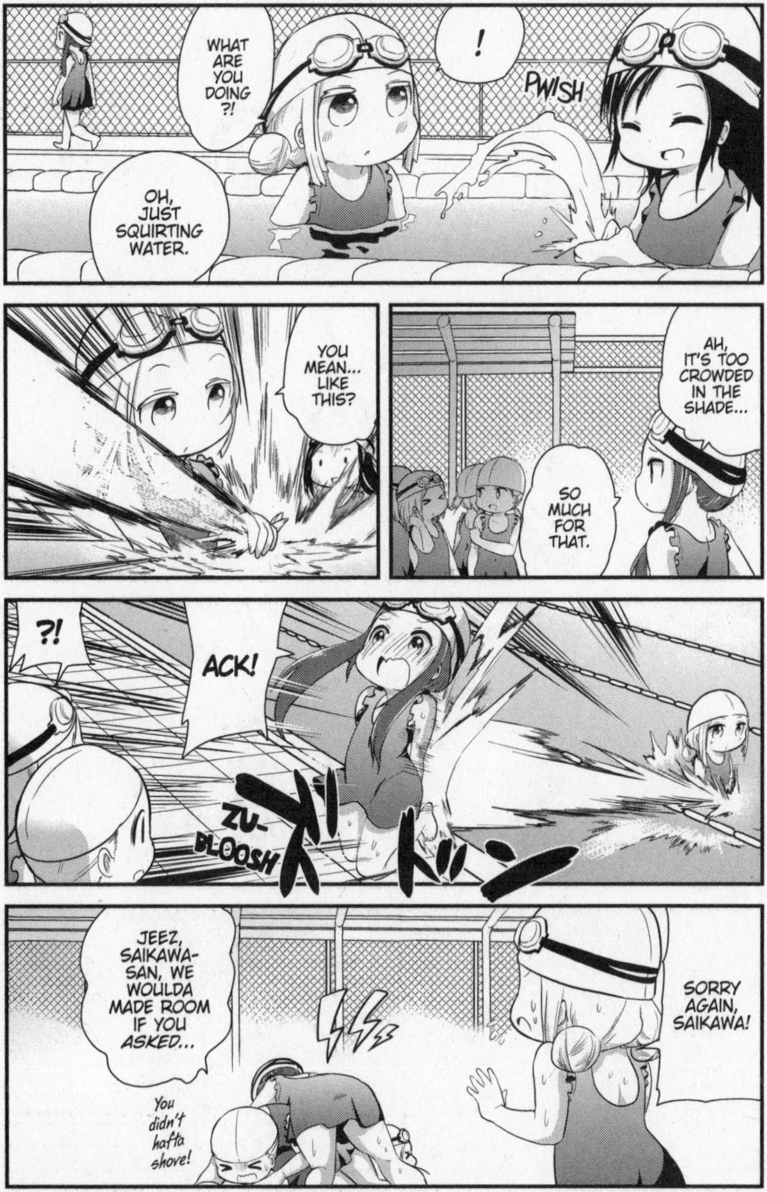
!
PWISH
WHAT ARE YOU DOING ?!
OH, JUST SQUIRTING WATER.
AH, IT'S TOO CROWDED IN THE SHADE...
SO MUCH FOR THAT.
YOU MEAN... LIKE THIS?
ACK!
?!
ZU-BLOOSH
SORRY AGAIN, SAIKAWA!
JEEZ, SAIKAWA-SAN, WE WOULDA MADE ROOM IF YOU ASKED...
You didn't hafta shove!

OOPS

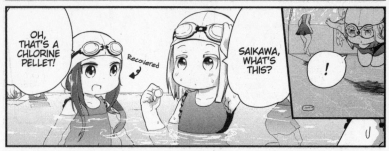

!
SAIKAWA, WHAT'S THIS?
Recovered
OH, THAT'S A CHLORINE PELLET!
IT'S WHAT GIVES THE POOL WATER THAT SMELL!
I HEARD IT "STERILIZES" THE POOL.
HUNH...
THERE'S A BUNCH OF 'EM LYING AROUND.
YOU'RE SUPPOSED TO LEAVE THEM THERE.
I'LL PUT IT BACK.
PLUNK
SHOOT! I TOOK MORE INSTEAD OF PUTTING THAT ONE BACK!
Heh.
I JUST COULDN'T HELP MYSELF!
DRAGONS LOVE HOARDING TREASURE.
CLINK...
Now I know how Lord Fafnir feels!

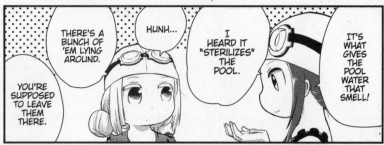

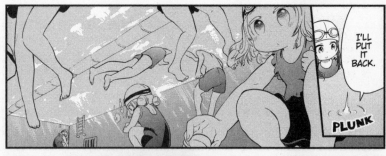

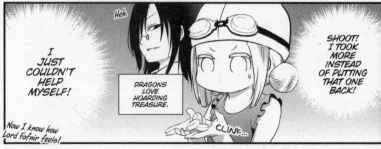

IT'S CONTAGIOUS

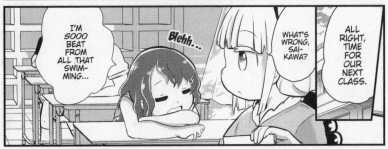

ALL RIGHT, TIME FOR OUR NEXT CLASS.
WHAT'S WRONG, SAI-KAWA?
Blehh...
I'M SOOO BEAT FROM ALL THAT SWIM-MING...
Don't worry, I'll...
NOD...
DAAAZE
NOD...
Zzz...
WAKE UP, YOU TWO.
I'M SORRY. THE POOL JUST MAKES ME SO SLEEPY...
WATCHING HER MADE ME SLEEPY, TOO.
I KNOW THE FEELING, SAIKAWA-SAN, BUT PLEASE STAY WITH US.
AND, KOBAYASHI-SAN, YOU SHOULD KNOW THAT'S NOT A VERY GOOD EXCUSE.

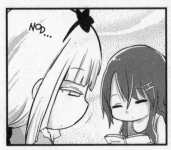

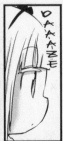

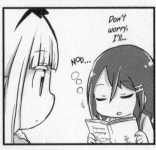

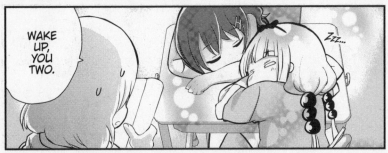

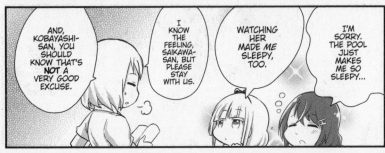

SLEEPY SUMMER AFTERNOON

Yeah!
Woo!
MIIIN
MIIIN
MIIIN...
MIIIIN
THE BREEZE FEELS NICE...
STILL SLEEPY TOO, HUH?
WHISPER
UH-HUH.
WHISPER
BUT THE TEACHER'D YELL AT US AGAIN...
CAN'T HELP YAWNING, THOUGH.
Hee hee!
Yaaaawn...
MIIIN
MIIIN

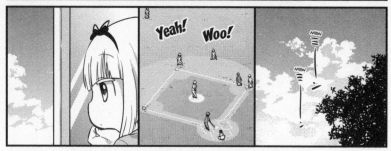

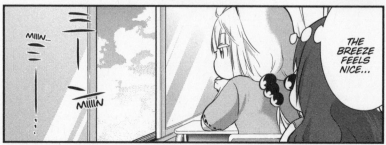

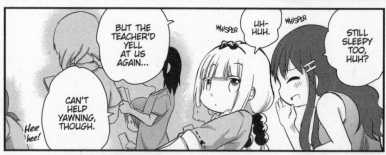

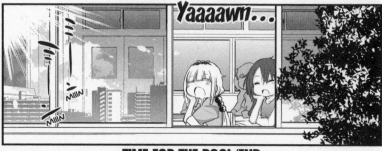

TIME FOR THE POOL/END

PF FT!

Miss Kobayashi's Dragon Maid

Kanna's Daily Life

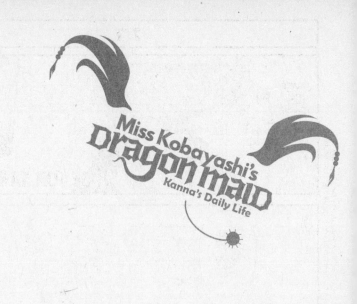

7/7

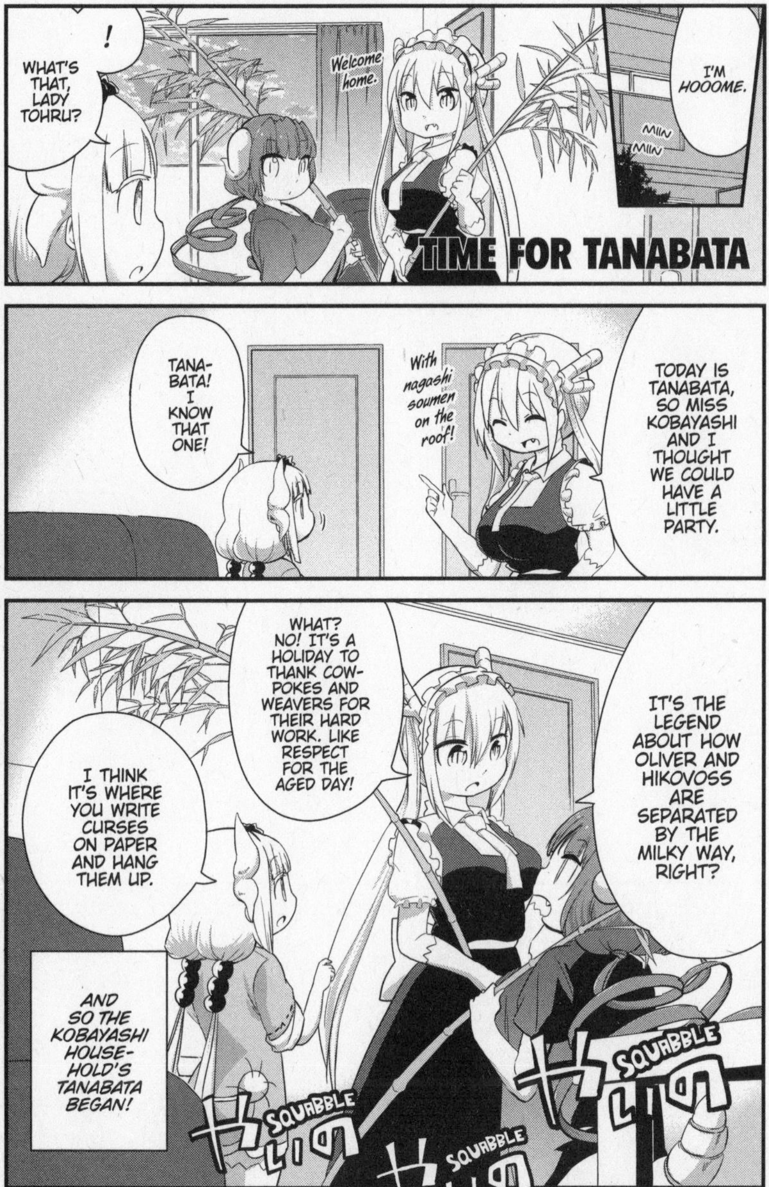
I'M HOOOME.
MIIN MIIN
Welcome home.
!
WHAT'S THAT, LADY TOHRU?
TIME FOR TANABATA
TODAY IS TANABATA, SO MISS KOBAYASHI AND I THOUGHT WE COULD HAVE A LITTLE PARTY.
With nagashi soumen on the roof!
TANA-BATA! I KNOW THAT ONE!
IT'S THE LEGEND ABOUT HOW OLIVER AND HIKOVOSS ARE SEPARATED BY THE MILKY WAY, RIGHT?
WHAT? NO! IT'S A HOLIDAY TO THANK COW-POKES AND WEAVERS FOR THEIR HARD WORK. LIKE RESPECT FOR THE AGED DAY!
I THINK IT'S WHERE YOU WRITE CURSES ON PAPER AND HANG THEM UP.
AND SO THE KOBAYASHI HOUSE-HOLD'S TANABATA BEGAN!
SQUABBLE
SQUABBLE
SQUABBLE

※ The real story of Tanabata celebrates a legend of two lovers, a cowherd (Hikoboshi) and a weaver (Orihime), who are separated by the Milky Way, and can only meet one day a year. Traditions include eating nagashi soumen (cold noodles flowed down a bamboo chute) and hanging wishes on bamboo.

WHERE'D SAIKAWA GO?

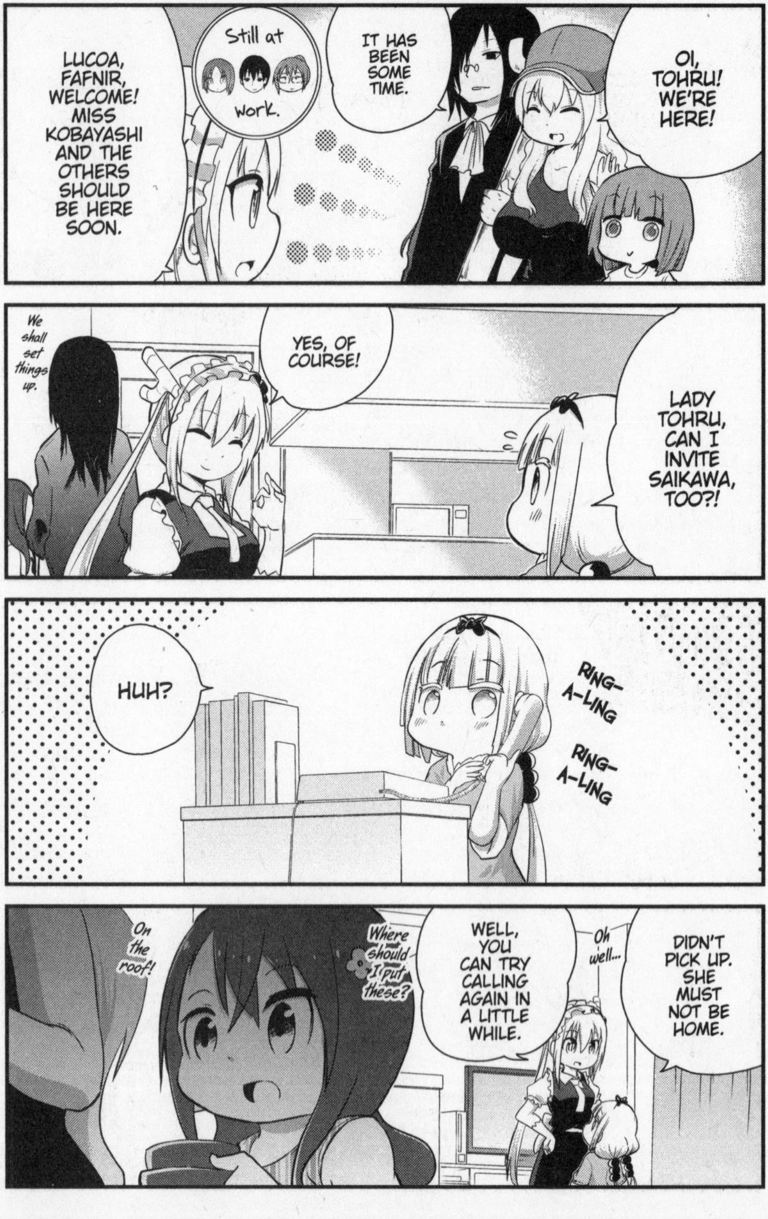
OI, TOHRU! WE'RE HERE!
IT HAS BEEN SOME TIME.
Still at work.
LUCOA, FAFNIR, WELCOME! MISS KOBAYASHI AND THE OTHERS SHOULD BE HERE SOON.
LADY TOHRU, CAN I INVITE SAIKAWA, TOO?!
YES, OF COURSE!
We shall set things up.
RING-A-LING
RING-A-LING
HUH?
DIDN'T PICK UP. SHE MUST NOT BE HOME.
Oh well...
WELL, YOU CAN TRY CALLING AGAIN IN A LITTLE WHILE.
Where should I put these?
On the roof!

THE HEART KNOWS

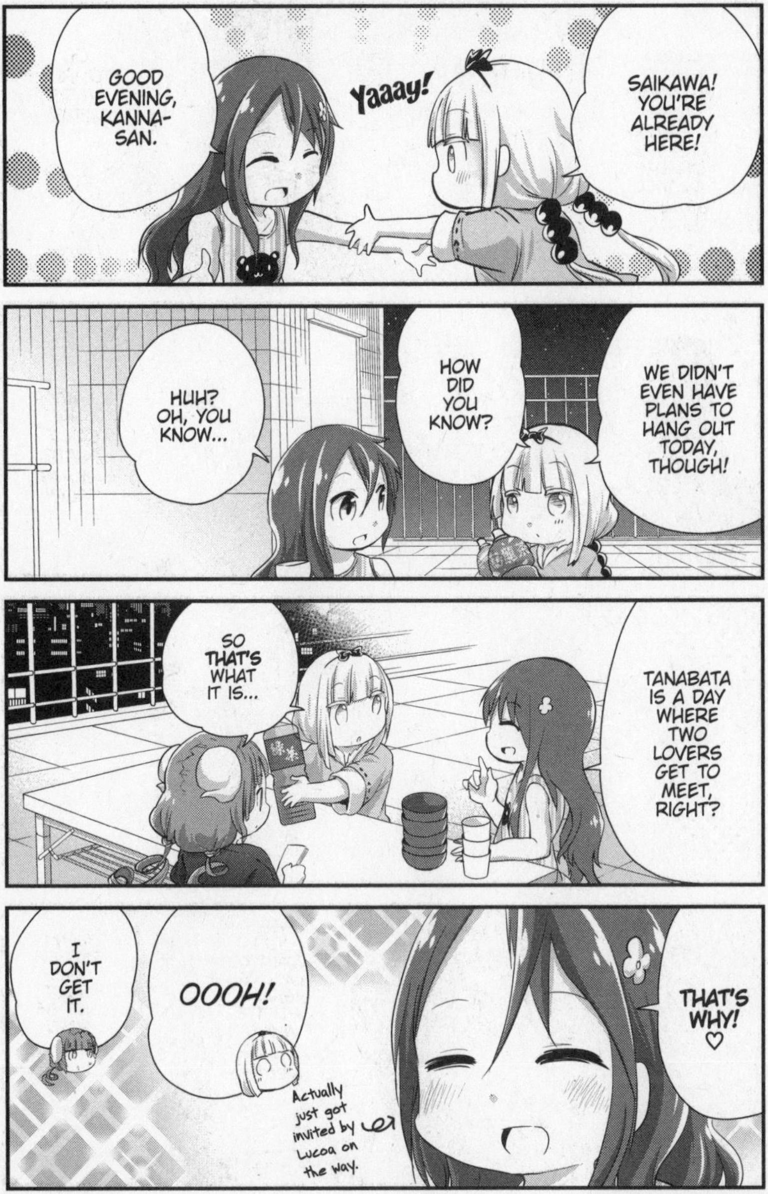
SAIKAWA! YOU'RE ALREADY HERE!
Yaaay!
GOOD EVENING, KANNA-SAN.
WE DIDN'T EVEN HAVE PLANS TO HANG OUT TODAY, THOUGH!
HOW DID YOU KNOW?
HUH? OH, YOU KNOW...
TANABATA IS A DAY WHERE TWO LOVERS GET TO MEET, RIGHT?
SO THAT'S WHAT IT IS...
THAT'S WHY! ♡
OOOH!
I DON'T GET IT.
Actually just got invited by Lucoa on the way.

DISASTER STRIKES!

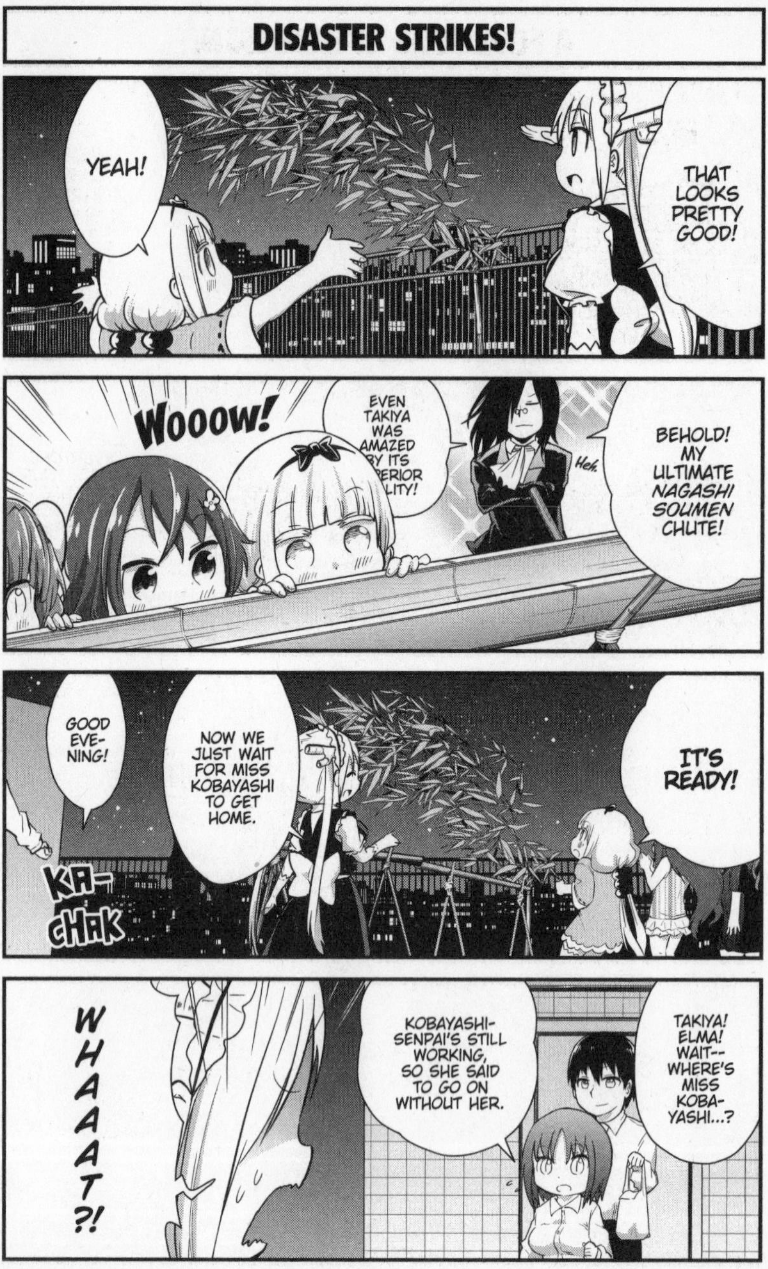
THAT LOOKS PRETTY GOOD!
YEAH!
BEHOLD! MY ULTIMATE NAGASHI SOUMEN CHUTE!
Heh.
EVEN TAKIYA WAS AMAZED BY ITS PERIOR LITY!
WOOOW!
IT'S READY!
NOW WE JUST WAIT FOR MISS KOBAYASHI TO GET HOME.
GOOD EVE-NING!
KA-CHAK
TAKIYA! ELMA! WAIT-- WHERE'S MISS KOBA-YASHI...?
KOBAYASHI-SENPAI'S STILL WORKING, SO SHE SAID TO GO ON WITHOUT HER.
WHAAAAT?!

A FOREGONE CONCLUSION!

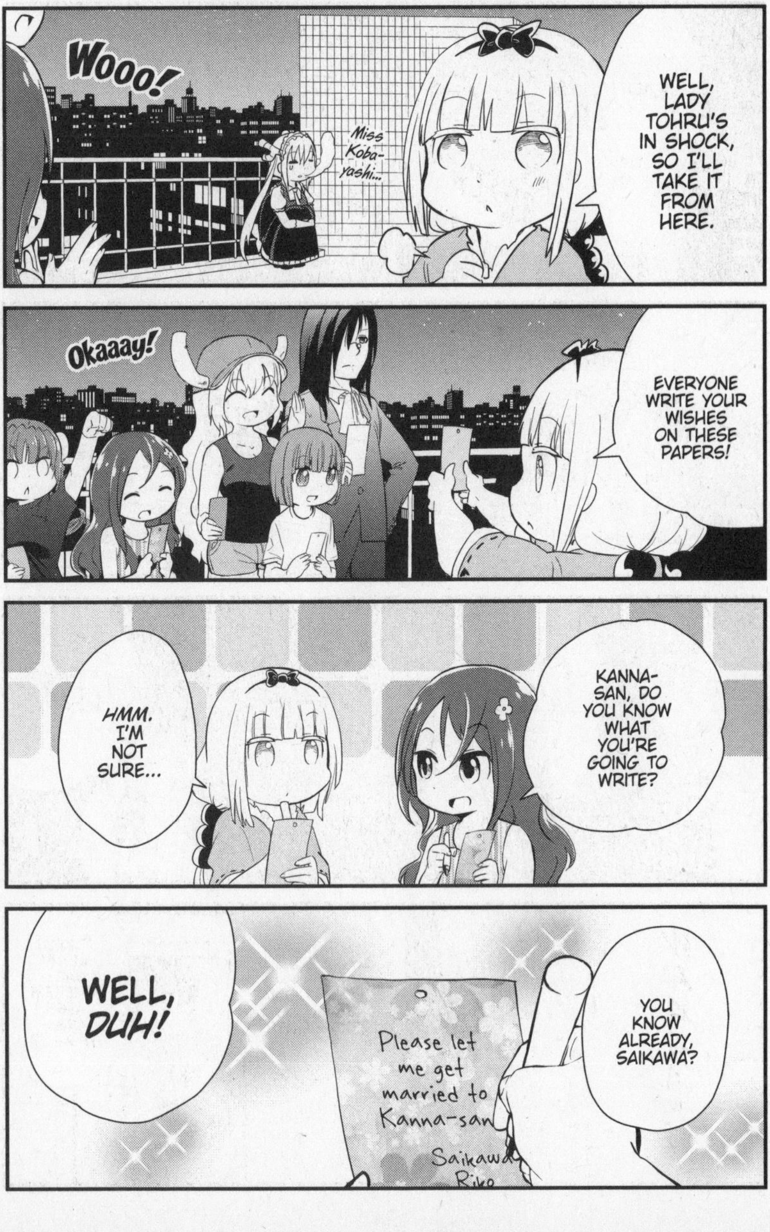
WELL, LADY TOHRU'S IN SHOCK, SO I'LL TAKE IT FROM HERE.
Miss Koba-yashi...
Wooo!
EVERYONE WRITE YOUR WISHES ON THESE PAPERS!
Okaaay!
KANNA-SAN, DO YOU KNOW WHAT YOU'RE GOING TO WRITE?
HMM. I'M NOT SURE...
YOU KNOW ALREADY, SAIKAWA?
Please let me get married to Kanna-san
Saikawa Riko
WELL, DUH!

SENSIBLE PRECAUTIONS

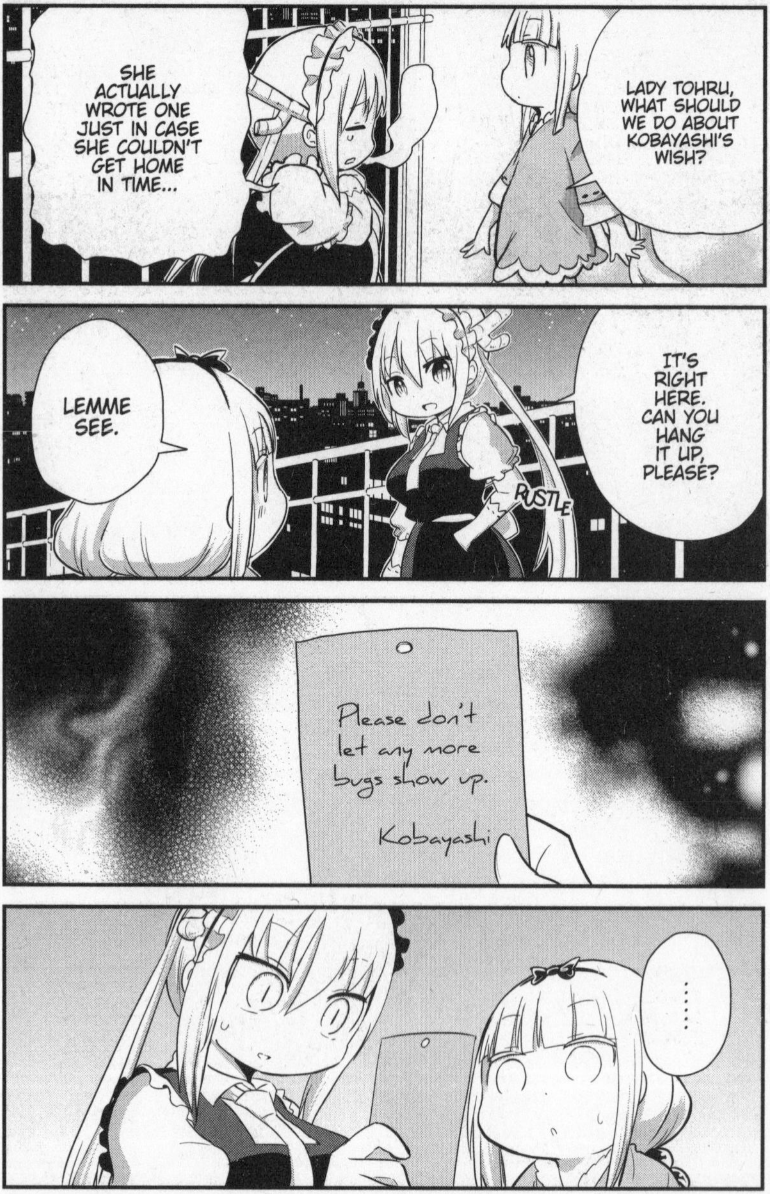
LADY TOHRU, WHAT SHOULD WE DO ABOUT KOBAYASHI'S WISH?
SHE ACTUALLY WROTE ONE JUST IN CASE SHE COULDN'T GET HOME IN TIME...
IT'S RIGHT HERE. CAN YOU HANG IT UP, PLEASE?
RUSTLE
LEMME SEE.
Please don't let any more bugs show up.
Kobayashi
......

TOHRU IN TURMOIL

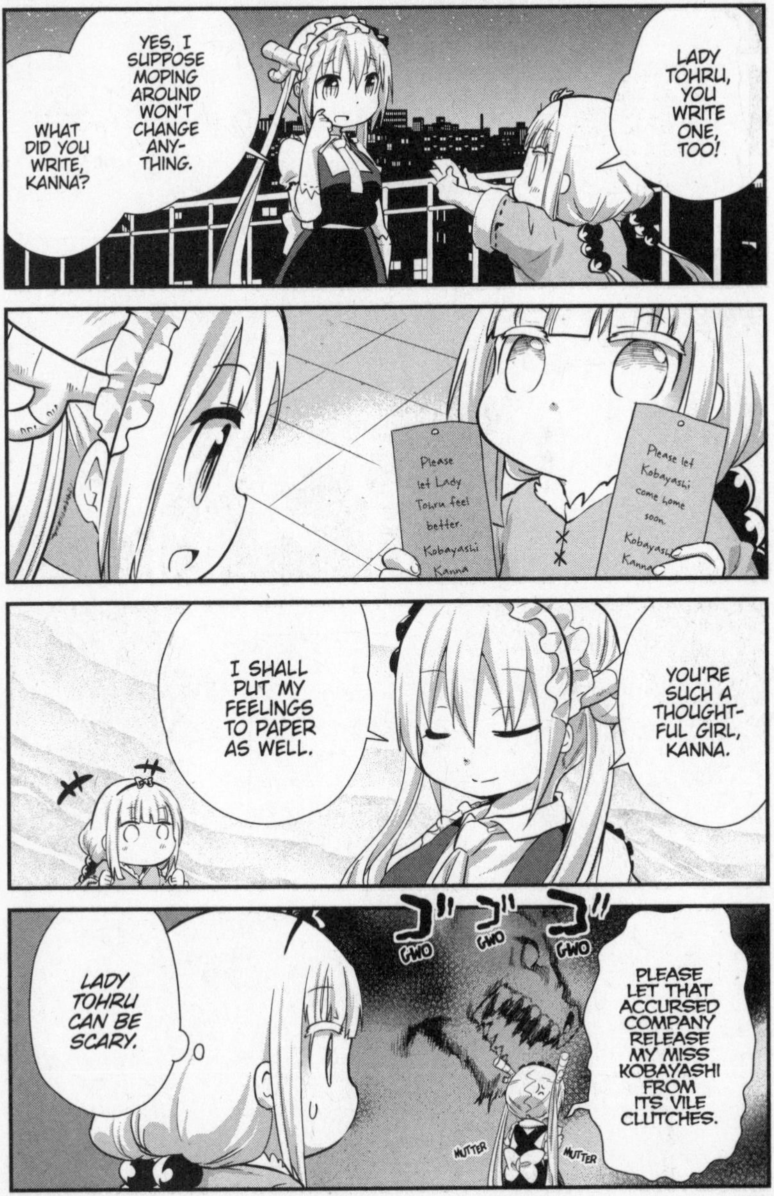
LADY TOHRU, YOU WRITE ONE, TOO!
YES, I SUPPOSE MOPING AROUND WON'T CHANGE ANY-THING.
WHAT DID YOU WRITE, KANNA?
Please let Kobayashi come home soon. Kobayashi Kanna
Please let Lady Tohru feel better. Kobayashi Kanna
YOU'RE SUCH A THOUGHT-FUL GIRL, KANNA.
I SHALL PUT MY FEELINGS TO PAPER AS WELL.
GWO GWO GWO
PLEASE LET THAT ACCURSED COMPANY RELEASE MY MISS KOBAYASHI FROM ITS VILE CLUTCHES.
MUTTER MUTTER
LADY TOHRU CAN BE SCARY.

IT'S ALL OVER YOUR FACE!

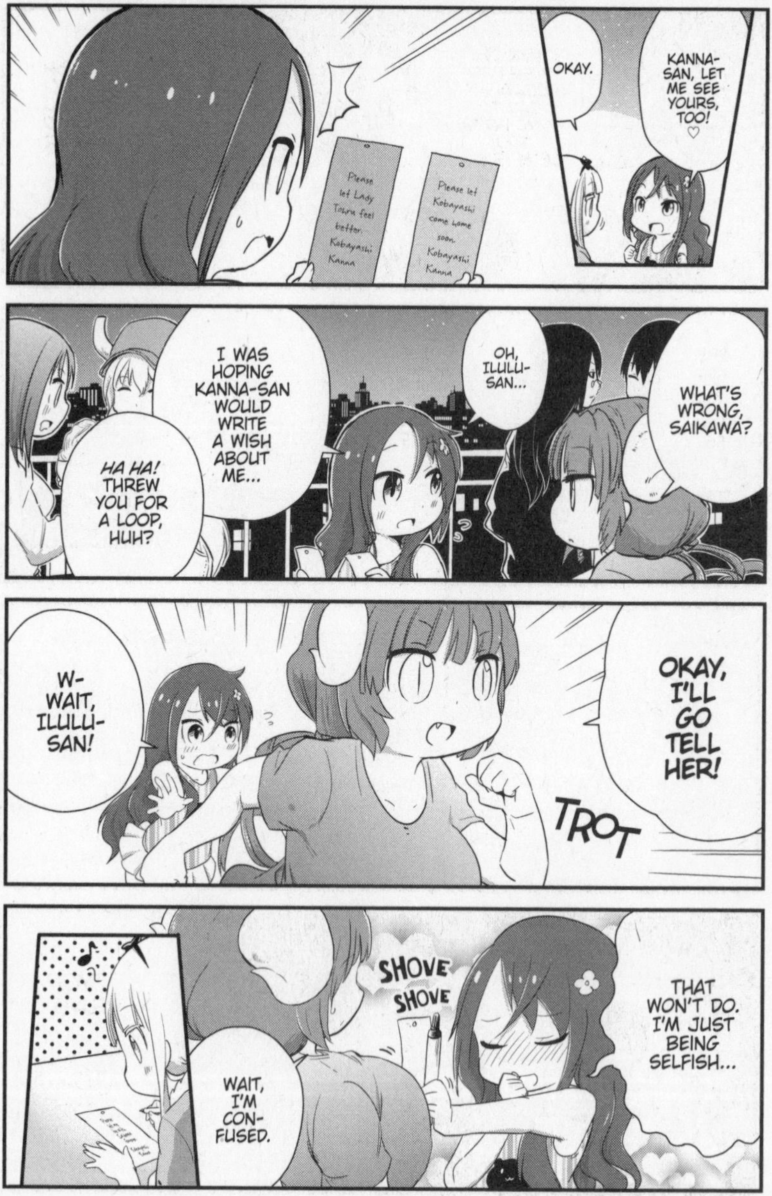
KANNA-SAN, LET ME SEE YOURS, TOO! ♡
OKAY.
Please let Kobayashi come home soon. Kobayashi Kanna
Please let Lady Tohru feel better. Kobayashi Kanna
WHAT'S WRONG, SAIKAWA?
OH, ILULU-SAN...
I WAS HOPING KANNA-SAN WOULD WRITE A WISH ABOUT ME...
HA HA! THREW YOU FOR A LOOP, HUH?
OKAY, I'LL GO TELL HER!
TROT
W-WAIT, ILULU-SAN!
THAT WON'T DO. I'M JUST BEING SELFISH...
SHOVE
SHOVE
WAIT, I'M CONFUSED.

DON'T FORGET ABOUT US!

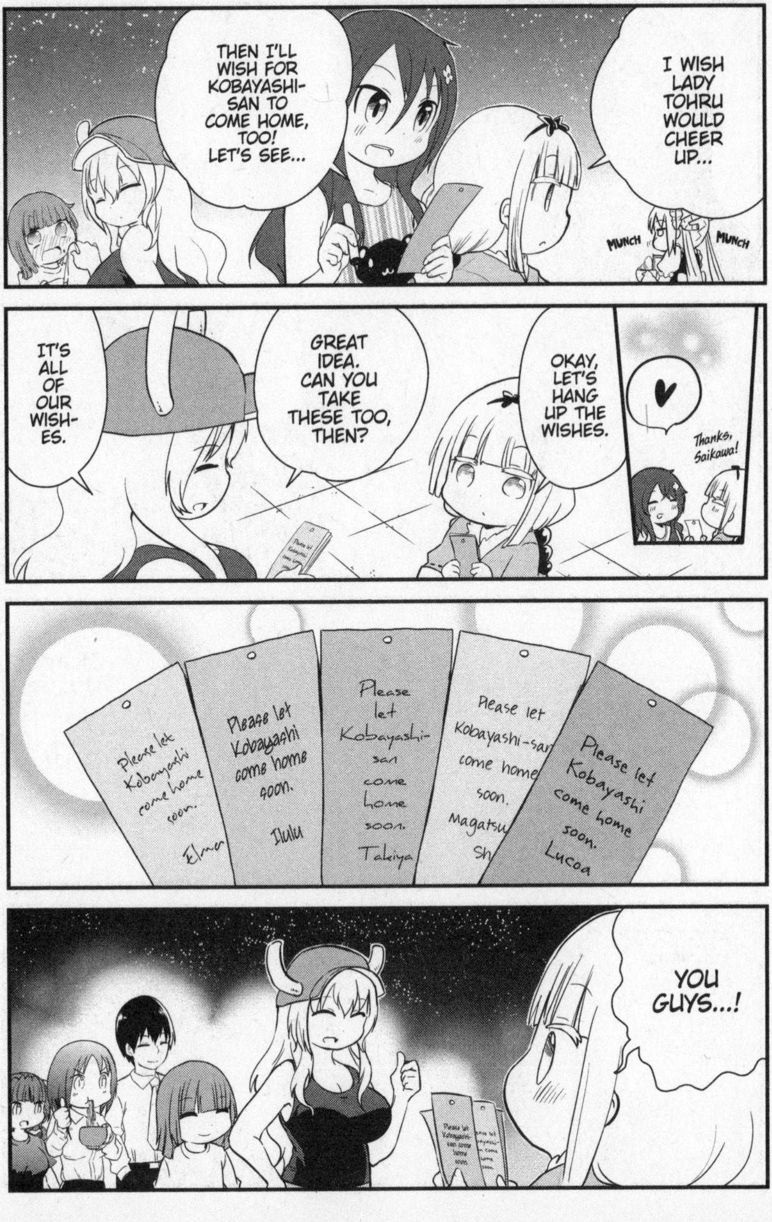
I WISH LADY TOHRU WOULD CHEER UP...
MUNCH
MUNCH
THEN I'LL WISH FOR KOBAYASHI-SAN TO COME HOME, TOO! LET'S SEE...
Thanks, Saikawa!
OKAY, LET'S HANG UP THE WISHES.
GREAT IDEA. CAN YOU TAKE THESE TOO, THEN?
IT'S ALL OF OUR WISH-ES.
Please let Kobayashi come home soon. Lucoa
Please let Kobayashi-san come home soon. Magatsu Sh
Please let Kobayashi-san come home soon. Takiya
Please let Kobayashi come home soon. Ilulu
Please let Kobayashi come home soon. Elma
YOU GUYS...!

AND THEN THERE'S FAFNIR...

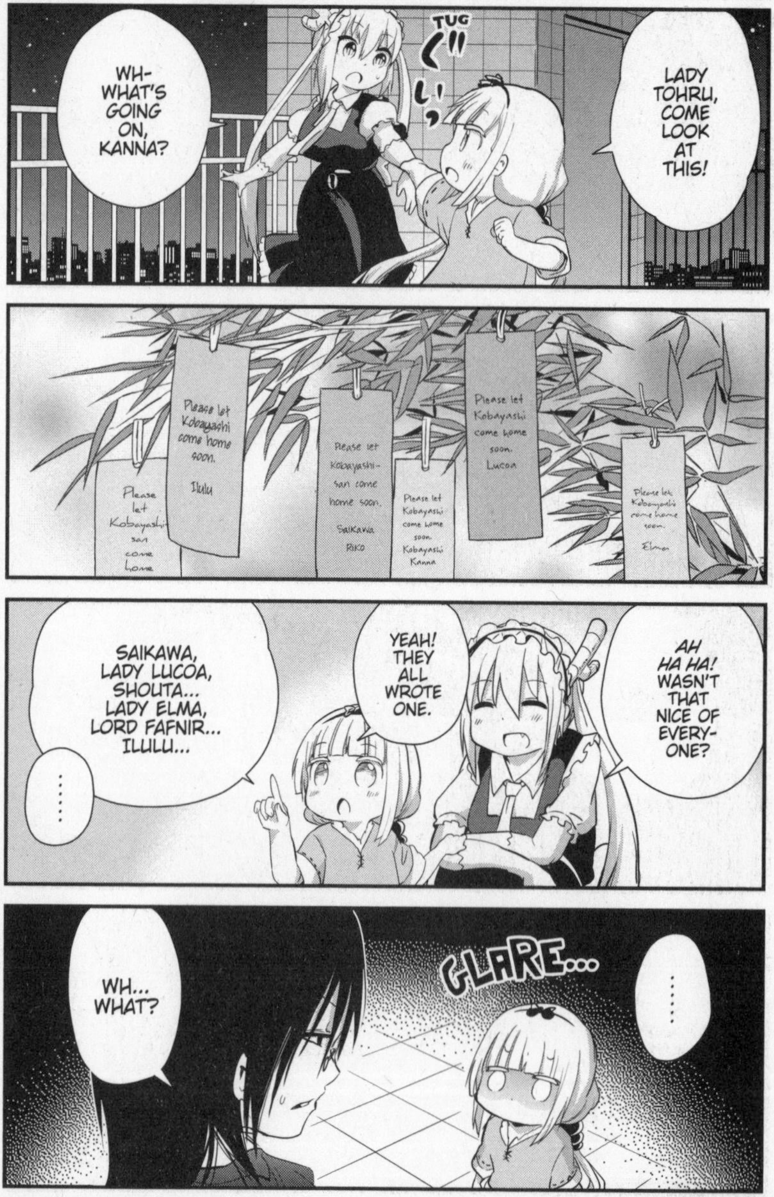
LADY TOHRU, COME LOOK AT THIS!
TUG
WH- WHAT'S GOING ON, KANNA?
Please let Kobayashi come home soon. Elma
Please let Kobayashi come home soon. Lucoa
Please let Kobayashi come home soon. Kobayashi Kanna
Please let Kobayashi-san come home soon. Saikawa Riko
Please let Kobayashi come home soon. Ilulu
Please let Kobayashi-san come home
AH HA HA! WASN'T THAT NICE OF EVERY-ONE?
YEAH! THEY ALL WROTE ONE.
SAIKAWA, LADY LUCOA, SHOUTA... LADY ELMA, LORD FAFNIR... ILULU...
......
......
GLARE...
WH... WHAT?

THE POWER OF INTENTION

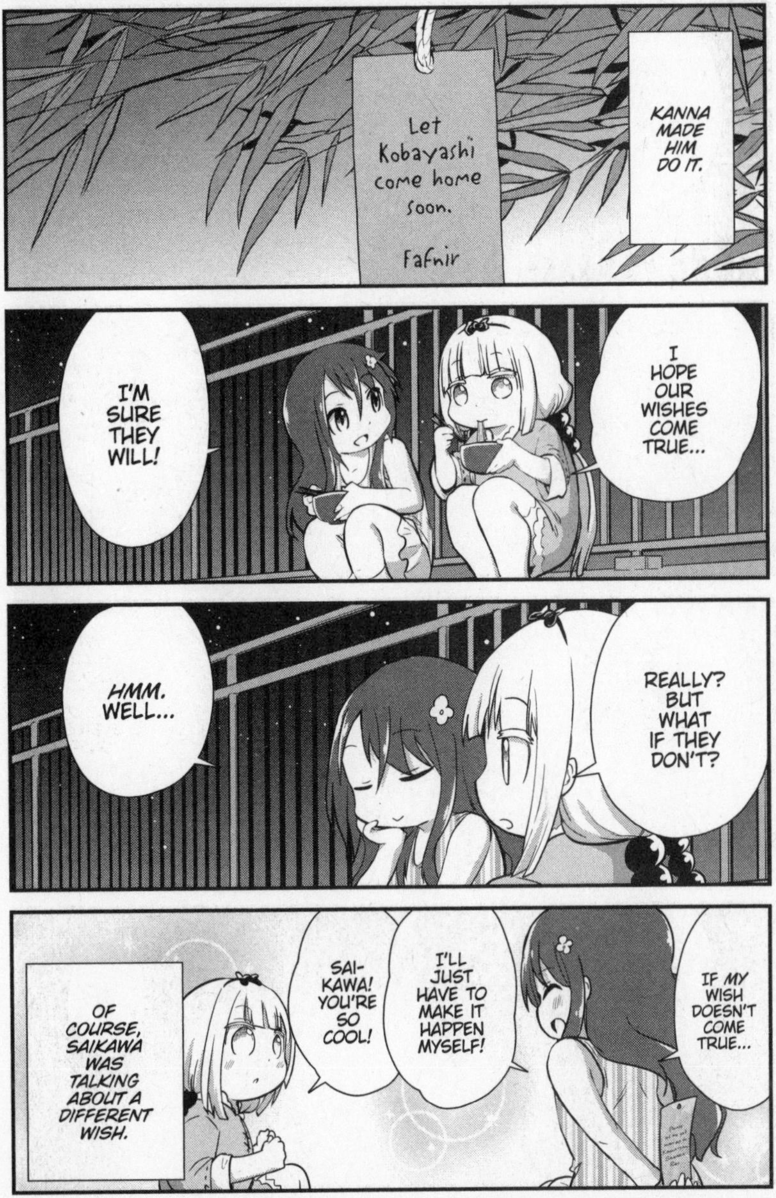
KANNA MADE HIM DO IT.
Let Kobayashi come home soon.
Fafnir
I HOPE OUR WISHES COME TRUE...
I'M SURE THEY WILL!
REALLY? BUT WHAT IF THEY DON'T?
HMM. WELL...
IF MY WISH DOESN'T COME TRUE...
I'LL JUST HAVE TO MAKE IT HAPPEN MYSELF!
SAI-KAWA! YOU'RE SO COOL!
OF COURSE, SAIKAWA WAS TALKING ABOUT A DIFFERENT WISH.

WISHES COME TRUE

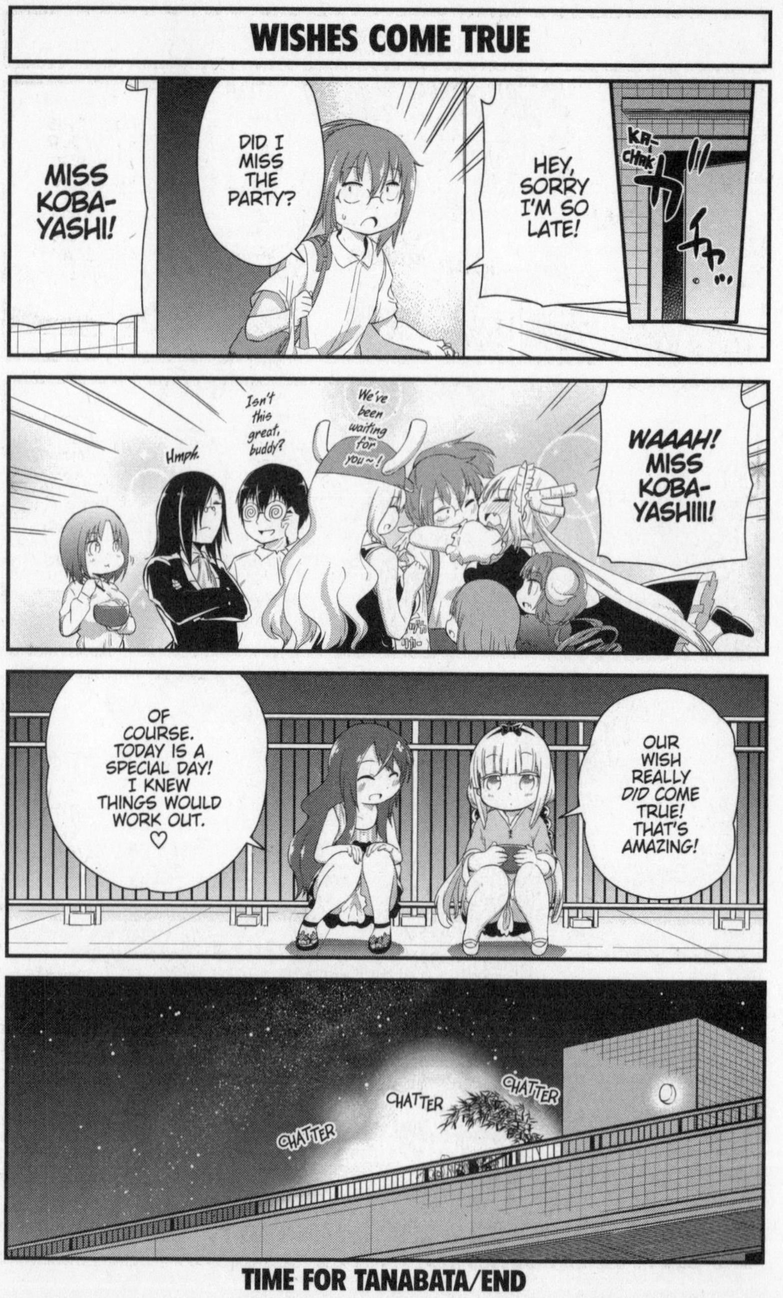
KA-CHAK
HEY, SORRY I'M SO LATE!
DID I MISS THE PARTY?
MISS KOBA-YASHI!
WAAAH! MISS KOBA-YASHIII!
We've been waiting for you~!
Isn't this great, buddy?
Hmph.
OUR WISH REALLY DID COME TRUE! THAT'S AMAZING!
OF COURSE. TODAY IS A SPECIAL DAY! I KNEW THINGS WOULD WORK OUT. ♡
CHATTER
CHATTER
CHATTER

TIME FOR TANABATA/END

AT LAST!

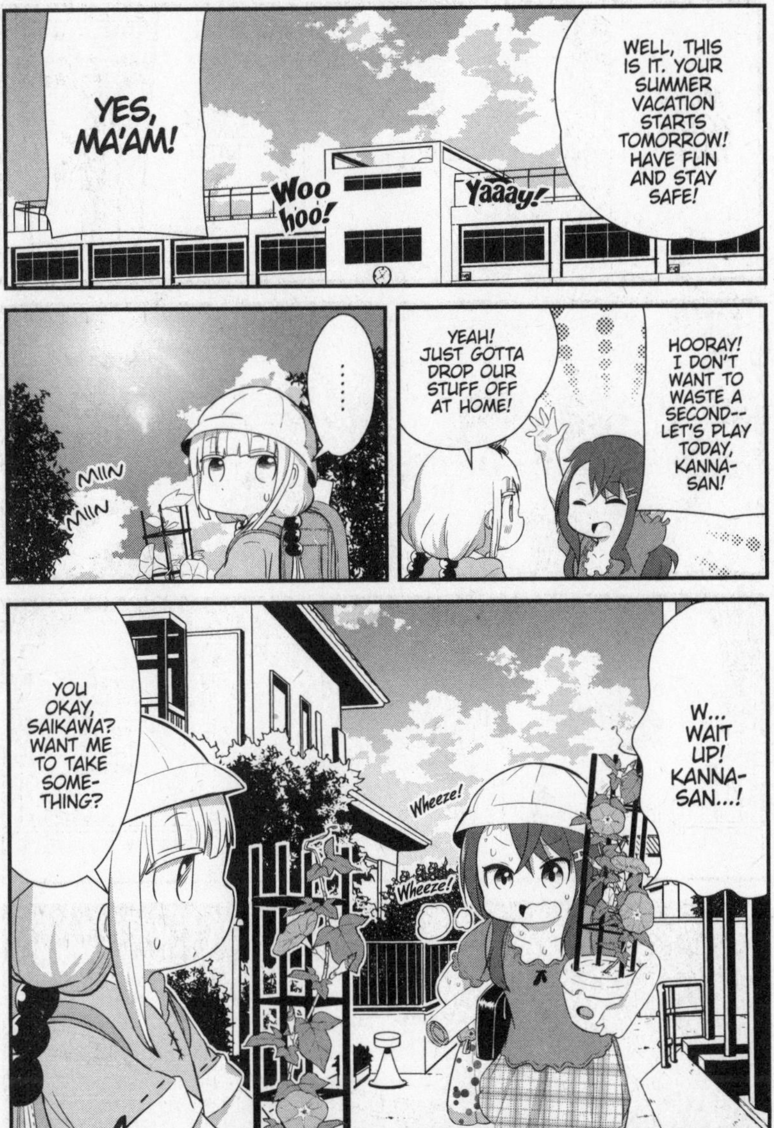
WELL, THIS IS IT. YOUR SUMMER VACATION STARTS TOMORROW! HAVE FUN AND STAY SAFE!
Yaaay!
Woo hoo!
YES, MA'AM!
HOORAY! I DON'T WANT TO WASTE A SECOND-- LET'S PLAY TODAY, KANNA-SAN!
YEAH! JUST GOTTA DROP OUR STUFF OFF AT HOME!
......
MIIN
MIIN
W... WAIT UP! KANNA-SAN...!
Wheeze!
Wheeze!
YOU OKAY, SAIKAWA? WANT ME TO TAKE SOME-THING?
TIME FOR SUMMER VACATION

FRESH COOKED SAIKAWA

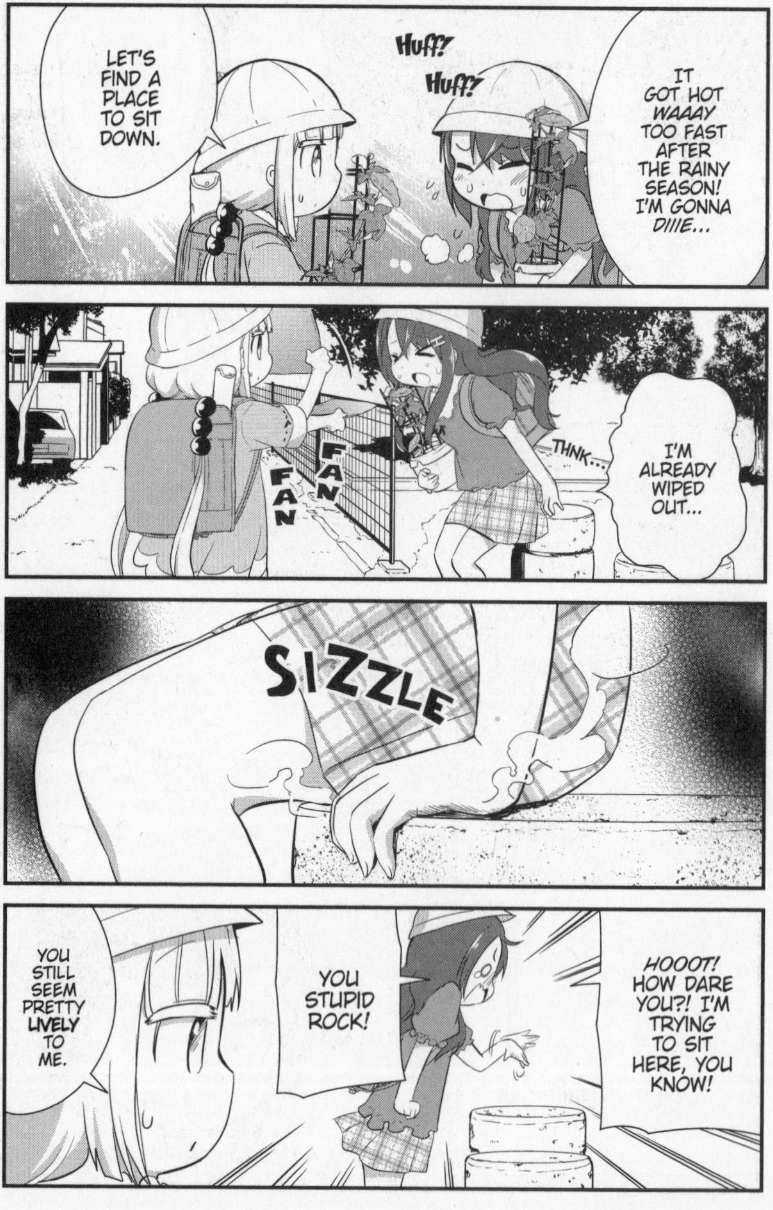
IT GOT HOT WAAAY TOO FAST AFTER THE RAINY SEASON! I'M GONNA DIIIE...
Huff?!
Huff?!
LET'S FIND A PLACE TO SIT DOWN.
I'M ALREADY WIPED OUT...
THNK...
FAN
FAN
SIZZLE
HOOOT! HOW DARE YOU?! I'M TRYING TO SIT HERE, YOU KNOW!
YOU STUPID ROCK!
YOU STILL SEEM PRETTY LIVELY TO ME.

SWEET TEMPTATION

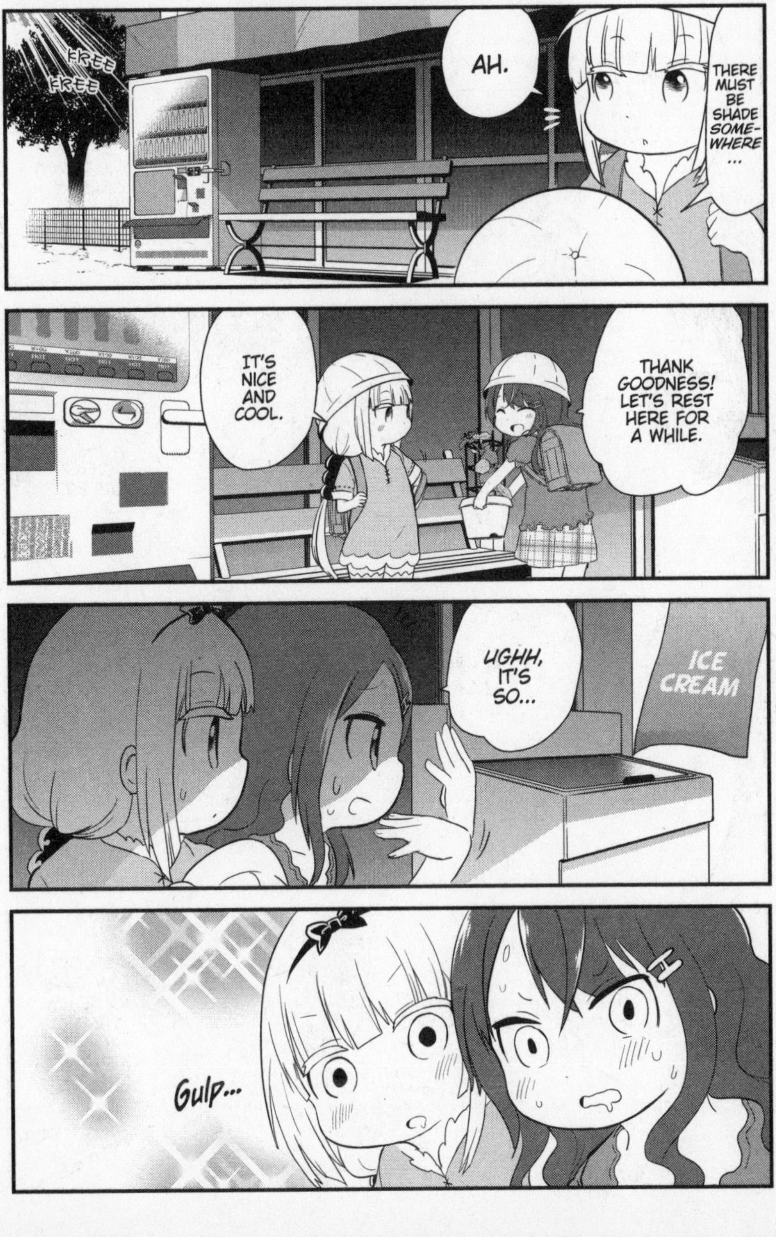
AH.
THERE MUST BE SHADE SOMEWHERE...
KREE KREE
THANK GOODNESS! LET'S REST HERE FOR A WHILE.
IT'S NICE AND COOL.
ICE CREAM
UGHH, IT'S SO...
Gulp...

IMPOSSIBLE

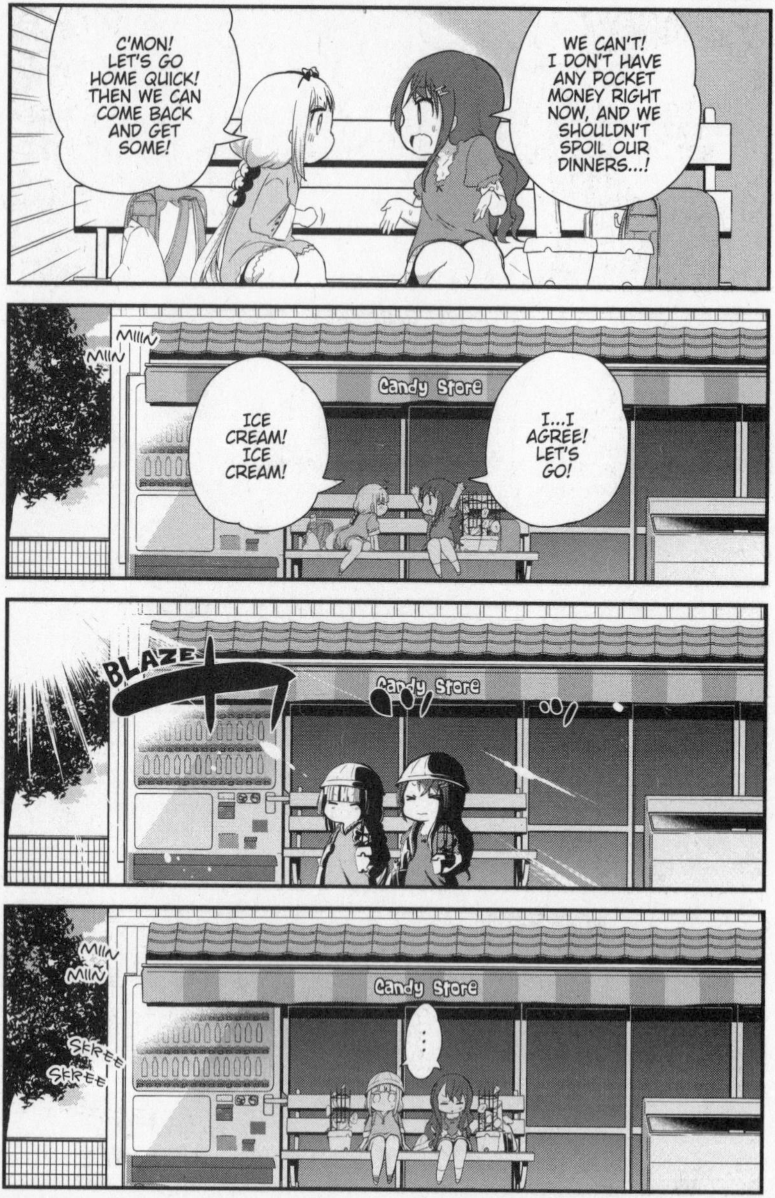
WE CAN'T! I DON'T HAVE ANY POCKET MONEY RIGHT NOW, AND WE SHOULDN'T SPOIL OUR DINNERS...!
C'MON! LET'S GO HOME QUICK! THEN WE CAN COME BACK AND GET SOME!
I...I AGREE! LET'S GO!
ICE CREAM! ICE CREAM!
MIIN
MIIN
Candy Store
Candy Store
BLAZE
Candy Store
...
MIIN
MIIN
SKREE
SKREE

EXTRA HEAT

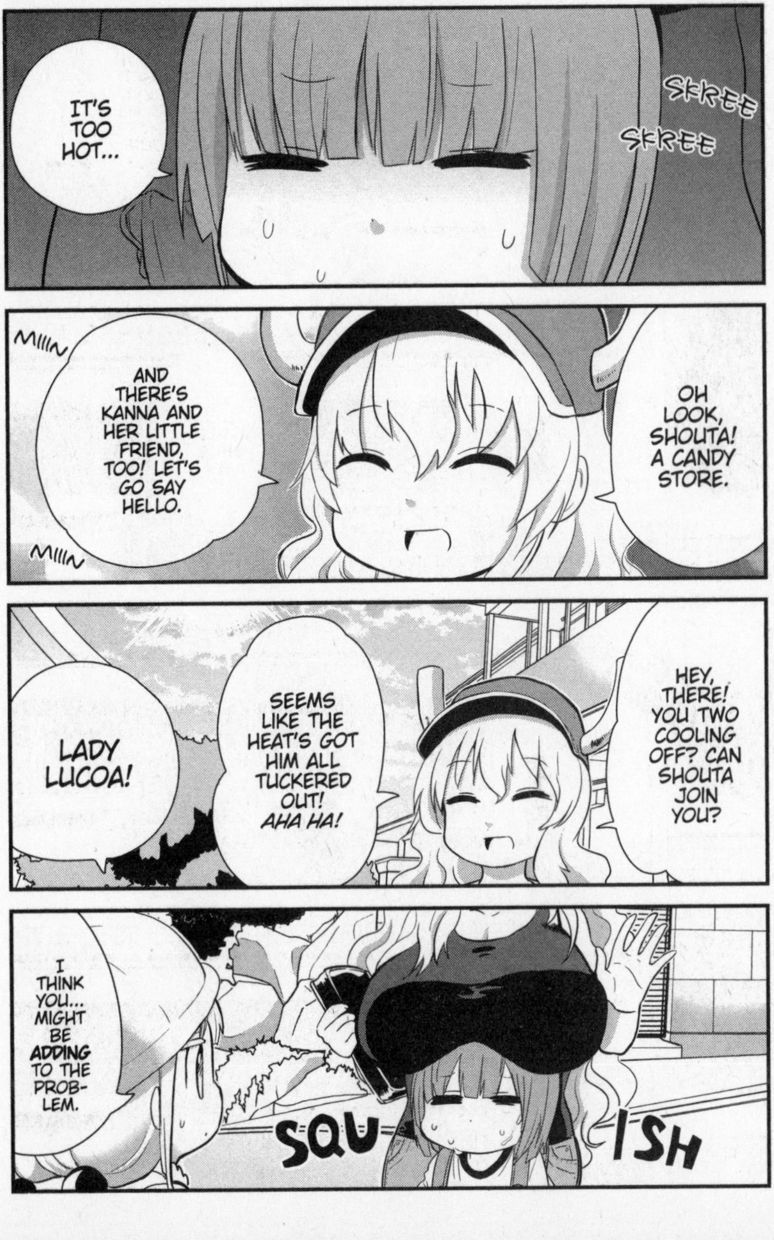
SKREE
SKREE
IT'S TOO HOT...
OH LOOK, SHOUTA! A CANDY STORE.
MIIIN
AND THERE'S KANNA AND HER LITTLE FRIEND, TOO! LET'S GO SAY HELLO.
MIIIN
HEY, THERE! YOU TWO COOLING OFF? CAN SHOUTA JOIN YOU?
SEEMS LIKE THE HEAT'S GOT HIM ALL TUCKERED OUT! AHA HA!
LADY LUCOA!
I THINK YOU... MIGHT BE ADDING TO THE PROB-LEM.
SQU ISH

SWEETS TO THE SWEET

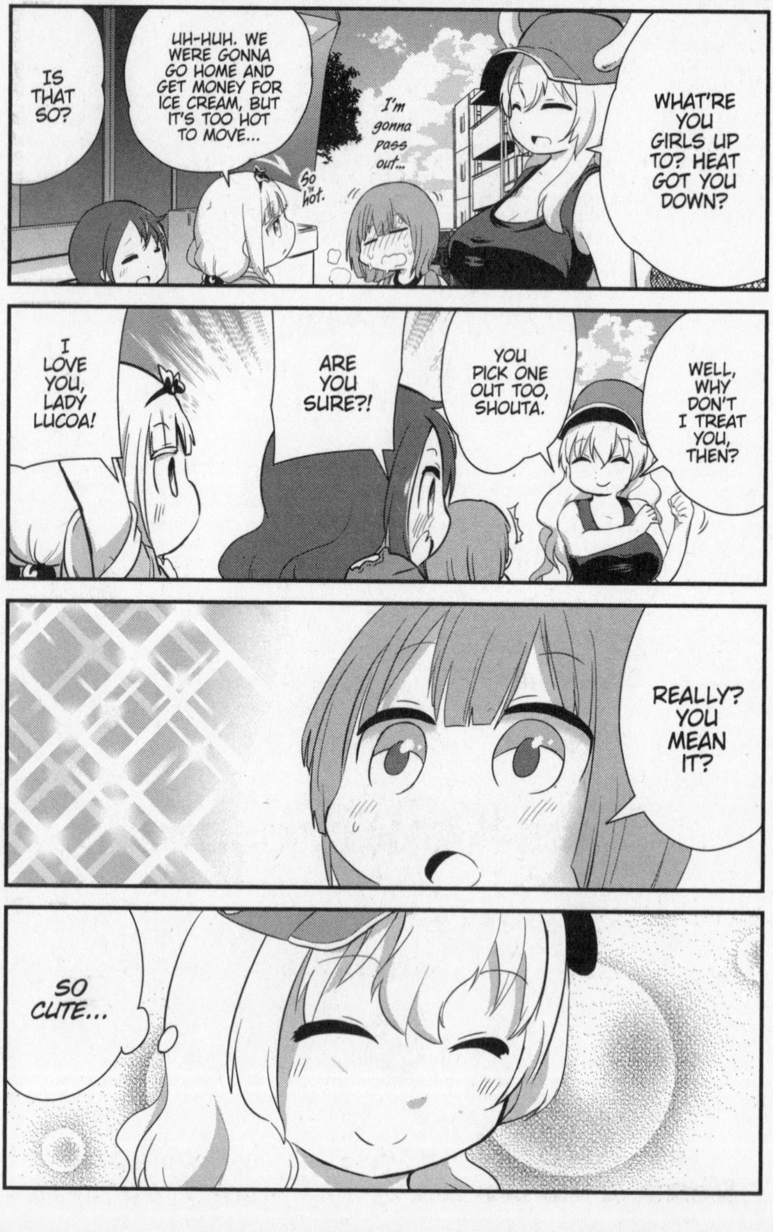
WHAT'RE YOU GIRLS UP TO? HEAT GOT YOU DOWN?
I'm gonna pass out...
So hot.
UH-HUH. WE WERE GONNA GO HOME AND GET MONEY FOR ICE CREAM, BUT IT'S TOO HOT TO MOVE...
IS THAT SO?
WELL, WHY DON'T I TREAT YOU, THEN?
YOU PICK ONE OUT TOO, SHOUTA.
ARE YOU SURE?!
I LOVE YOU, LADY LUCOA!
REALLY? YOU MEAN IT?
SO CUTE...

ALMOST FORGOT

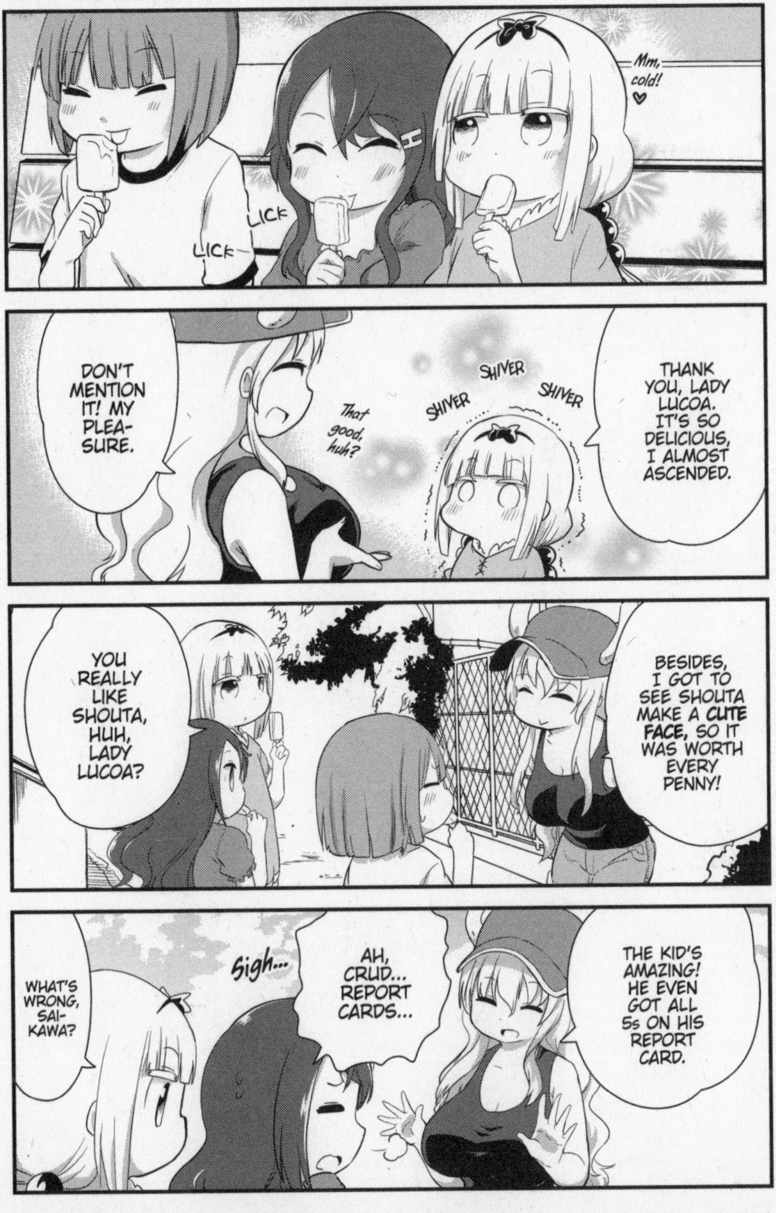
Mm, cold! ♥
LICK
LICK
THANK YOU, LADY LUCOA. IT'S SO DELICIOUS, I ALMOST ASCENDED.
SHIVER
SHIVER
SHIVER
That good, huh?
DON'T MENTION IT! MY PLEA-SURE.
BESIDES, I GOT TO SEE SHOUTA MAKE A **CUTE FACE,** SO IT WAS WORTH EVERY PENNY!
YOU REALLY LIKE SHOUTA, HUH, LADY LUCOA?
THE KID'S AMAZING! HE EVEN GOT ALL 5s ON HIS REPORT CARD.
AH, CRUD... REPORT CARDS...
Sigh...
WHAT'S WRONG, SAI-KAWA?

NO HESITATION!

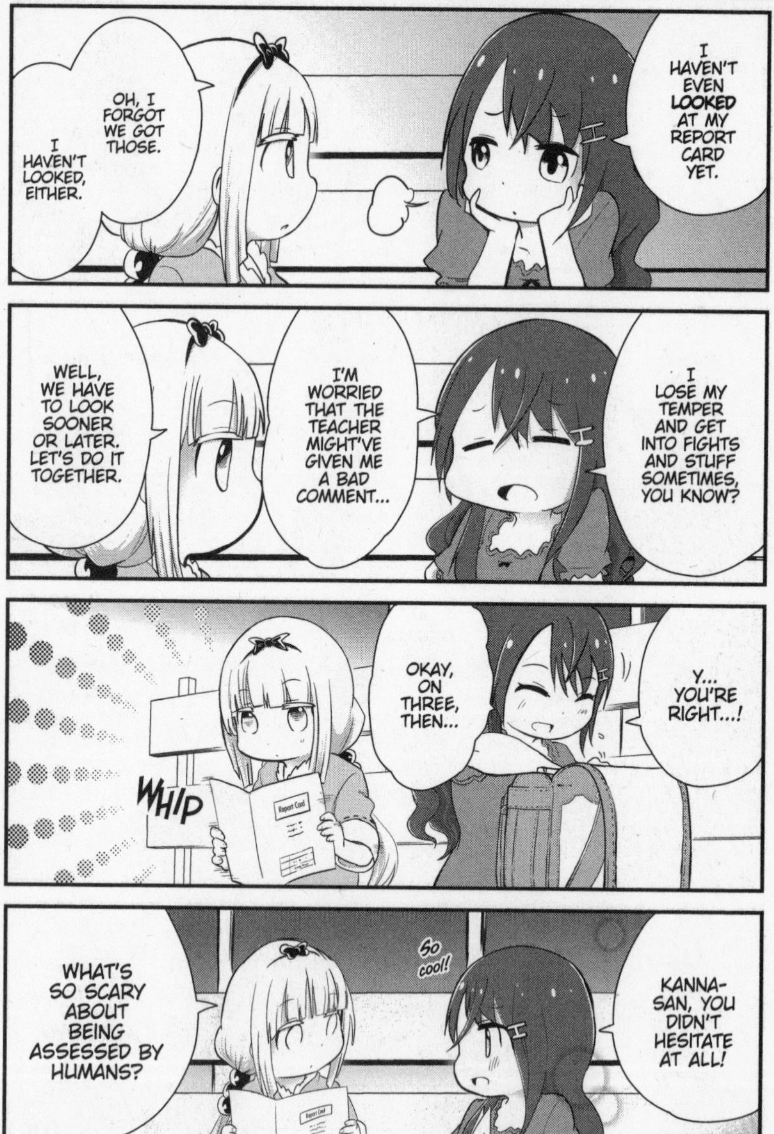
I HAVEN'T EVEN LOOKED AT MY REPORT CARD YET.
OH, I FORGOT WE GOT THOSE.
I HAVEN'T LOOKED, EITHER.
I LOSE MY TEMPER AND GET INTO FIGHTS AND STUFF SOMETIMES, YOU KNOW?
I'M WORRIED THAT THE TEACHER MIGHT'VE GIVEN ME A BAD COMMENT...
WELL, WE HAVE TO LOOK SOONER OR LATER. LET'S DO IT TOGETHER.
Y... YOU'RE RIGHT...!
OKAY, ON THREE, THEN...
WHIP
Report Card
KANNA-SAN, YOU DIDN'T HESITATE AT ALL!
So cool!
WHAT'S SO SCARY ABOUT BEING ASSESSED BY HUMANS?

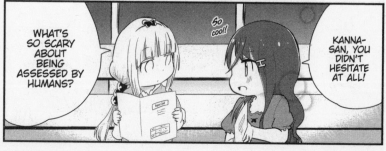

I KNOW HER BEST

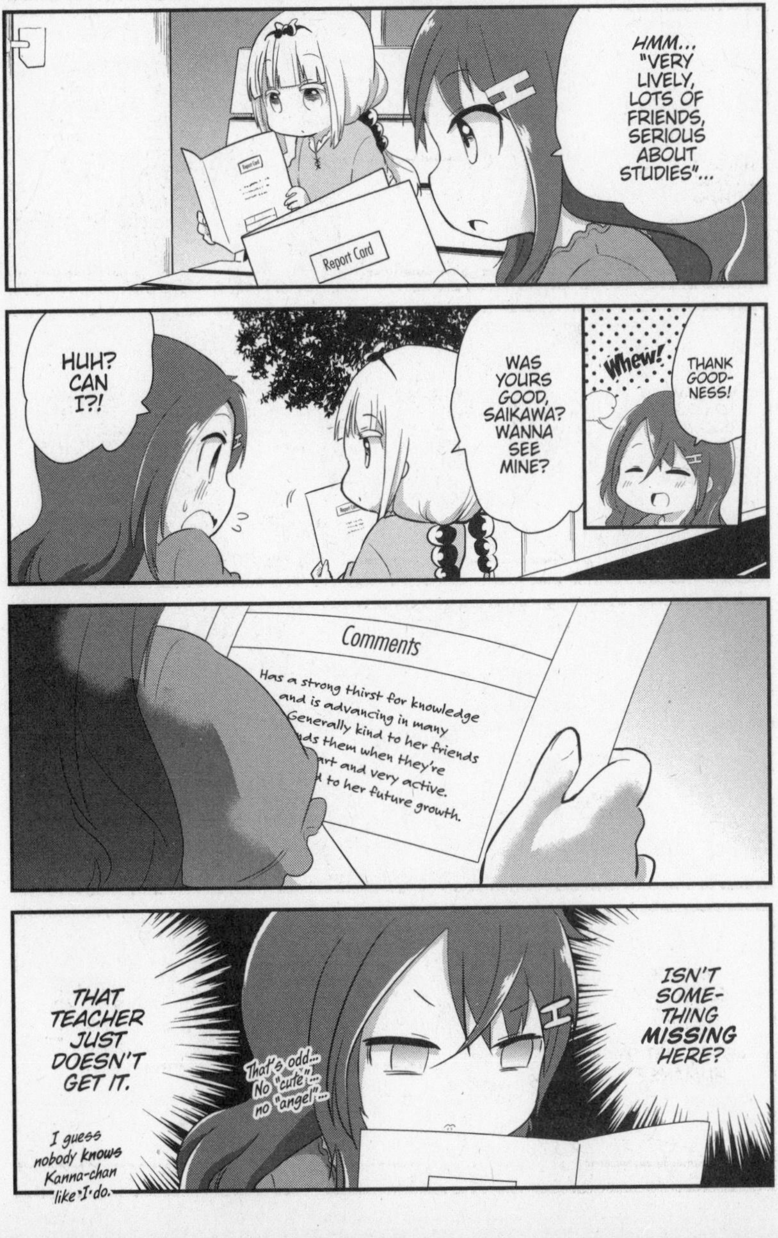

HMM... "VERY LIVELY, LOTS OF FRIENDS, SERIOUS ABOUT STUDIES"...
Report Card
THANK GOODNESS!
Whew!
WAS YOURS GOOD, SAIKAWA? WANNA SEE MINE?
HUH? CAN I?!
Comments
Has a strong thirst for knowledge
and is advancing in many
Generally kind to her friends
nds them when they're
art and very active.
d to her future growth.
ISN'T SOMETHING MISSING HERE?
That's odd... No "cute"... no "angel"...
THAT TEACHER JUST DOESN'T GET IT.
I guess nobody knows Kanna-chan like I do.

WILL IT BE DONE BY 8/31?

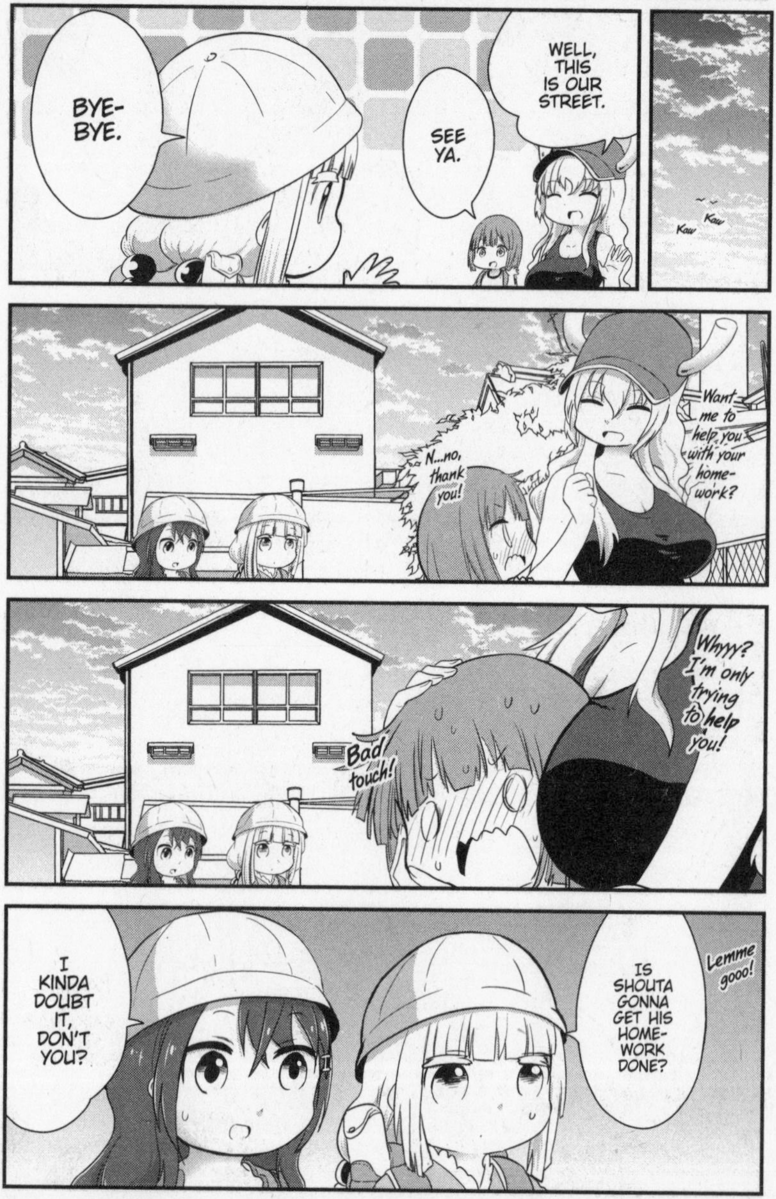
Kaw
Kaw
WELL, THIS IS OUR STREET.
SEE YA.
BYE-BYE.
Want me to help you with your home-work?
N...no, thank you!
Whyyy? I'm only trying to help you!
Bad touch!
Lemme gooo!
IS SHOUTA GONNA GET HIS HOME-WORK DONE?
I KINDA DOUBT IT, DON'T YOU?

PARTING IS SUCH SWEET SORROW...

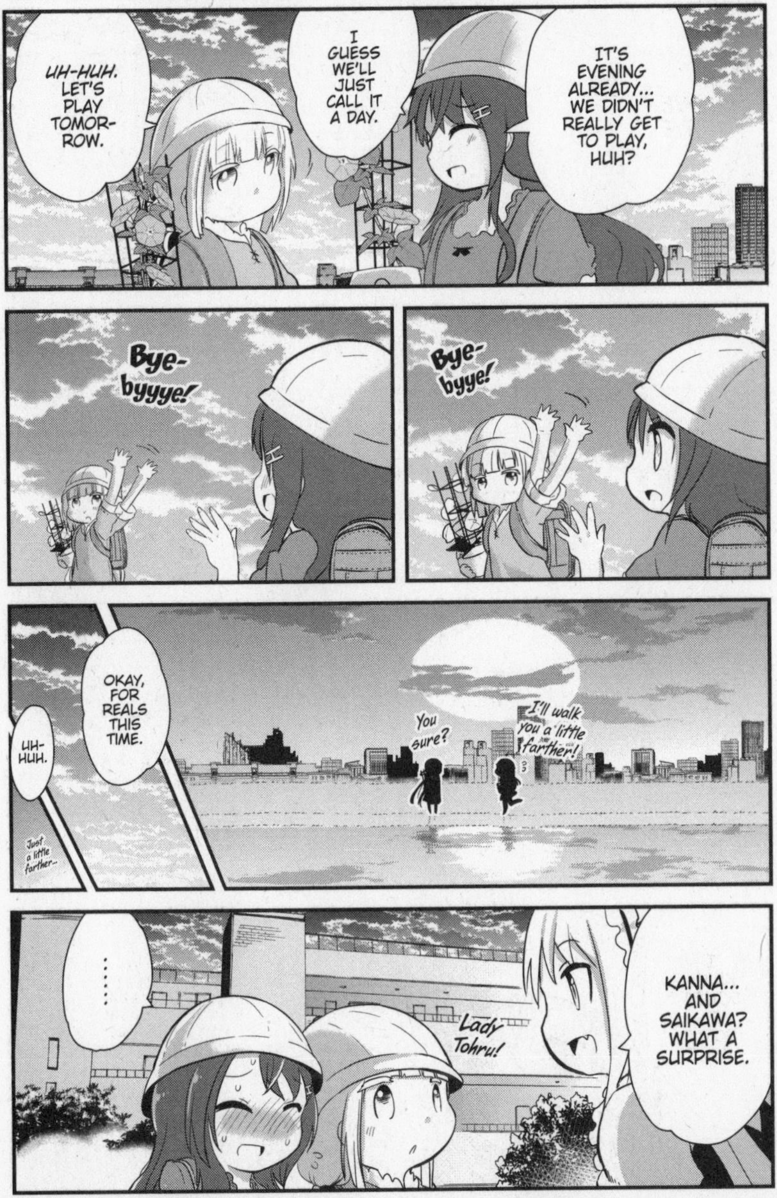
IT'S EVENING ALREADY... WE DIDN'T REALLY GET TO PLAY, HUH?
I GUESS WE'LL JUST CALL IT A DAY.
UH-HUH. LET'S PLAY TOMOR-ROW.
Bye-byye!
Bye-byyye!
I'll walk you a little farther!
You sure?
OKAY, FOR REALS THIS TIME.
UH-HUH.
Just a little farther...
KANNA... AND SAIKAWA? WHAT A SURPRISE.
Lady Tohru!
......

EXCITING SUMMER VACATION

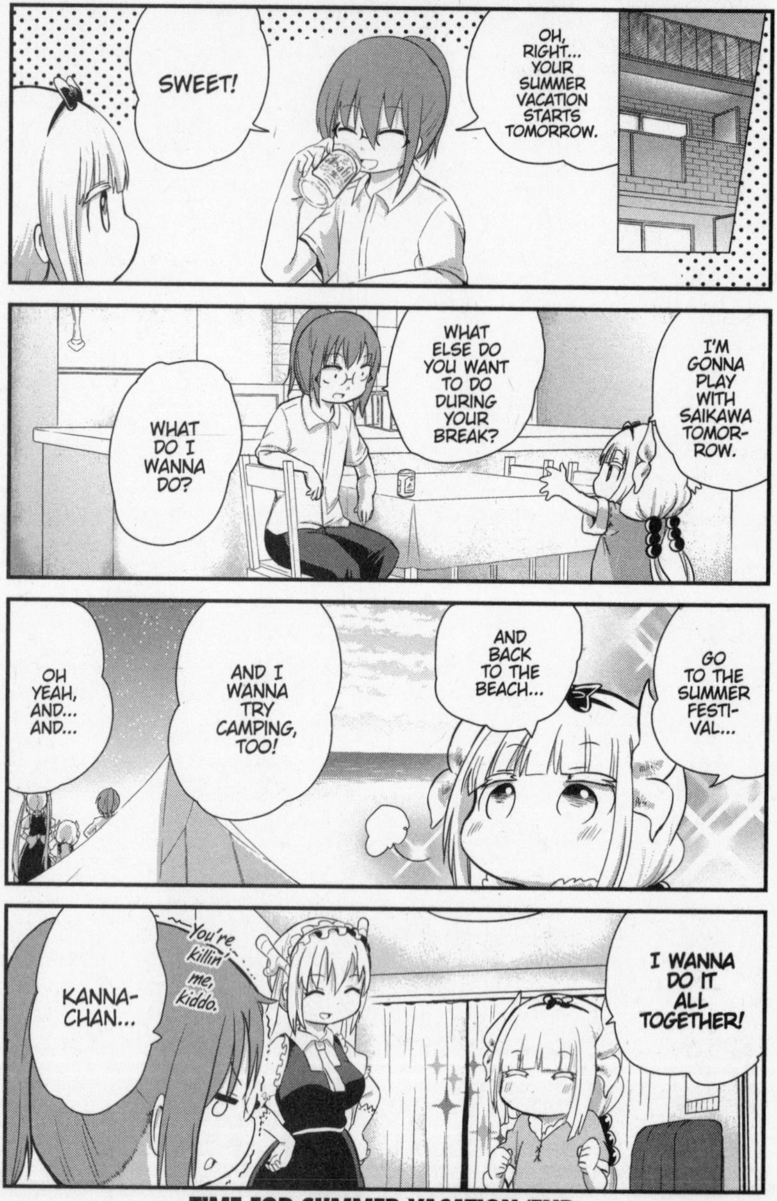
OH, RIGHT... YOUR SUMMER VACATION STARTS TOMORROW.
SWEET!
I'M GONNA PLAY WITH SAIKAWA TOMORROW.
WHAT ELSE DO YOU WANT TO DO DURING YOUR BREAK?
WHAT DO I WANNA DO?
GO TO THE SUMMER FESTIVAL...
AND BACK TO THE BEACH...
AND I WANNA TRY CAMPING, TOO!
OH YEAH, AND... AND...
I WANNA DO IT ALL TOGETHER!
You're killin' me, kiddo.
KANNA-CHAN...

TIME FOR SUMMER VACATION/END

I hope
tomorrow
comes
soon...

Miss Kobayashi's Dragon Maid

Kanna's Daily Life

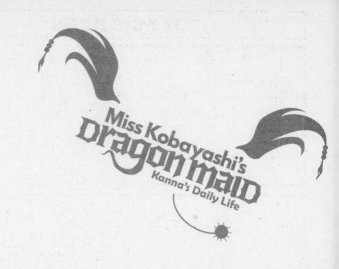

THE WORD IS "TAN"

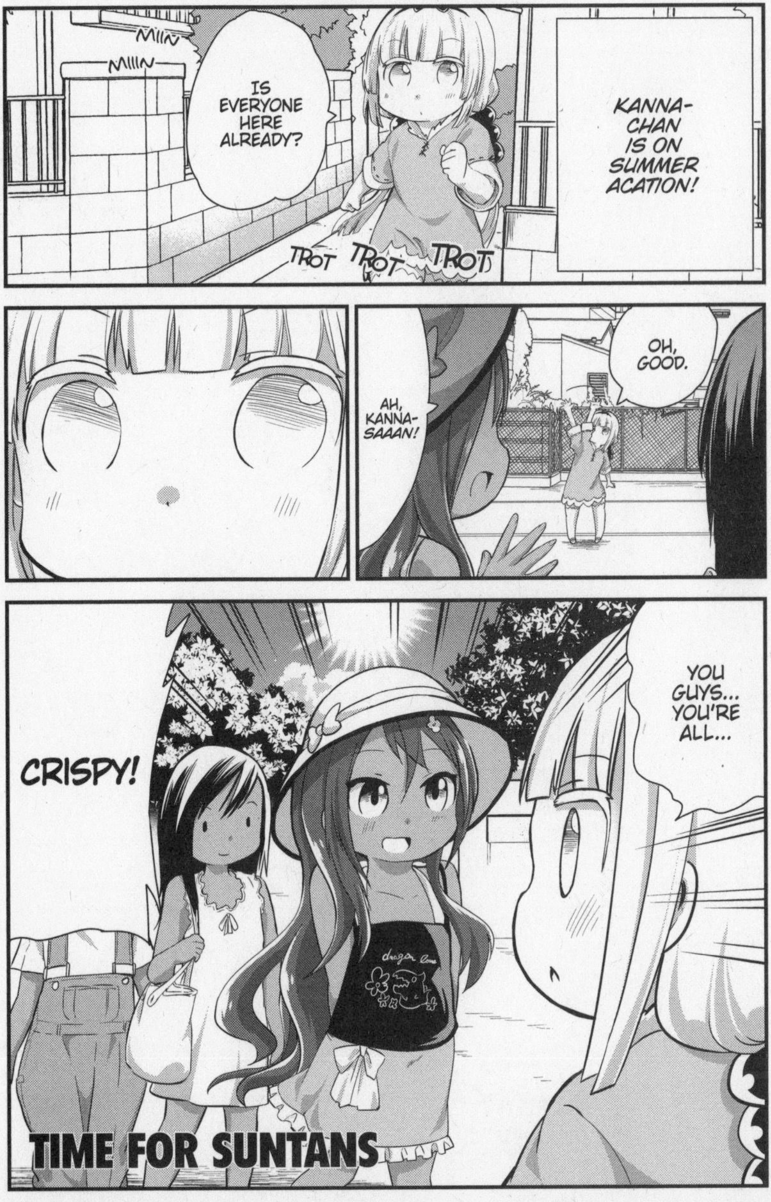
KANNA-CHAN IS ON SUMMER ACATION!
MIIN
MIIN
IS EVERYONE HERE ALREADY?
TROT TROT TROT
OH, GOOD.
AH, KANNA-SAAAN!
YOU GUYS... YOU'RE ALL...
CRISPY!
TIME FOR SUNTANS

I WANNA BE TAN, TOO!

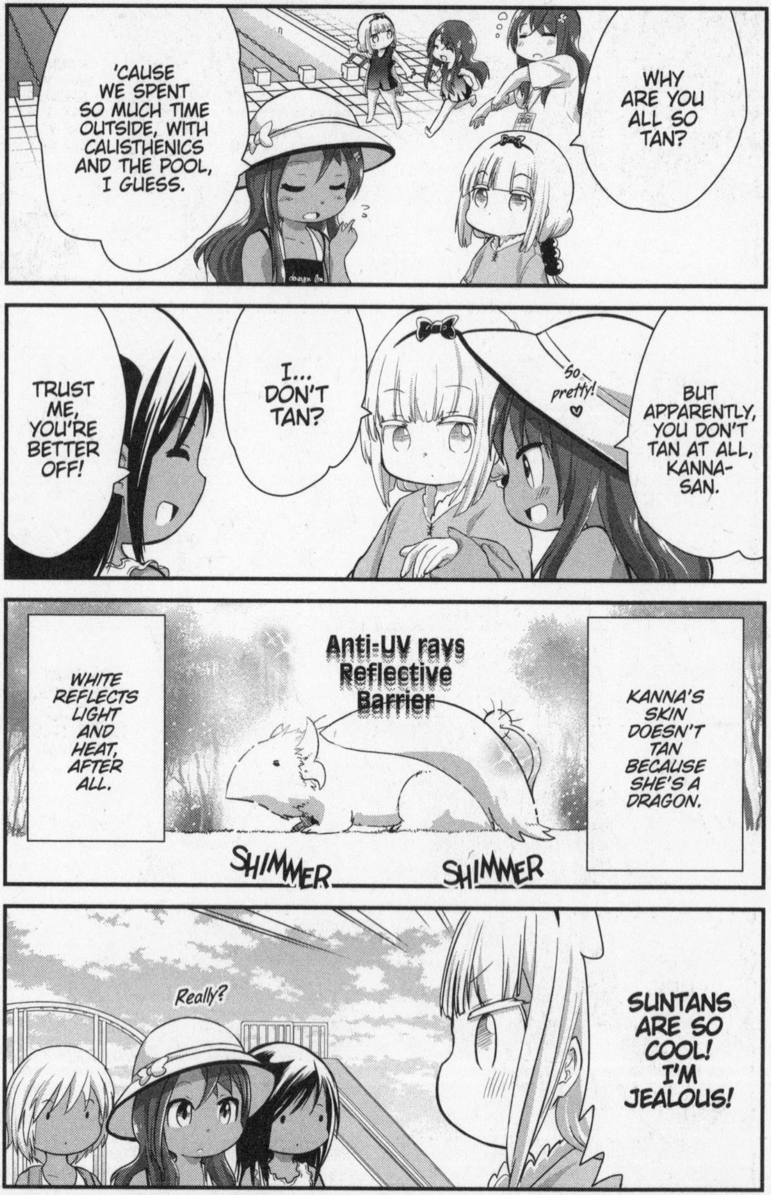
WHY ARE YOU ALL SO TAN?
'CAUSE WE SPENT SO MUCH TIME OUTSIDE, WITH CALISTHENICS AND THE POOL, I GUESS.
BUT APPARENTLY, YOU DON'T TAN AT ALL, KANNA-SAN.
So pretty! ♥
I... DON'T TAN?
TRUST ME, YOU'RE BETTER OFF!
KANNA'S SKIN DOESN'T TAN BECAUSE SHE'S A DRAGON.
Anti-UV rays Reflective Barrier
WHITE REFLECTS LIGHT AND HEAT, AFTER ALL.
SHIMMER
SHIMMER
SUNTANS ARE SO COOL! I'M JEALOUS!
Really?

STROKE OF GENIUS

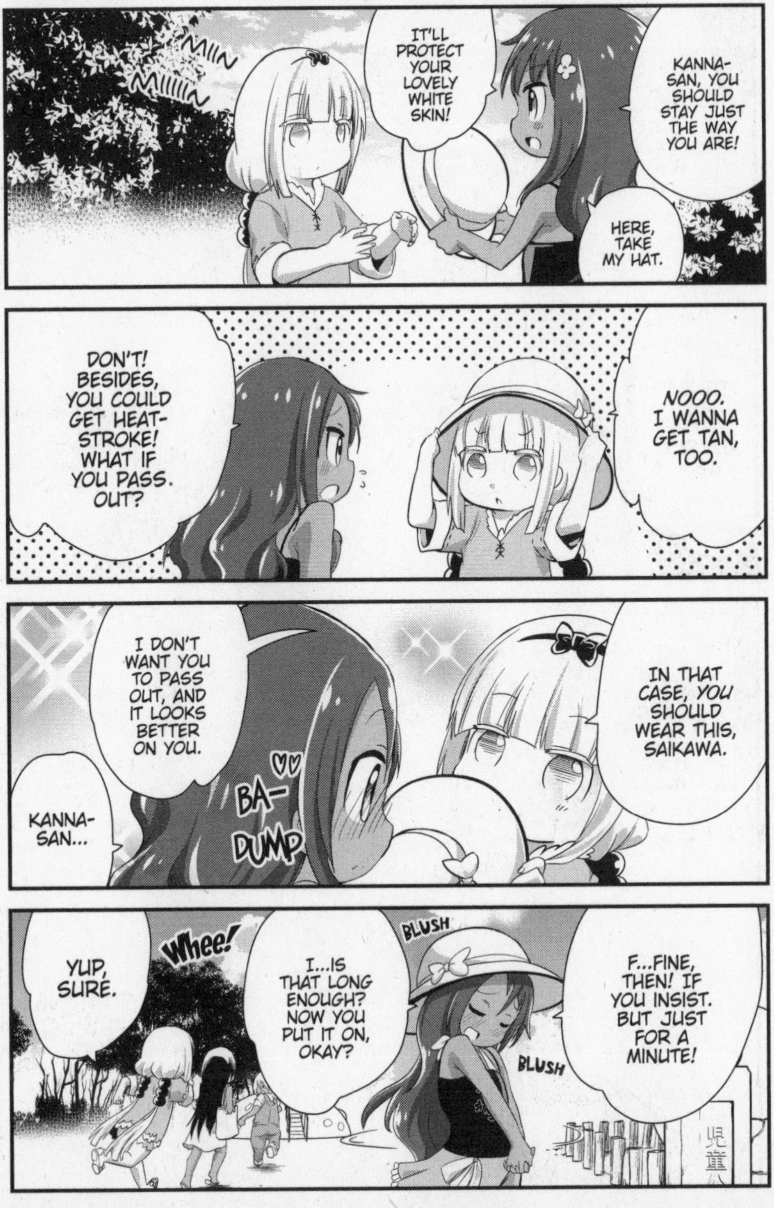

KANNA-SAN, YOU SHOULD STAY JUST THE WAY YOU ARE!
HERE, TAKE MY HAT.
IT'LL PROTECT YOUR LOVELY WHITE SKIN!
MIIN
MIIIIN
NOOO. I WANNA GET TAN, TOO.
DON'T! BESIDES, YOU COULD GET HEAT-STROKE! WHAT IF YOU PASS. OUT?
IN THAT CASE, YOU SHOULD WEAR THIS, SAIKAWA.
I DON'T WANT YOU TO PASS OUT, AND IT LOOKS BETTER ON YOU.
BA-DUMP
KANNA-SAN...
F...FINE, THEN! IF YOU INSIST. BUT JUST FOR A MINUTE!
児童公
BLUSH
BLUSH
I...IS THAT LONG ENOUGH? NOW YOU PUT IT ON, OKAY?
Whee!
YUP, SURE.

AP-PEELING SITUATION

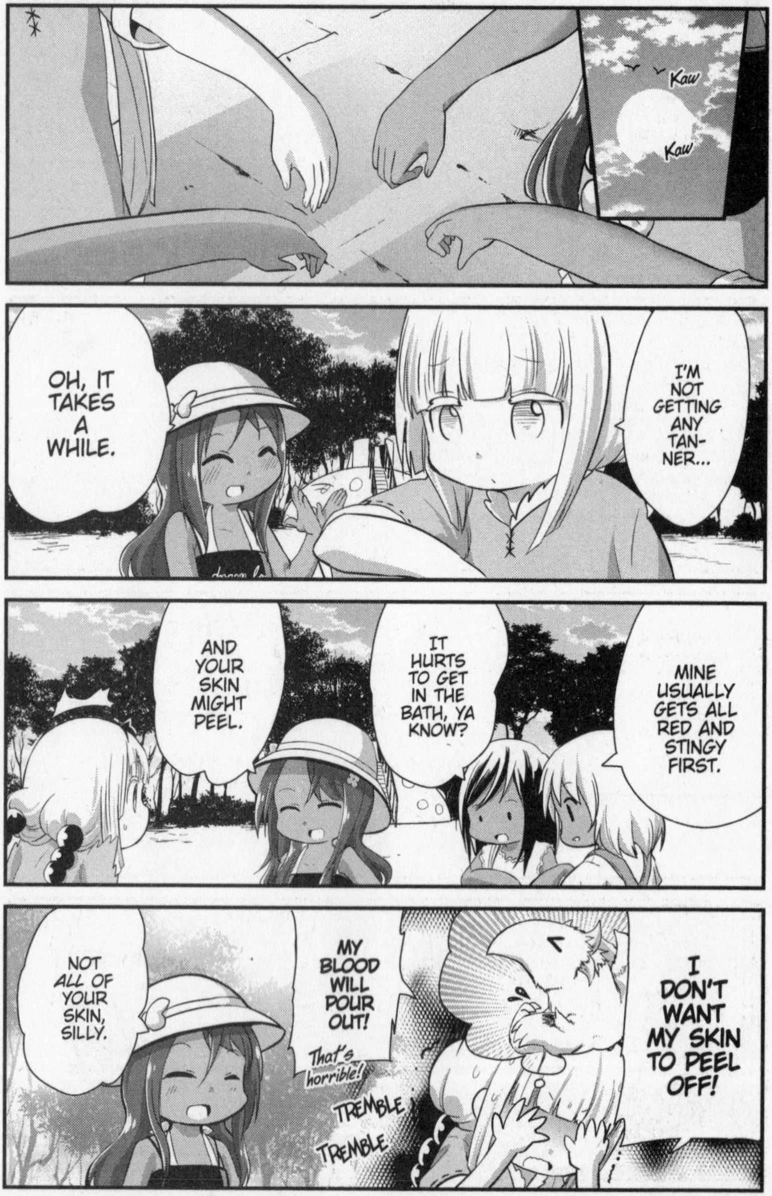
Kaw
Kaw
I'M NOT GETTING ANY TAN-NER...
OH, IT TAKES A WHILE.
MINE USUALLY GETS ALL RED AND STINGY FIRST.
IT HURTS TO GET IN THE BATH, YA KNOW?
AND YOUR SKIN MIGHT PEEL.
I DON'T WANT MY SKIN TO PEEL OFF!
TREMBLE
TREMBLE
MY BLOOD WILL POUR OUT!
That's horrible!
NOT ALL OF YOUR SKIN, SILLY.

YOU DON'T GET IT, KOBAYASHI!

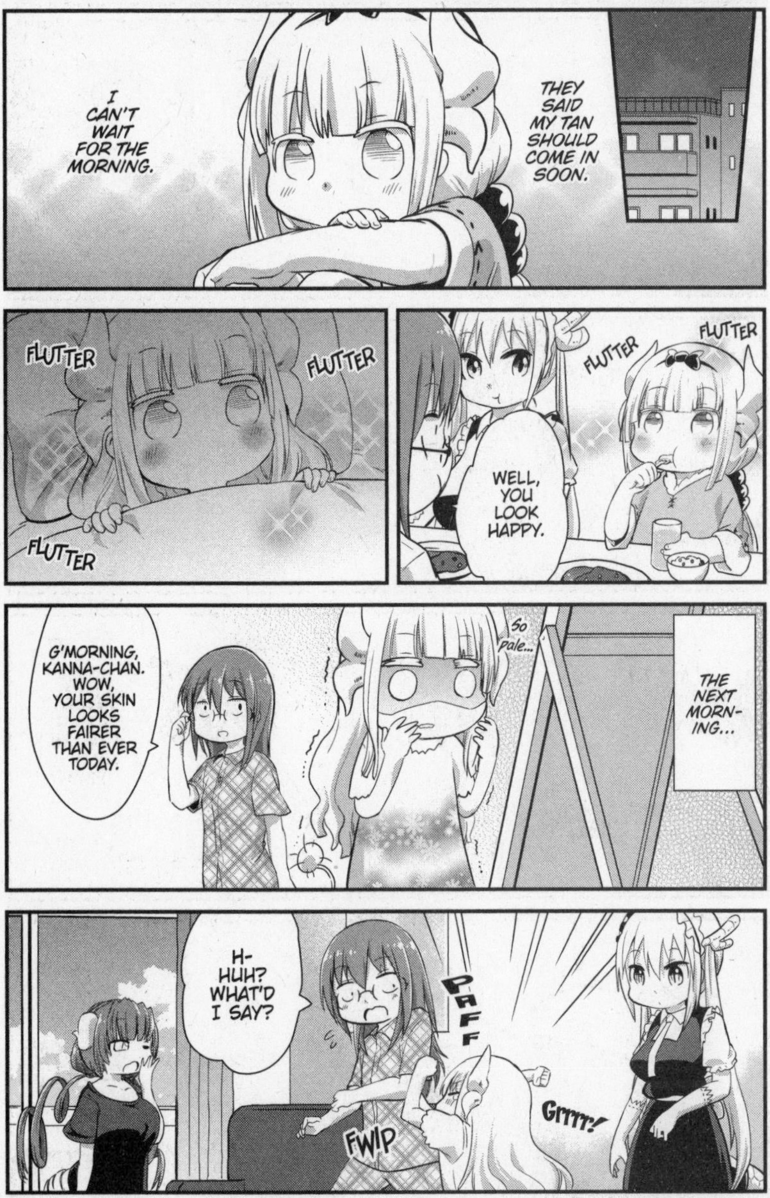
THEY SAID MY TAN SHOULD COME IN SOON.
I CAN'T WAIT FOR THE MORNING.
FLUTTER
FLUTTER
WELL, YOU LOOK HAPPY.
FLUTTER
FLUTTER
FLUTTER
THE NEXT MORNING...
So pale...
G'MORNING, KANNA-CHAN. WOW, YOUR SKIN LOOKS FAIRER THAN EVER TODAY.
Grrrr!
PAFF
FWIP
H-HUH? WHAT'D I SAY?

MISSION A-TAN-ABLE?

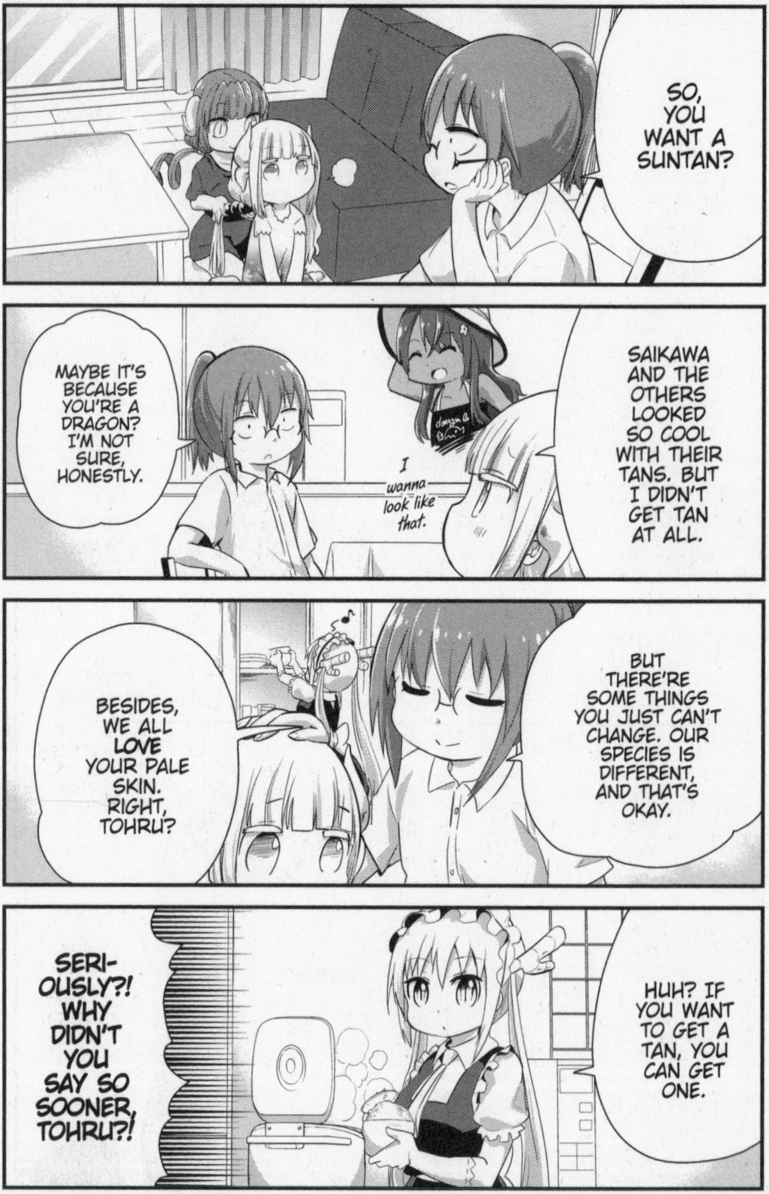
SO, YOU WANT A SUNTAN?
SAIKAWA AND THE OTHERS LOOKED SO COOL WITH THEIR TANS. BUT I DIDN'T GET TAN AT ALL.
I wanna look like that.
MAYBE IT'S BECAUSE YOU'RE A DRAGON? I'M NOT SURE, HONESTLY.
BUT THERE'RE SOME THINGS YOU JUST CAN'T CHANGE. OUR SPECIES IS DIFFERENT, AND THAT'S OKAY.
BESIDES, WE ALL LOVE YOUR PALE SKIN. RIGHT, TOHRU?
HUH? IF YOU WANT TO GET A TAN, YOU CAN GET ONE.
SERI-OUSLY?! WHY DIDN'T YOU SAY SO SOONER, TOHRU?!

TOHRU THE TAN

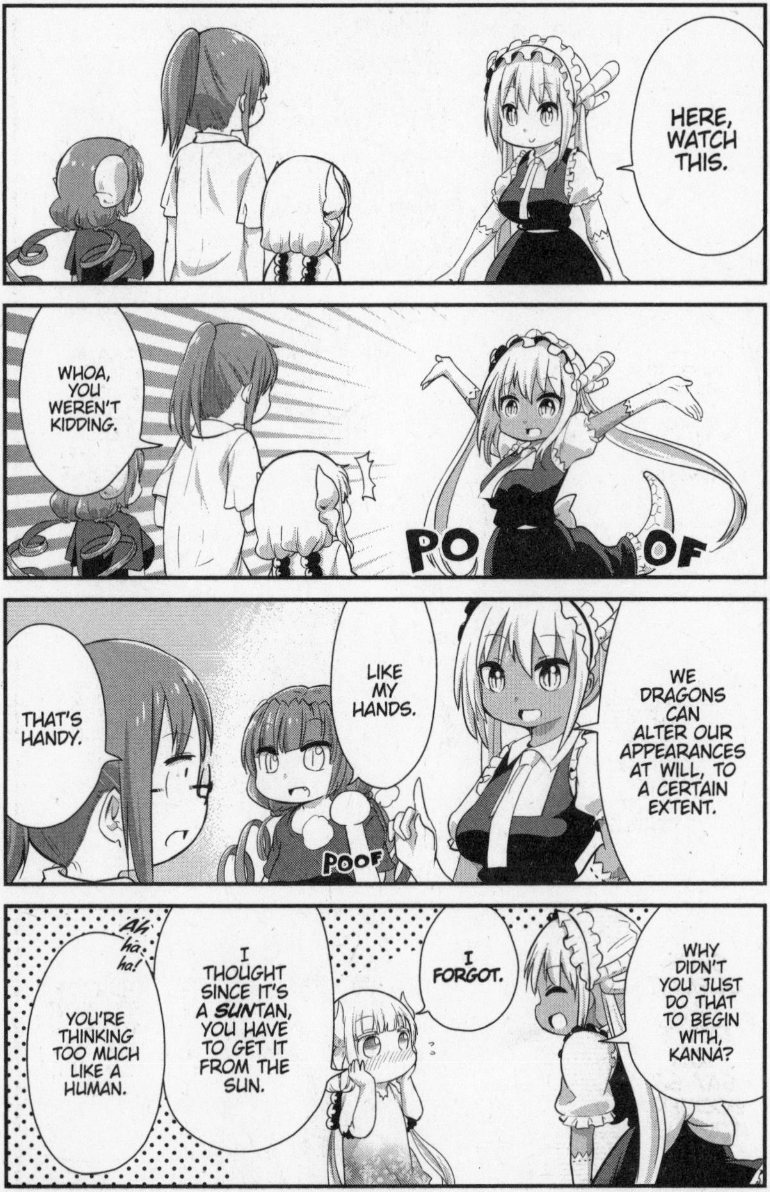
HERE, WATCH THIS.
POO OF
WHOA, YOU WEREN'T KIDDING.
WE DRAGONS CAN ALTER OUR APPEARANCES AT WILL, TO A CERTAIN EXTENT.
LIKE MY HANDS.
POOF
THAT'S HANDY.
WHY DIDN'T YOU JUST DO THAT TO BEGIN WITH, KANNA?
I FORGOT.
I THOUGHT SINCE IT'S A SUNTAN, YOU HAVE TO GET IT FROM THE SUN.
Ah ha ha!
YOU'RE THINKING TOO MUCH LIKE A HUMAN.

THE HORROR!

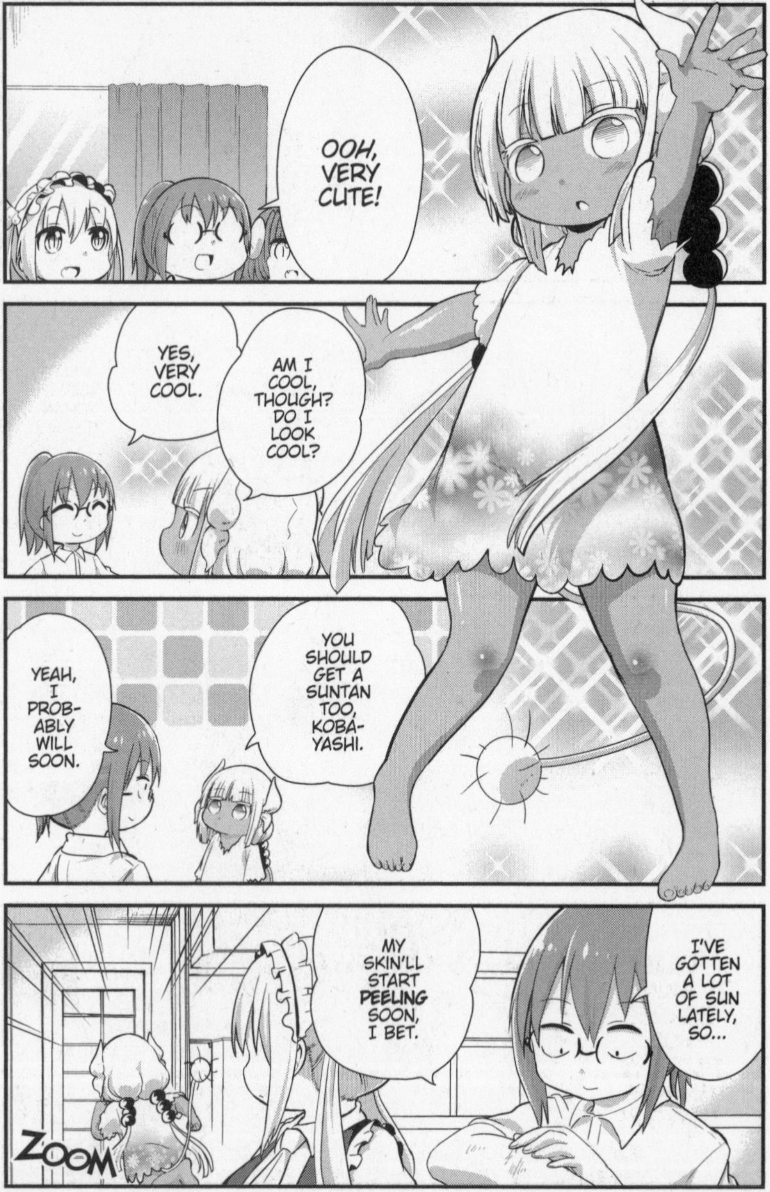
OOH, VERY CUTE!
AM I COOL, THOUGH? DO I LOOK COOL?
YES, VERY COOL.
YOU SHOULD GET A SUNTAN TOO, KOBA-YASHI.
YEAH, I PROBABLY WILL SOON.
I'VE GOTTEN A LOT OF SUN LATELY, SO...
MY SKIN'LL START PEELING SOON, I BET.
ZOOM

THAT'S WAY SCARIER

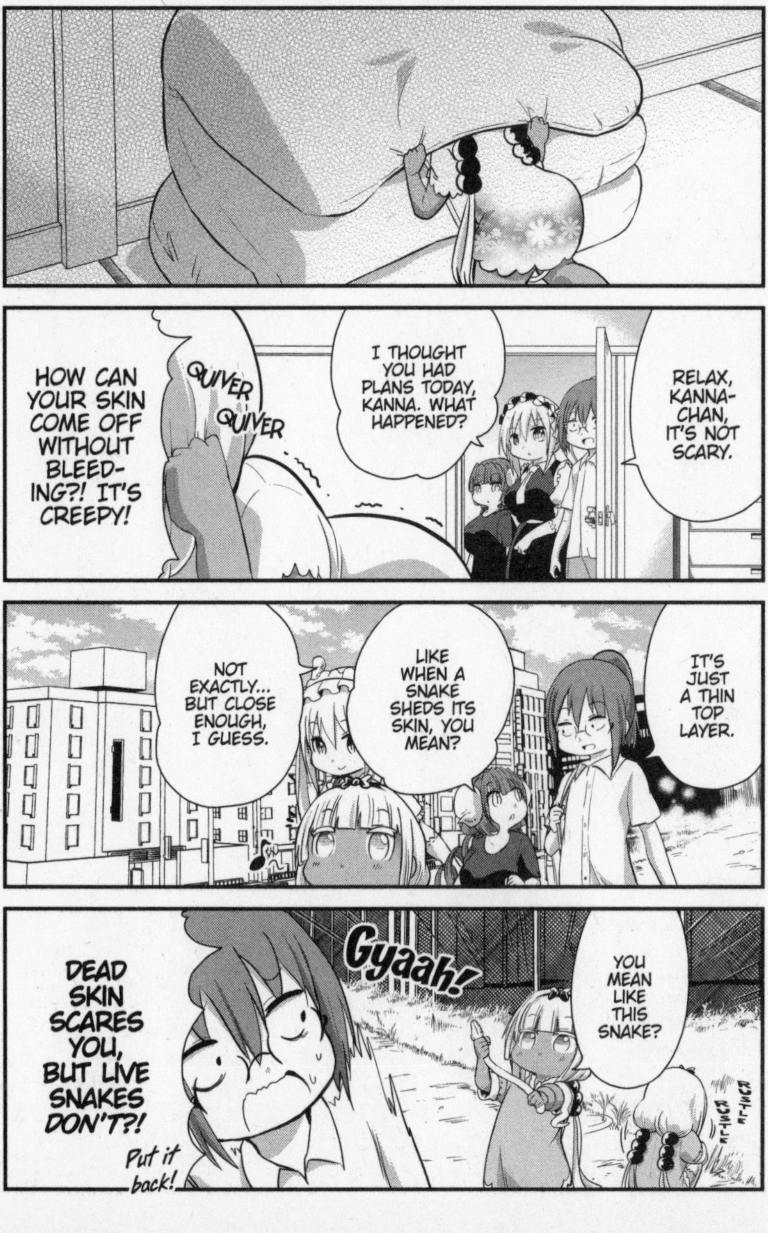
RELAX, KANNA-CHAN, IT'S NOT SCARY.
I THOUGHT YOU HAD PLANS TODAY, KANNA. WHAT HAPPENED?
QUIVER QUIVER
HOW CAN YOUR SKIN COME OFF WITHOUT BLEED-ING?! IT'S CREEPY!
IT'S JUST A THIN TOP LAYER.
LIKE WHEN A SNAKE SHEDS ITS SKIN, YOU MEAN?
NOT EXACTLY... BUT CLOSE ENOUGH, I GUESS.
RUSTLE RUSTLE
YOU MEAN LIKE THIS SNAKE?
Gyaah!
DEAD SKIN SCARES YOU, BUT LIVE SNAKES DON'T?!
Put it back!

JUST ANOTHER TYPICAL DAY

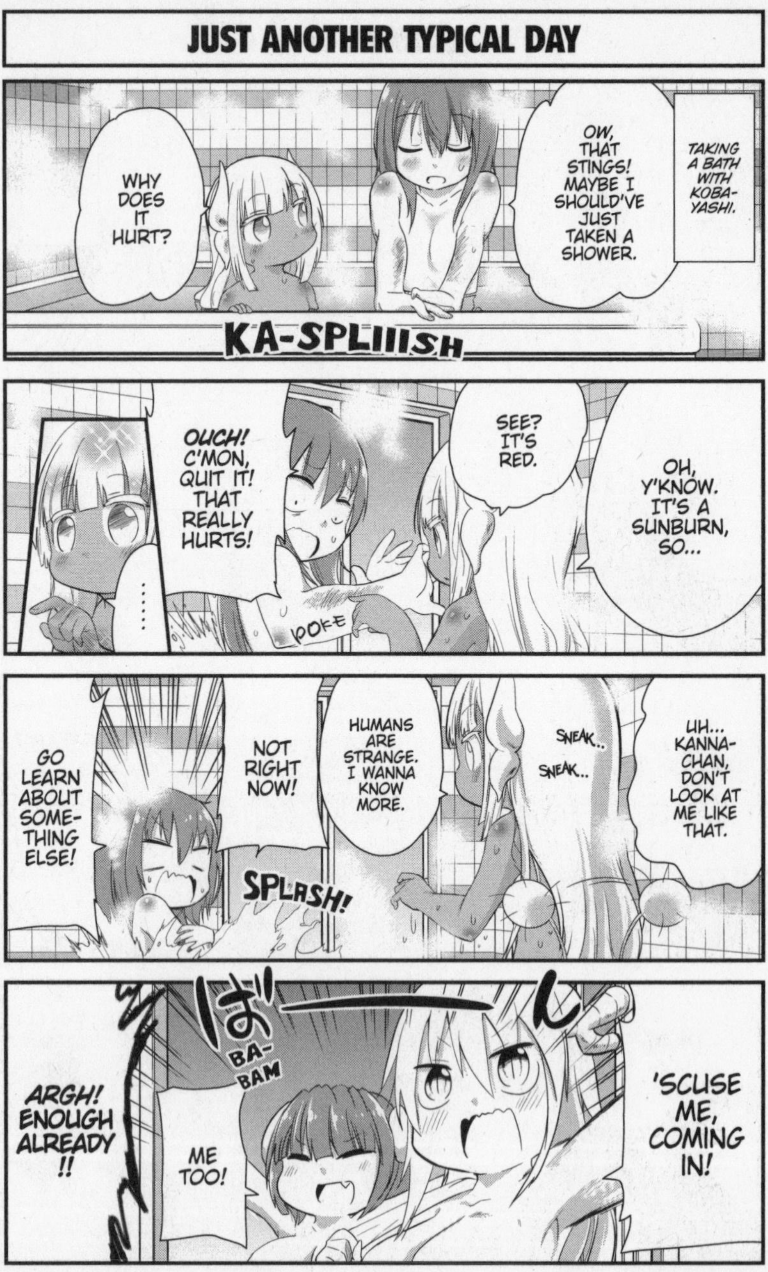
TAKING A BATH WITH KOBAYASHI.
OW, THAT STINGS! MAYBE I SHOULD'VE JUST TAKEN A SHOWER.
WHY DOES IT HURT?
KA-SPLIIISH
OH, Y'KNOW. IT'S A SUNBURN, SO...
SEE? IT'S RED.
OUCH! C'MON, QUIT IT! THAT REALLY HURTS!
POKE
......
UH... KANNA-CHAN, DON'T LOOK AT ME LIKE THAT.
SNEAK..
SNEAK..
HUMANS ARE STRANGE. I WANNA KNOW MORE.
NOT RIGHT NOW!
GO LEARN ABOUT SOMETHING ELSE!
SPLASH!
ば———ん
BA-BAM
'SCUSE ME, COMING IN!
ME TOO!
ARGH! ENOUGH ALREADY!!

THANKS...!

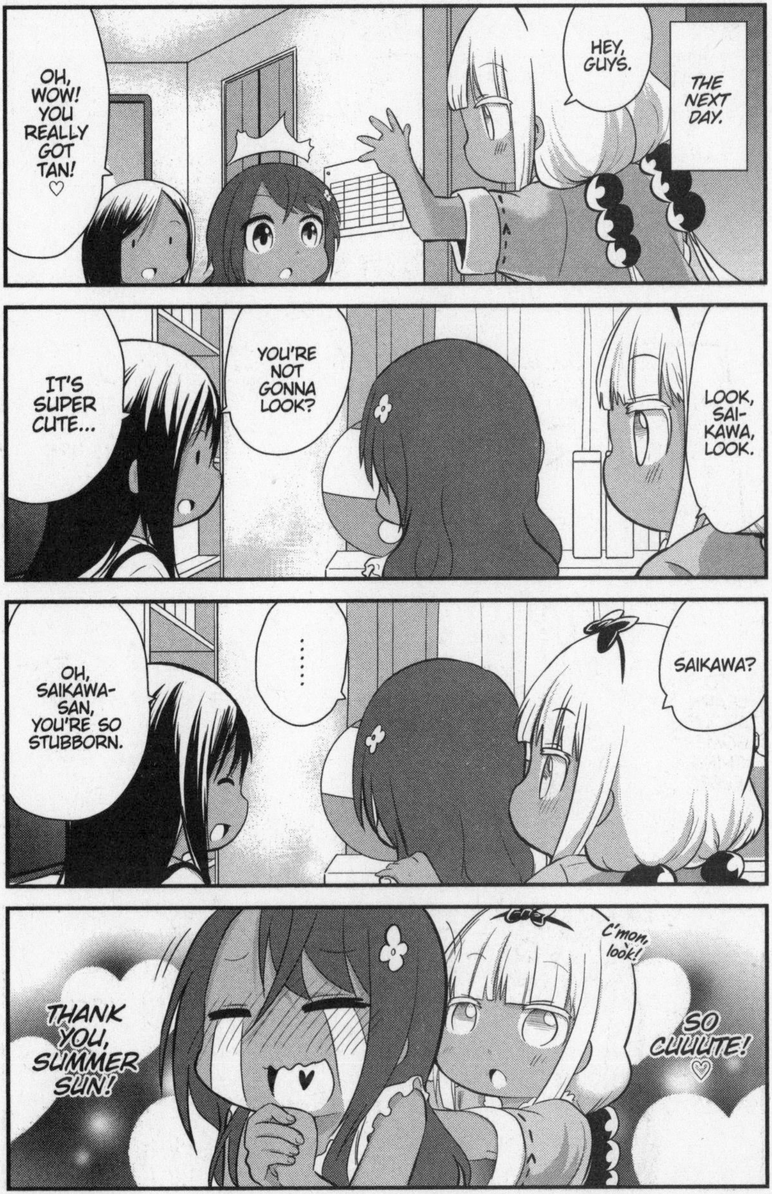
THE NEXT DAY.
HEY, GUYS.
OH, WOW! YOU REALLY GOT TAN! ♡
LOOK, SAIKAWA, LOOK.
YOU'RE NOT GONNA LOOK?
IT'S SUPER CUTE...
SAIKAWA?
......
OH, SAIKAWA-SAN, YOU'RE SO STUBBORN.
C'mon, look!
SO CUUUTE! ♡
THANK YOU, SUMMER SUN!

TIME FOR A FASHION SHOW

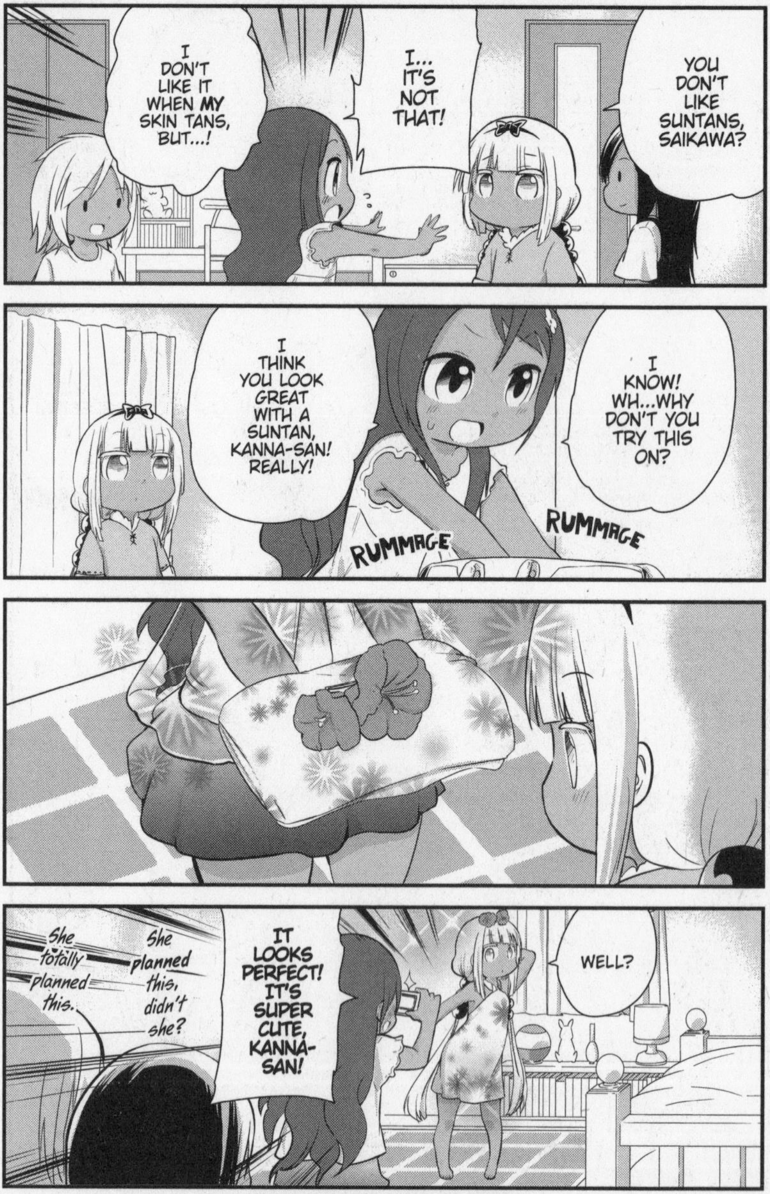

YOU DON'T LIKE SUNTANS, SAIKAWA?
I... IT'S NOT THAT!
I DON'T LIKE IT WHEN MY SKIN TANS, BUT...!
I KNOW! WH...WHY DON'T YOU TRY THIS ON?
I THINK YOU LOOK GREAT WITH A SUNTAN, KANNA-SAN! REALLY!
RUMMAGE
RUMMAGE
WELL?
IT LOOKS PERFECT! IT'S SUPER CUTE, KANNA-SAN!
She planned this, didn't she?
She totally planned this.

TIME FOR SUNTANS/END

SUMMER MORNING

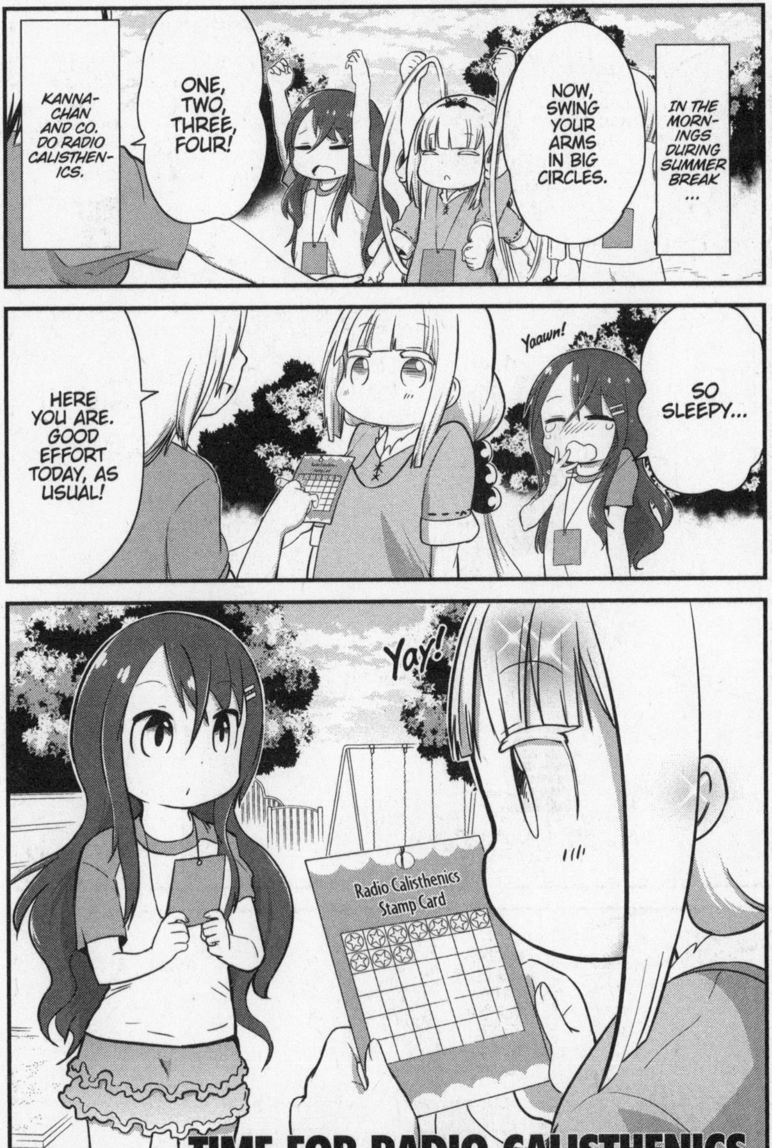
IN THE MORNINGS DURING SUMMER BREAK...
NOW, SWING YOUR ARMS IN BIG CIRCLES.
ONE, TWO, THREE, FOUR!
KANNA-CHAN AND CO. DO RADIO CALISTHENICS.
SO SLEEPY...
Yaawn!
HERE YOU ARE. GOOD EFFORT TODAY, AS USUAL!
Yay!
Radio Calisthenics Stamp Card
TIME FOR RADIO CALISTHENICS

SORT OF A SHABBY PRIZE

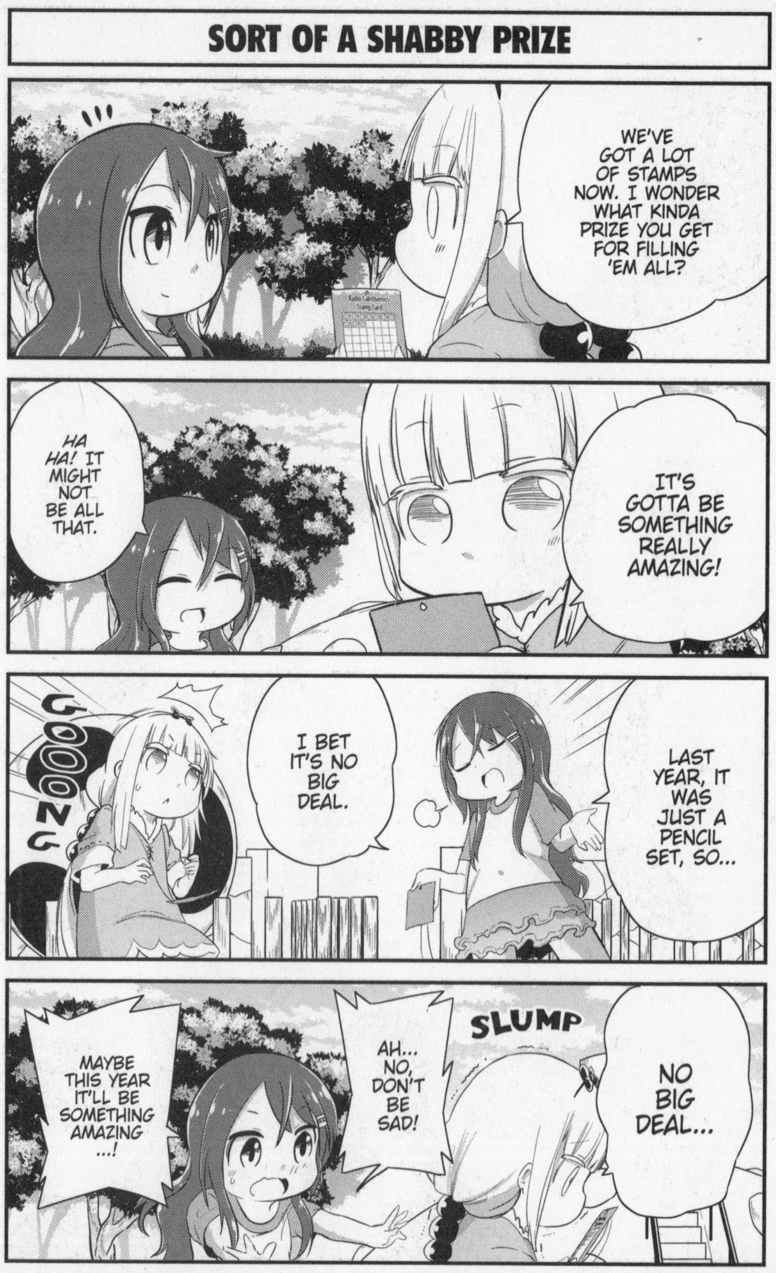
WE'VE GOT A LOT OF STAMPS NOW. I WONDER WHAT KINDA PRIZE YOU GET FOR FILLING 'EM ALL?
Radio Calisthenics Stamp Card
IT'S GOTTA BE SOMETHING REALLY AMAZING!
HA HA! IT MIGHT NOT BE ALL THAT.
LAST YEAR, IT WAS JUST A PENCIL SET, SO...
I BET IT'S NO BIG DEAL.
GOOOONG
NO BIG DEAL...
SLUMP
AH... NO, DON'T BE SAD!
MAYBE THIS YEAR IT'LL BE SOMETHING AMAZING ...!

HE RARELY GOES OUT

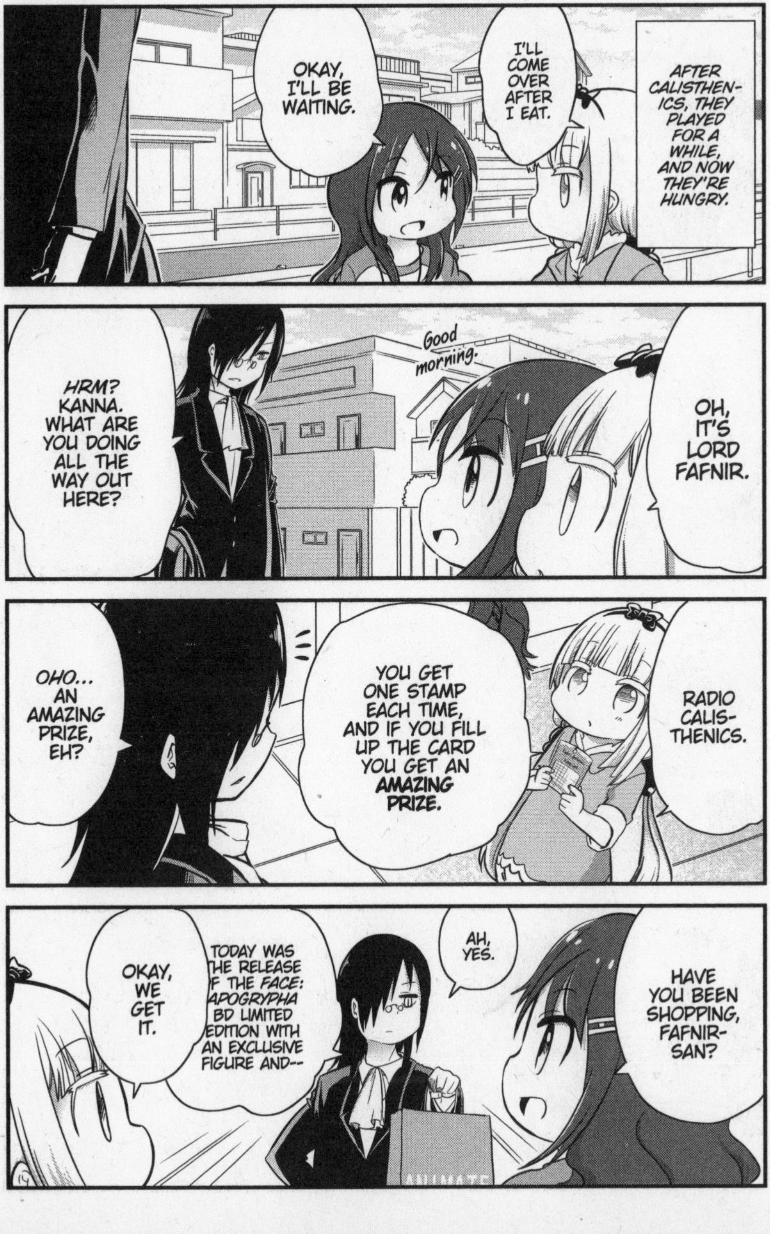
AFTER CALISTHENICS, THEY PLAYED FOR A WHILE, AND NOW THEY'RE HUNGRY.
I'LL COME OVER AFTER I EAT.
OKAY, I'LL BE WAITING.
OH, IT'S LORD FAFNIR.
Good morning.
HRM? KANNA. WHAT ARE YOU DOING ALL THE WAY OUT HERE?
RADIO CALISTHENICS.
YOU GET ONE STAMP EACH TIME, AND IF YOU FILL UP THE CARD YOU GET AN AMAZING PRIZE.
OHO... AN AMAZING PRIZE, EH?
HAVE YOU BEEN SHOPPING, FAFNIR-SAN?
AH, YES.
TODAY WAS THE RELEASE F THE FACE: APOCRYPHA BD LIMITED EDITION WITH AN EXCLUSIVE FIGURE AND--
OKAY, WE GET IT.
ANIMATE

NON SEQUITUR

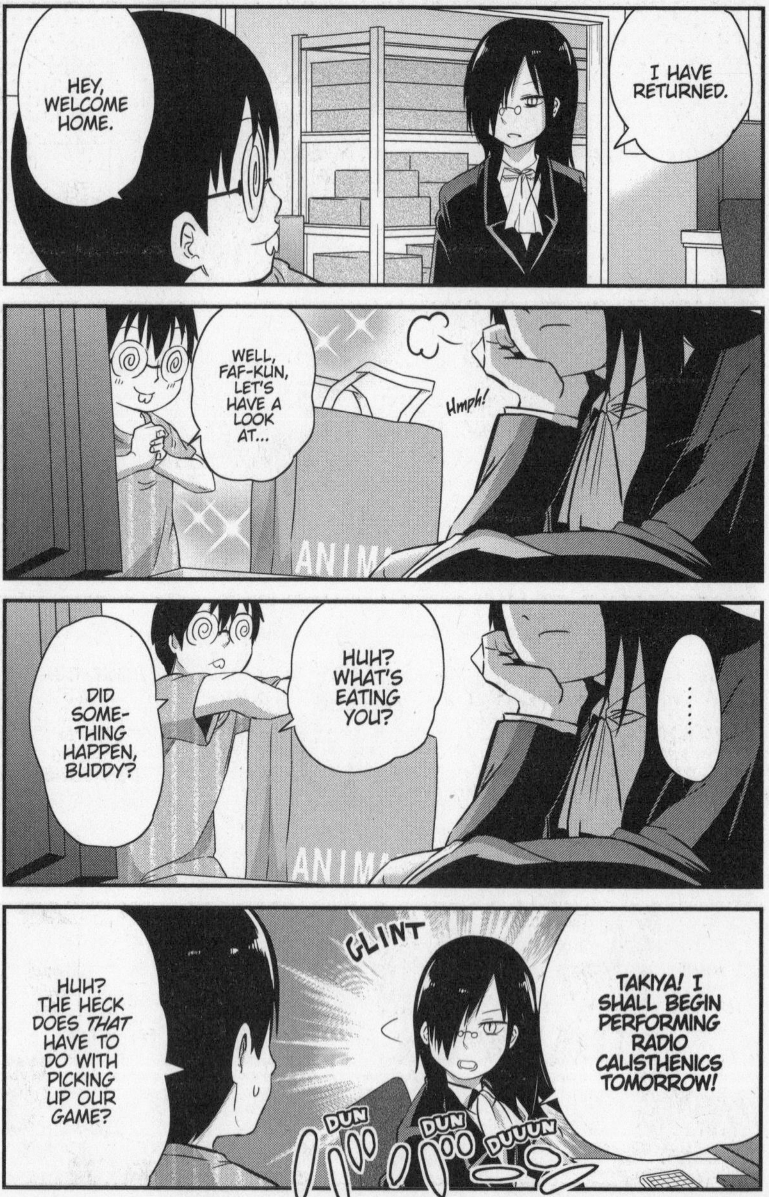
I HAVE RETURNED.
HEY, WELCOME HOME.
Hmph!
WELL, FAF-KUN, LET'S HAVE A LOOK AT...
......
HUH? WHAT'S EATING YOU?
DID SOMETHING HAPPEN, BUDDY?
TAKIYA! I SHALL BEGIN PERFORMING RADIO CALISTHENICS TOMORROW!
GLINT
HUH? THE HECK DOES *THAT* HAVE TO DO WITH PICKING UP OUR GAME?
DUUUN
DUN
DUN

FAFNIR'S NATURE

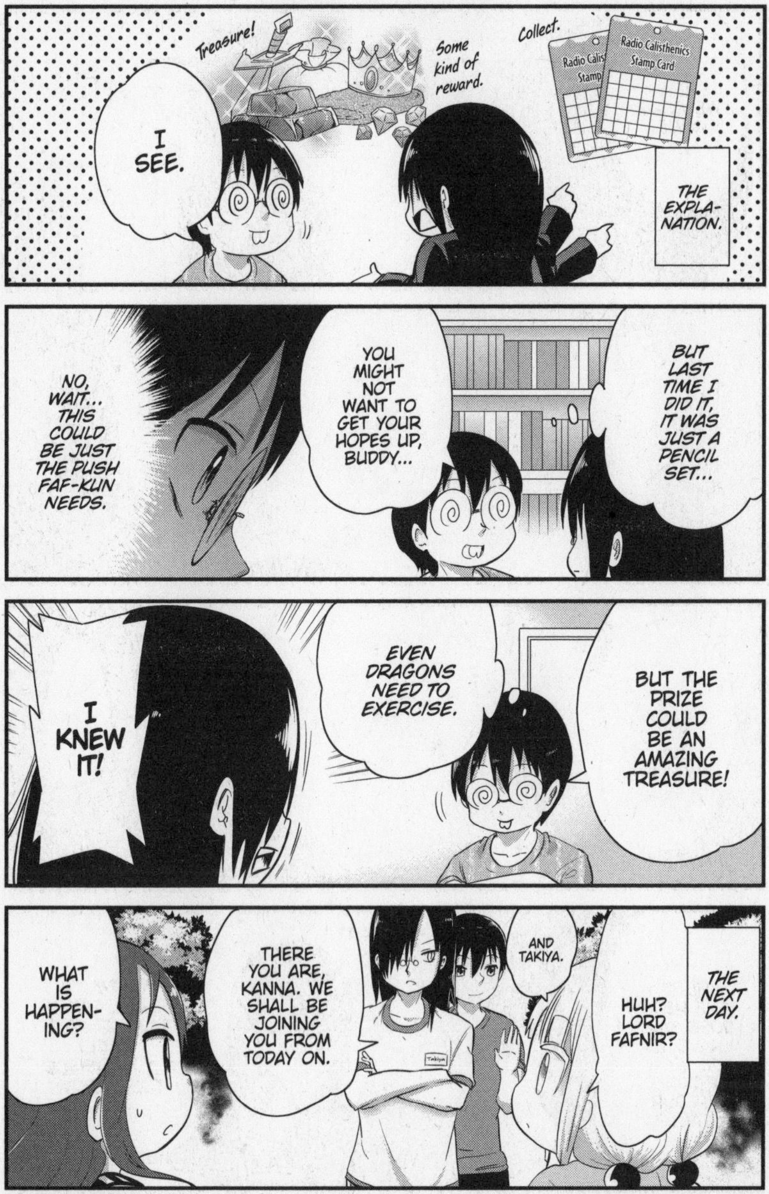
THE EXPLANATION.
Collect.
Radio Calisthenics Stamp Card
Some kind of reward.
Treasure!
I SEE.
BUT LAST TIME I DID IT, IT WAS JUST A PENCIL SET...
YOU MIGHT NOT WANT TO GET YOUR HOPES UP, BUDDY...
NO, WAIT... THIS COULD BE JUST THE PUSH FAF-KUN NEEDS.
BUT THE PRIZE COULD BE AN AMAZING TREASURE!
EVEN DRAGONS NEED TO EXERCISE.
I KNEW IT!
THE NEXT DAY.
HUH? LORD FAFNIR?
AND TAKIYA.
THERE YOU ARE, KANNA. WE SHALL BE JOINING YOU FROM TODAY ON.
Takiya
WHAT IS HAPPENING?

NO USE TRYING TO HIDE IT!

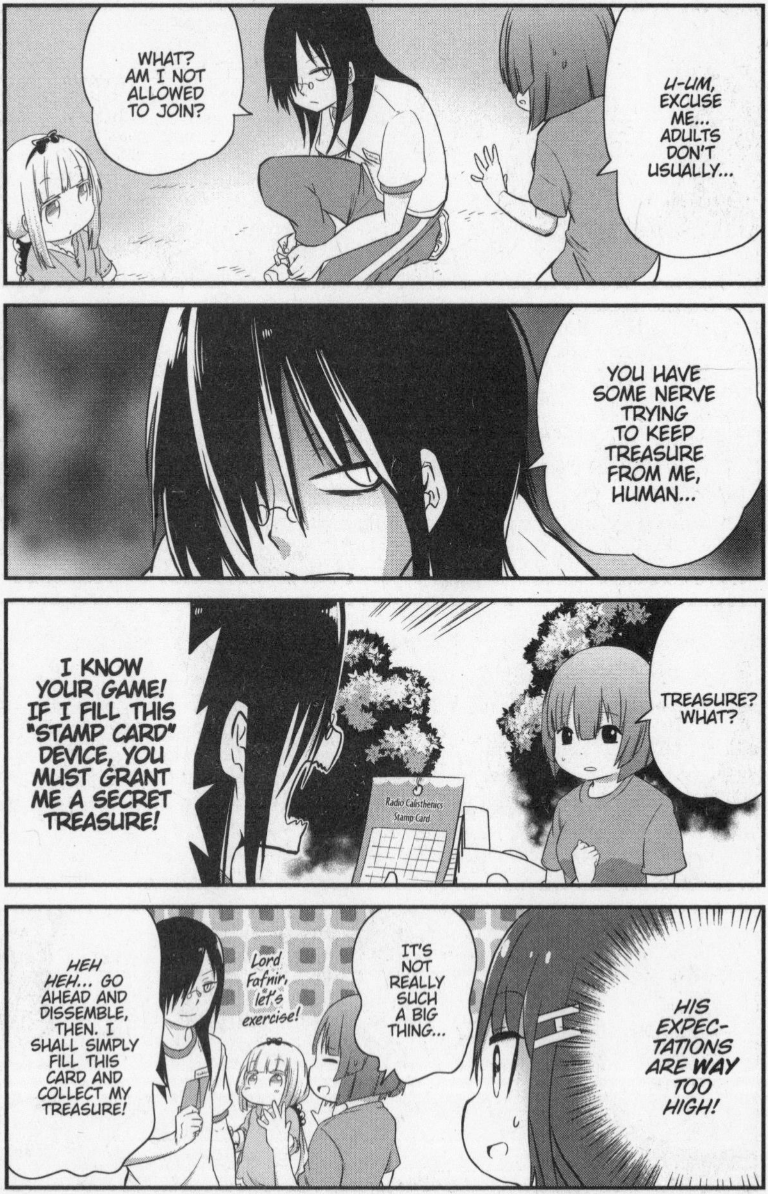

U-UM, EXCUSE ME... ADULTS DON'T USUALLY...
WHAT? AM I NOT ALLOWED TO JOIN?
YOU HAVE SOME NERVE TRYING TO KEEP TREASURE FROM ME, HUMAN...
TREASURE? WHAT?
I KNOW YOUR GAME! IF I FILL THIS "STAMP CARD" DEVICE, YOU MUST GRANT ME A SECRET TREASURE!
Radio Calisthenics Stamp Card
IT'S NOT REALLY SUCH A BIG THING...
Lord Fafnir, let's exercise!
HEH HEH... GO AHEAD AND DISSEMBLE, THEN. I SHALL SIMPLY FILL THIS CARD AND COLLECT MY TREASURE!
HIS EXPECTATIONS ARE WAY TOO HIGH!

SAIKAWA'S SCHEME

HMM, LET ME SEE...

HOW CAN WE HELP HIM?

SAIKAWA, LORD FAFNIR REALLY WANTS TO DO RADIO CALISTHENICS.

It's true. I can't find anyone to help with calisthenics every morning.

Right?

Summer break sure is tough for parents and guardians.

AT HOME.

OOH, GREAT IDEA! SAIKAWA, YOU'RE SO SMART!

YOU'RE SHORT ON HELPERS, RIGHT?

I KNOW! FAFNIR-SAN'S AN ADULT, SO WHY NOT HAVE HIM PARTICIPATE AS A GUARDIAN?

I... I SEE... WELL, IF YOU'RE FRIENDS OF SAIKAWA-SAN, I SUPPOSE...

Me too, please.

WHAT SHE SAID. LET ME JOIN!

Takiya

FAFNIR, THAT'S FOR IDOL FANS!

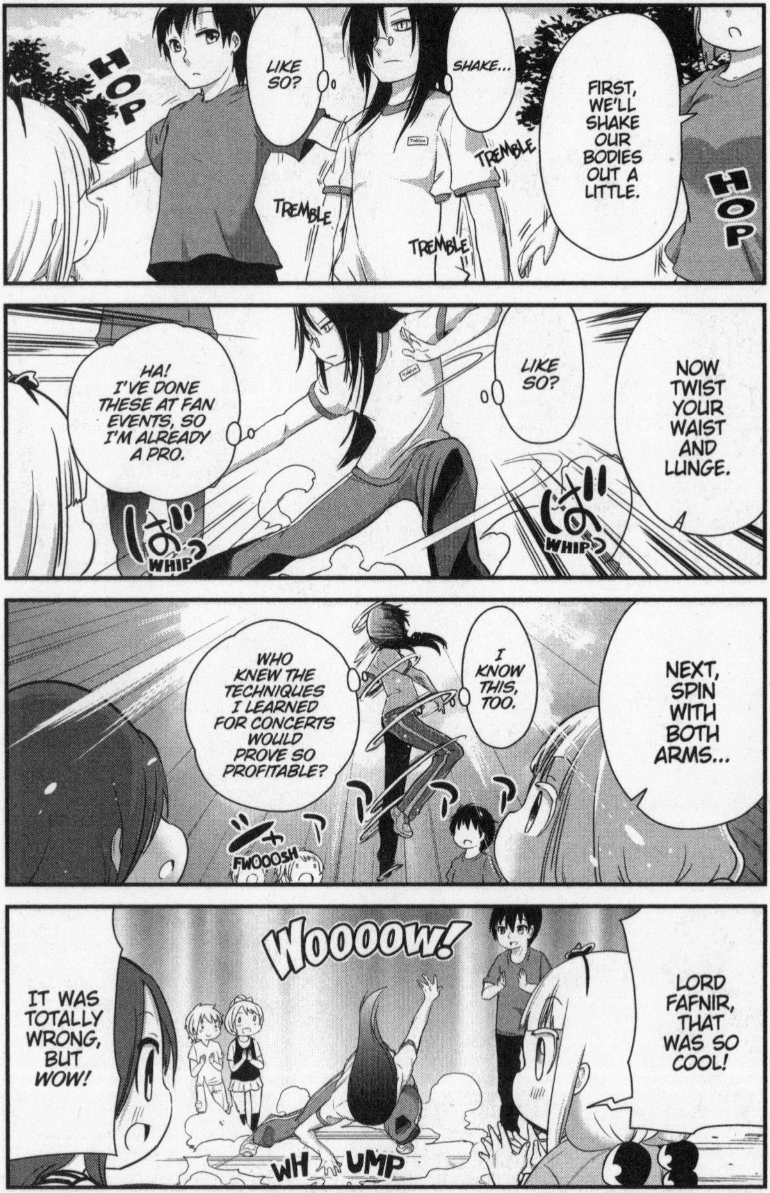
FIRST, WE'LL SHAKE OUR BODIES OUT A LITTLE.
HOP
SHAKE...
TREMBLE
TREMBLE
TREMBLE
LIKE SO?
HOP
NOW TWIST YOUR WAIST AND LUNGE.
ばっ
WHIP
LIKE SO?
HA! I'VE DONE THESE AT FAN EVENTS, SO I'M ALREADY A PRO.
ばっ
WHIP
NEXT, SPIN WITH BOTH ARMS...
I KNOW THIS, TOO.
WHO KNEW THE TECHNIQUES I LEARNED FOR CONCERTS WOULD PROVE SO PROFITABLE?
FWOOOSH
LORD FAFNIR, THAT WAS SO COOL!
WOOOOW!
WH UMP
IT WAS TOTALLY WRONG, BUT WOW!

MAJOR MISCALCULATION

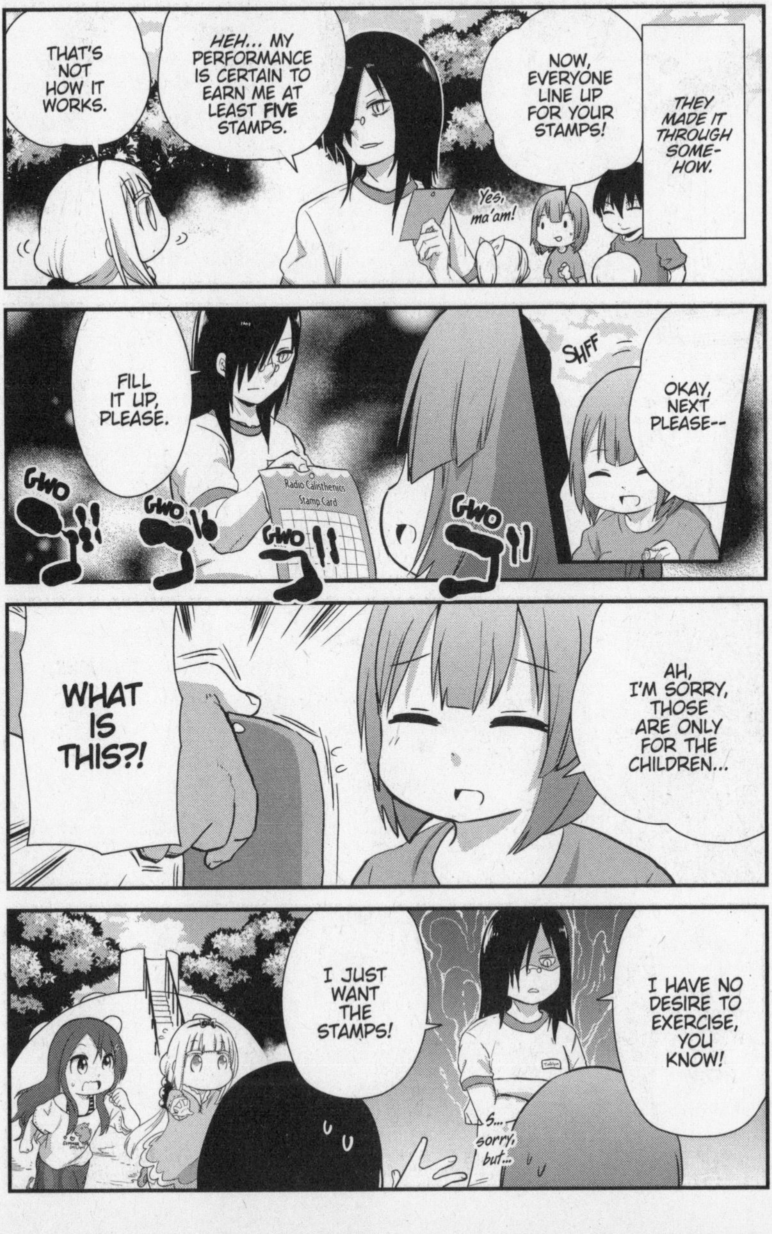
THEY MADE IT THROUGH SOME-HOW.
NOW, EVERYONE LINE UP FOR YOUR STAMPS!
Yes, ma'am!
HEH... MY PERFORMANCE IS CERTAIN TO EARN ME AT LEAST FIVE STAMPS.
THAT'S NOT HOW IT WORKS.
OKAY, NEXT PLEASE--
SHFF
FILL IT UP, PLEASE.
Radio Calisthenics Stamp Card
GWO
GWO
GWO
GWO
AH, I'M SORRY, THOSE ARE ONLY FOR THE CHILDREN...
WHAT IS THIS?!
I HAVE NO DESIRE TO EXERCISE, YOU KNOW!
S... sorry, but...
I JUST WANT THE STAMPS!

KANNA'S PLAN

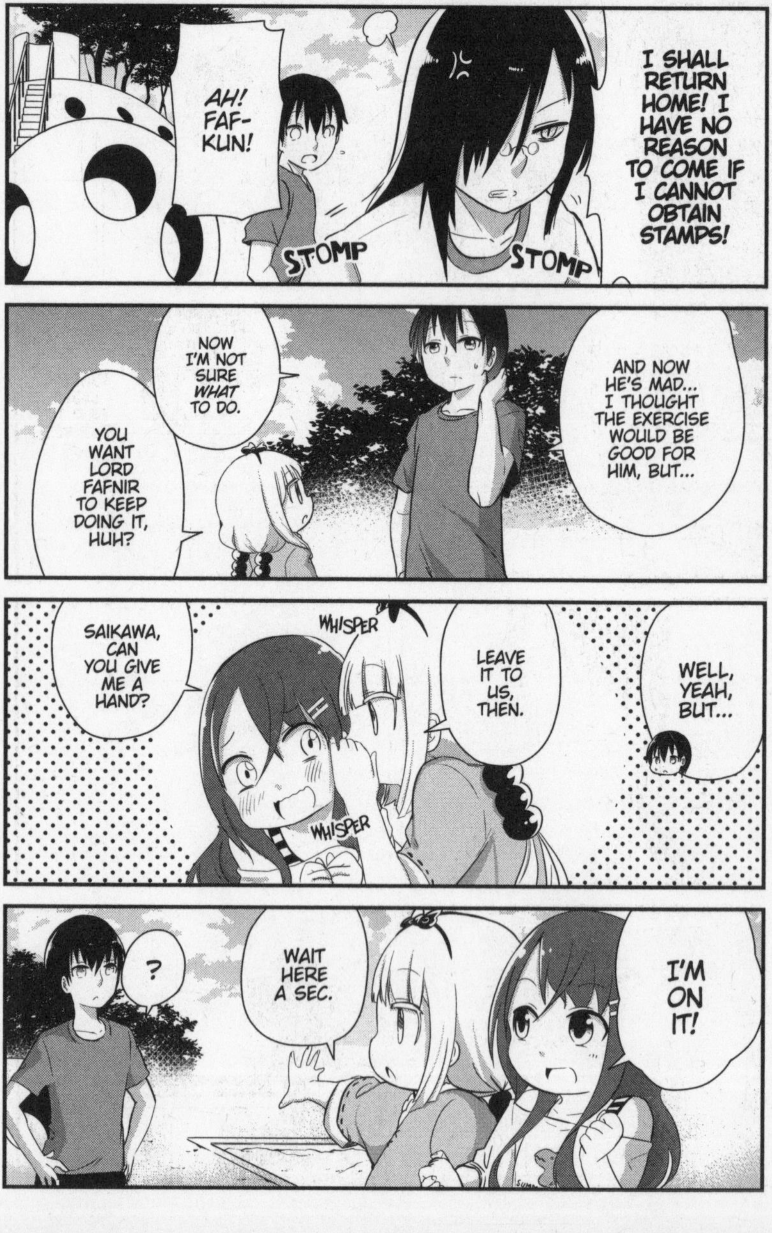
I SHALL RETURN HOME! I HAVE NO REASON TO COME IF I CANNOT OBTAIN STAMPS!
STOMP
STOMP
AH! FAF-KUN!
AND NOW HE'S MAD... I THOUGHT THE EXERCISE WOULD BE GOOD FOR HIM, BUT...
NOW I'M NOT SURE *WHAT* TO DO.
YOU WANT LORD FAFNIR TO KEEP DOING IT, HUH?
WELL, YEAH, BUT...
LEAVE IT TO US, THEN.
WHISPER
SAIKAWA, CAN YOU GIVE ME A HAND?
WHISPER
I'M ON IT!
WAIT HERE A SEC.
?

THE PRIZE BETTER BE GOOD

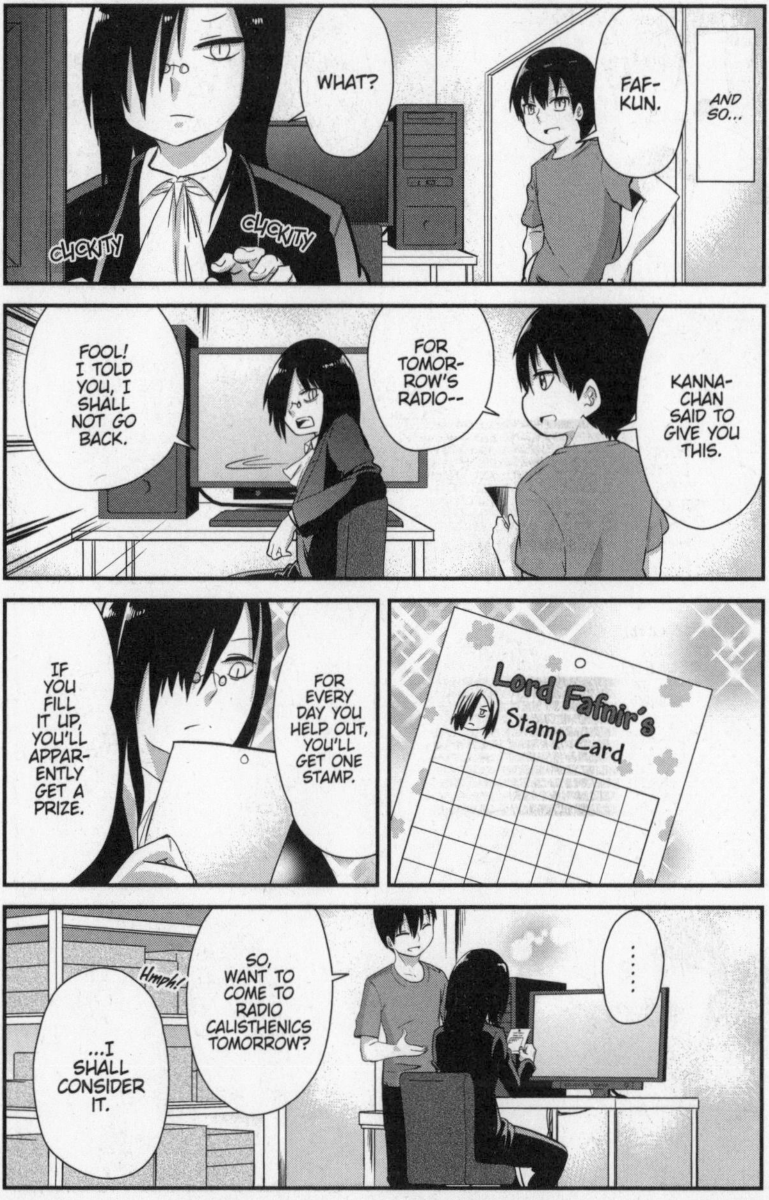
AND SO...
FAF-KUN.
WHAT?
CLICKITY
CLICKITY
KANNA-CHAN SAID TO GIVE YOU THIS.
FOR TOMORROW'S RADIO--
FOOL! I TOLD YOU, I SHALL NOT GO BACK.
Lord Fafnir's Stamp Card
FOR EVERY DAY YOU HELP OUT, YOU'LL GET ONE STAMP.
IF YOU FILL IT UP, YOU'LL APPARENTLY GET A PRIZE.
......
SO, WANT TO COME TO RADIO CALISTHENICS TOMORROW?
Hmph!
...I SHALL CONSIDER IT.

RADIO CALISTHENICS: TAKE TWO!

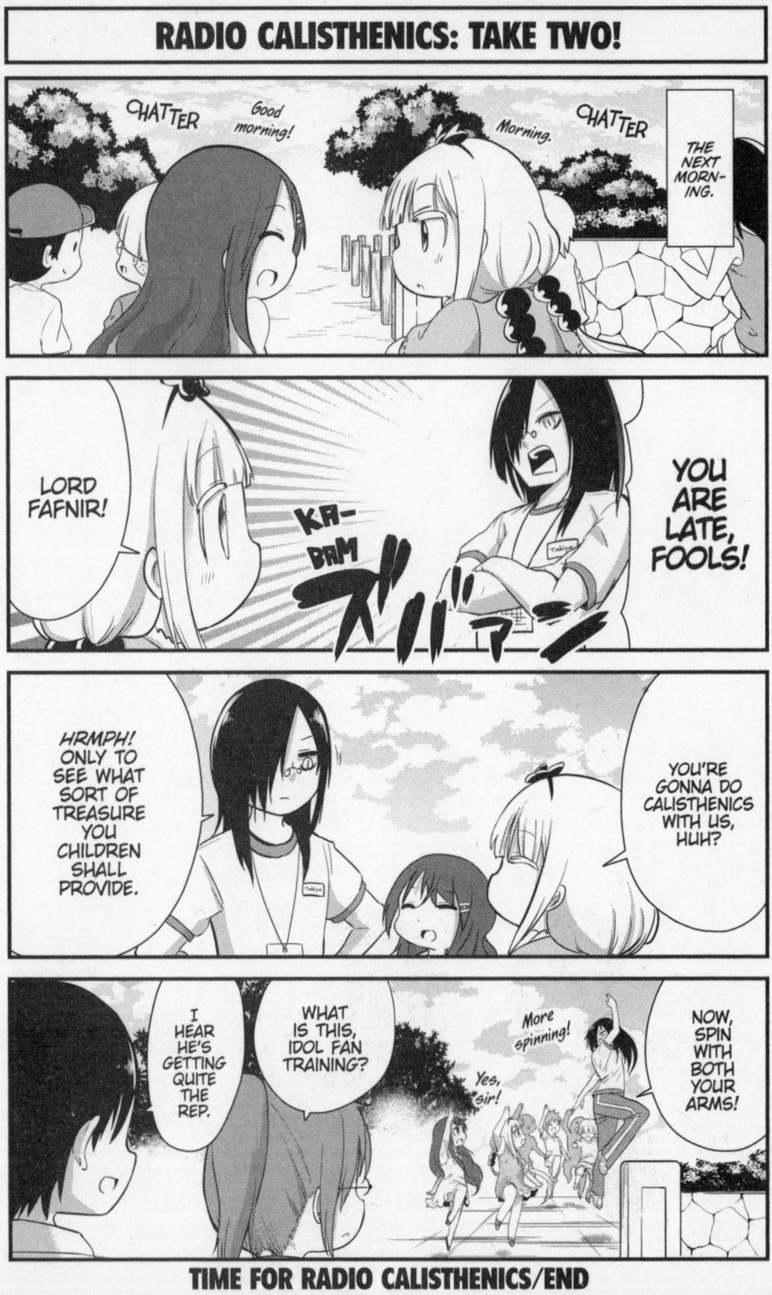
THE NEXT MORNING.
CHATTER
Morning.
Good morning!
CHATTER
YOU ARE LATE, FOOLS!
KA-BAM
LORD FAFNIR!
YOU'RE GONNA DO CALISTHENICS WITH US, HUH?
HRMPH! ONLY TO SEE WHAT SORT OF TREASURE YOU CHILDREN SHALL PROVIDE.
NOW, SPIN WITH BOTH YOUR ARMS!
More spinning!
Yes, sir!
WHAT IS THIS, IDOL FAN TRAINING?
I HEAR HE'S GETTING QUITE THE REP.

TIME FOR RADIO CALISTHENICS/END

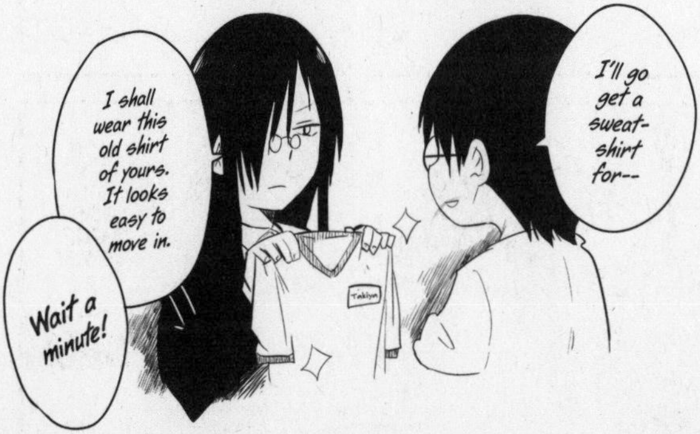
I'll go get a sweat-shirt for--
I shall wear this old shirt of yours. It looks easy to move in.
Wait a minute!

Miss Kobayashi's Dragon Maid

Kanna's Daily Life

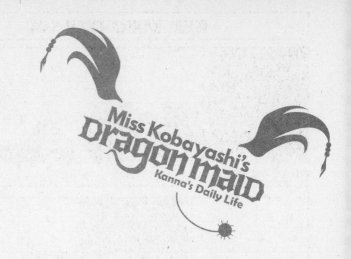

WHAT KANNA-CHAN SAW

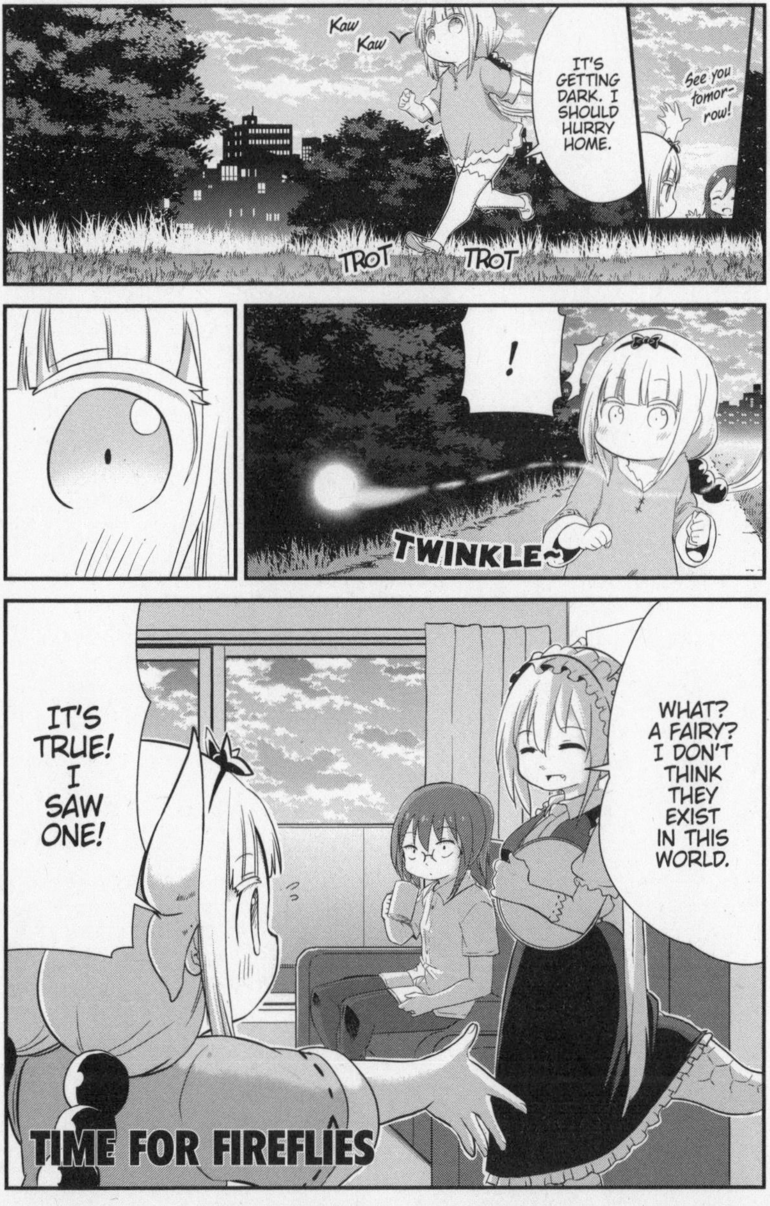
See you tomor-row!
IT'S GETTING DARK. I SHOULD HURRY HOME.
Kaw Kaw
TROT TROT
!
TWINKLE~
WHAT? A FAIRY? I DON'T THINK THEY EXIST IN THIS WORLD.
IT'S TRUE! I SAW ONE!

TIME FOR FIREFLIES

REALITY CHECK

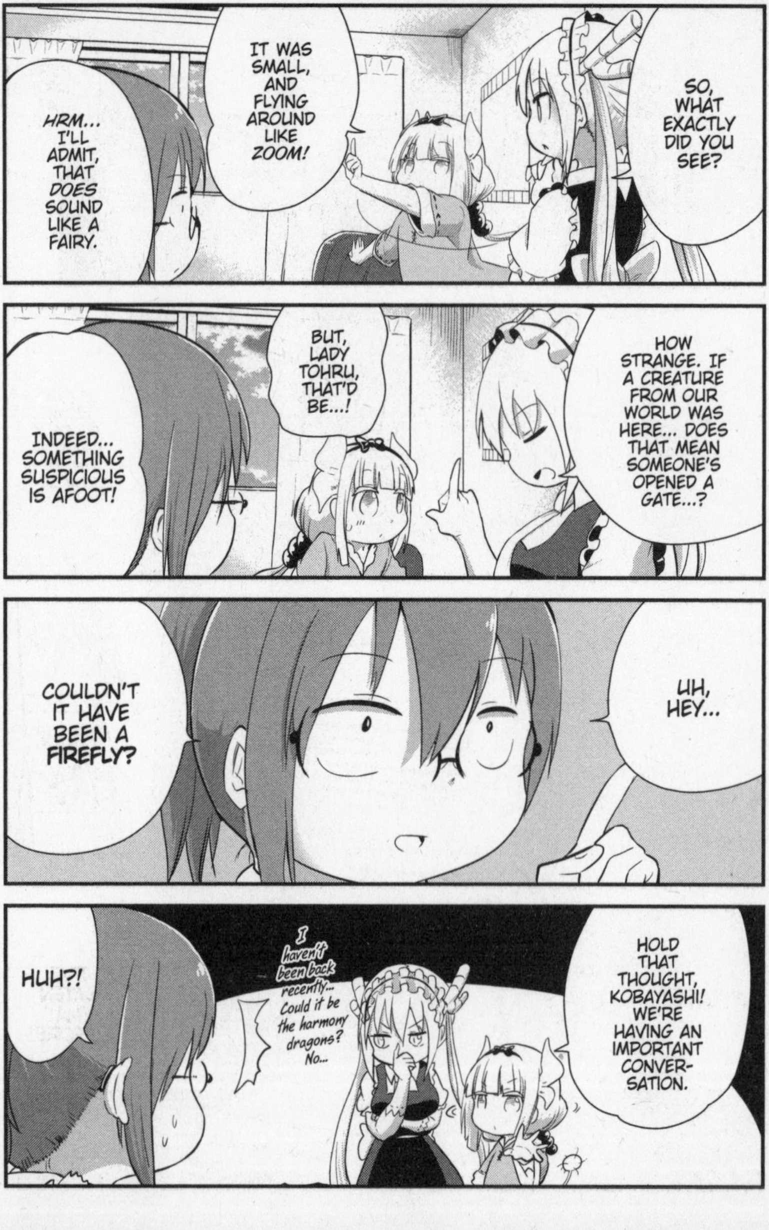
SO, WHAT EXACTLY DID YOU SEE?
IT WAS SMALL, AND FLYING AROUND LIKE ZOOM!
HRM... I'LL ADMIT, THAT DOES SOUND LIKE A FAIRY.
HOW STRANGE. IF A CREATURE FROM OUR WORLD WAS HERE... DOES THAT MEAN SOMEONE'S OPENED A GATE...?
BUT, LADY TOHRU, THAT'D BE...!
INDEED... SOMETHING SUSPICIOUS IS AFOOT!
UH, HEY...
COULDN'T IT HAVE BEEN A FIREFLY?
HOLD THAT THOUGHT, KOBAYASHI! WE'RE HAVING AN IMPORTANT CONVER-SATION.
I haven't been back recently... Could it be the harmony dragons? No...
HUH?!

I KNOW THIS ONE

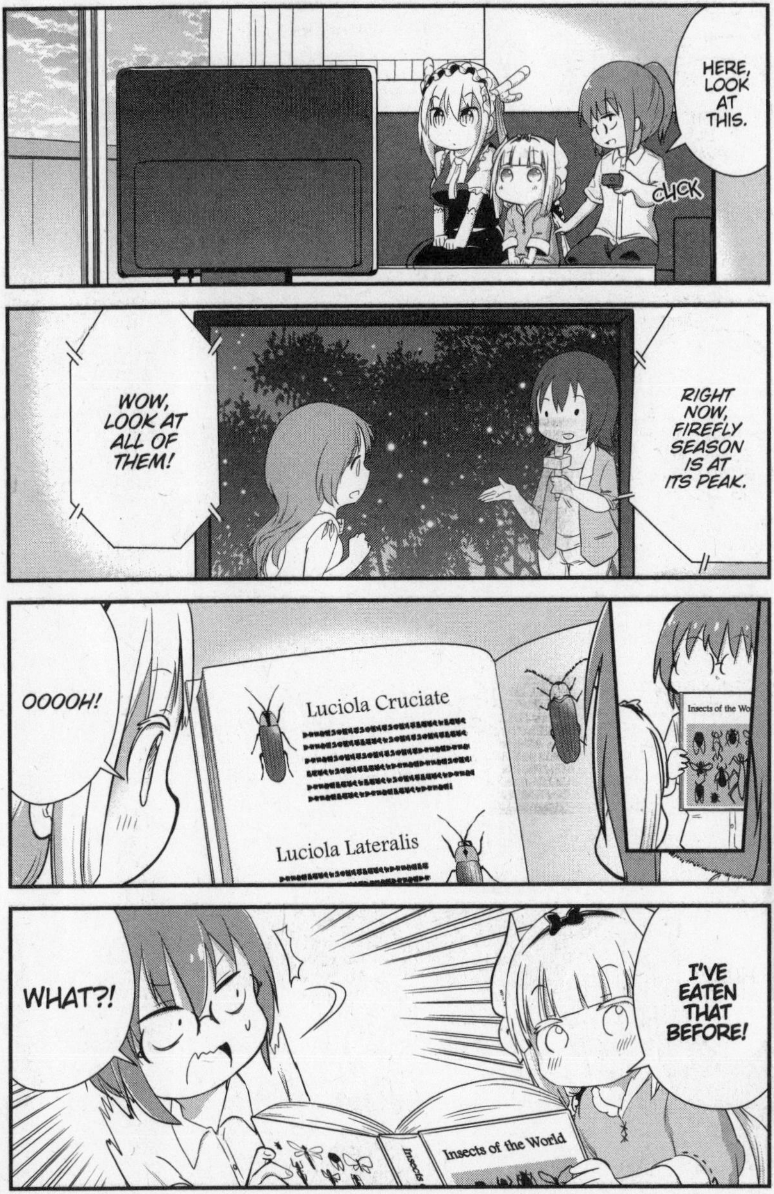
HERE, LOOK AT THIS.
CLICK
RIGHT NOW, FIREFLY SEASON IS AT ITS PEAK.
WOW, LOOK AT ALL OF THEM!
Luciola Cruciate
OOOOH!
Luciola Lateralis
I'VE EATEN THAT BEFORE!
WHAT?!
Insects of the World

BON APPÉTIT

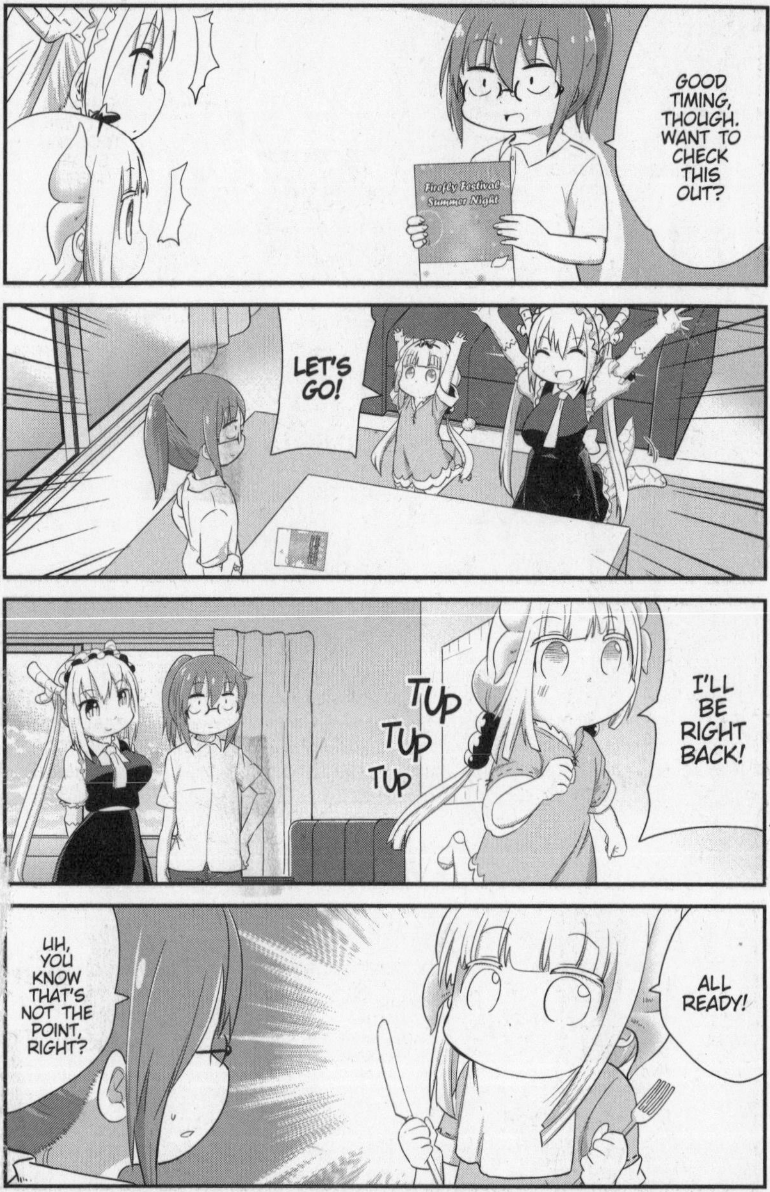
GOOD TIMING, THOUGH. WANT TO CHECK THIS OUT?
Firefly Festival Summer Night
LET'S GO!
I'LL BE RIGHT BACK!
TUP TUP TUP
ALL READY!
UH, YOU KNOW THAT'S NOT THE POINT, RIGHT?

A FATHER'S FEARS?

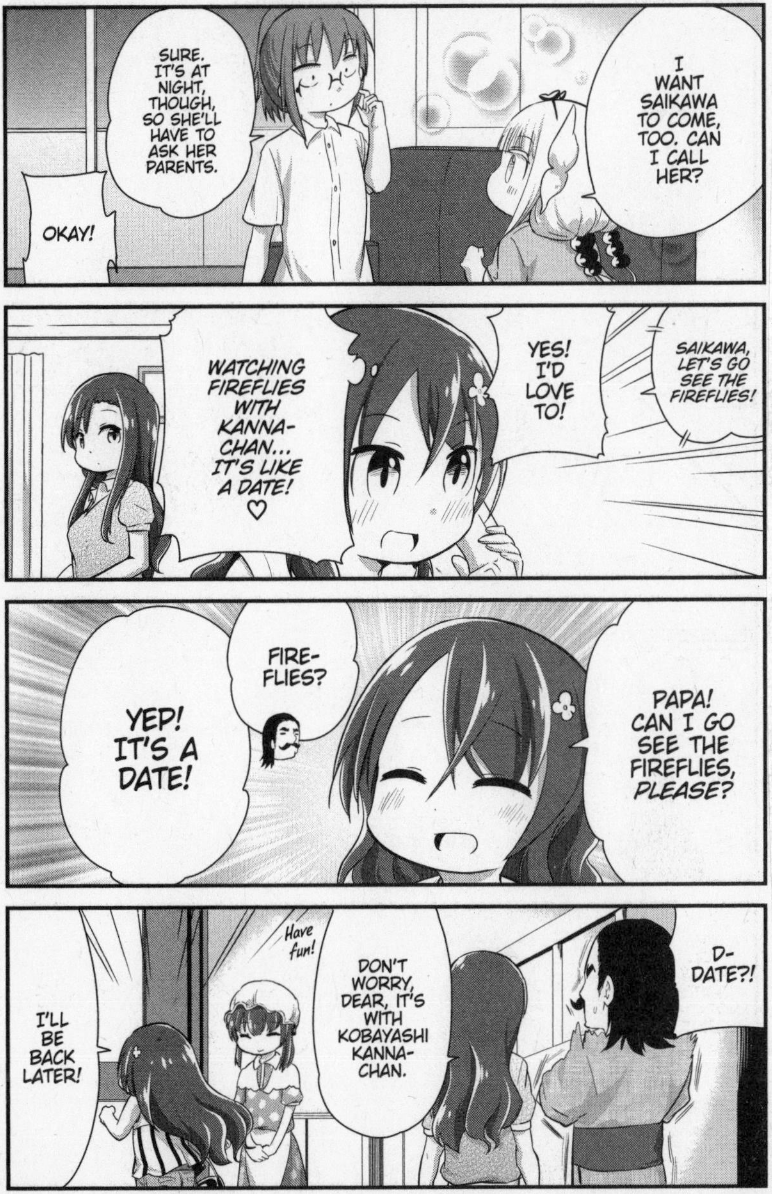
I WANT SAIKAWA TO COME, TOO. CAN I CALL HER?
SURE. IT'S AT NIGHT, THOUGH, SO SHE'LL HAVE TO ASK HER PARENTS.
OKAY!
SAIKAWA, LET'S GO SEE THE FIREFLIES!
YES! I'D LOVE TO!
WATCHING FIREFLIES WITH KANNA-CHAN... IT'S LIKE A DATE! ♡
PAPA! CAN I GO SEE THE FIREFLIES, PLEASE?
FIRE-FLIES?
YEP! IT'S A DATE!
D-DATE?!
DON'T WORRY, DEAR, IT'S WITH KOBAYASHI KANNA-CHAN.
Have fun!
I'LL BE BACK LATER!

REALITY CHECK

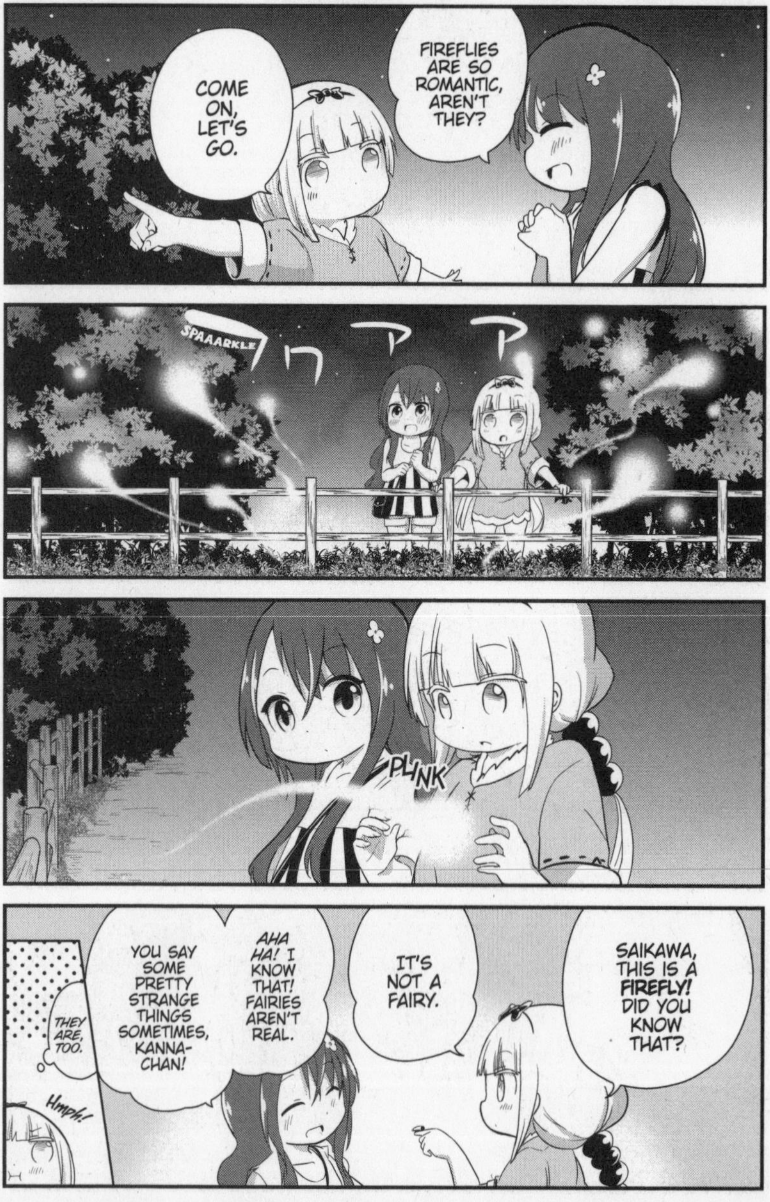
FIREFLIES ARE SO ROMANTIC, AREN'T THEY?
COME ON, LET'S GO.
SPAAARKLE
PLINK
SAIKAWA, THIS IS A **FIREFLY!** DID YOU KNOW THAT?
IT'S NOT A FAIRY.
AHA HA! I KNOW THAT! FAIRIES AREN'T REAL.
YOU SAY SOME PRETTY STRANGE THINGS SOMETIMES, KANNA-CHAN!
THEY ARE, TOO.
Hmph!

KANNA THE RADIANT

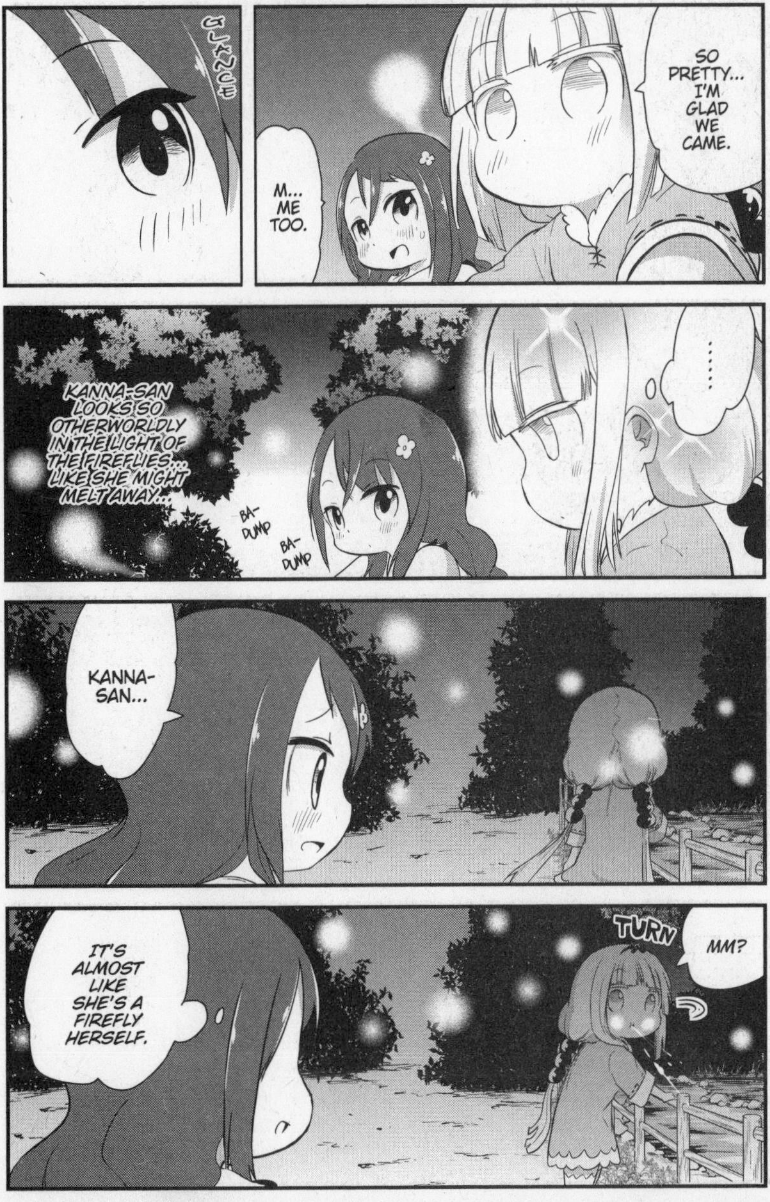
SO PRETTY... I'M GLAD WE CAME.
M... ME TOO.
GLANCE
......
KANNA-SAN LOOKS SO OTHERWORLDLY IN THE LIGHT OF THE FIREFLIES... LIKE SHE MIGHT MELT AWAY...
BA-DUMP
BA-DUMP
KANNA-SAN...
MM?
TURN
IT'S ALMOST LIKE SHE'S A FIREFLY HERSELF.

BELLFLOWER FIREFLY

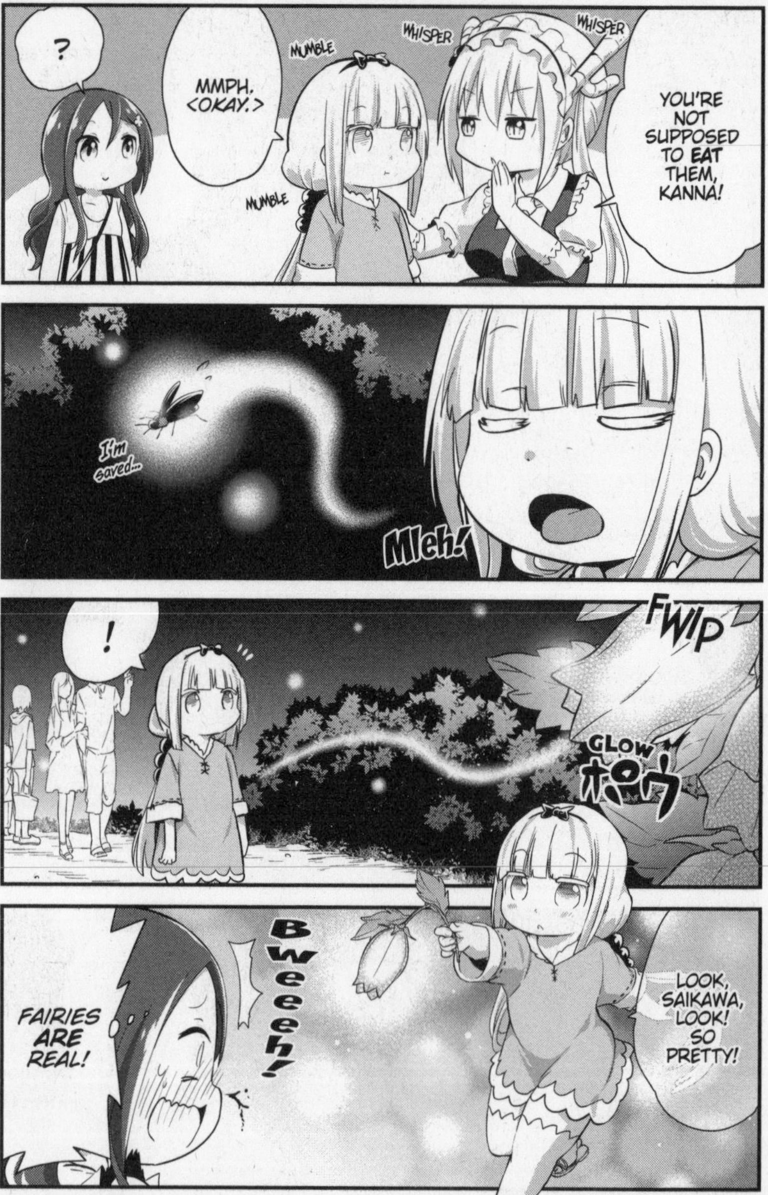
YOU'RE NOT SUPPOSED TO EAT THEM, KANNA!
WHISPER
WHISPER
MUMBLE
MMPH. <OKAY.>
MUMBLE
?
Mleh!
I'm saved...
FWIP
GLOW
!
LOOK, SAIKAWA, LOOK! SO PRETTY!
Bweeeh!
FAIRIES ARE REAL!

TIME SPENT TOGETHER

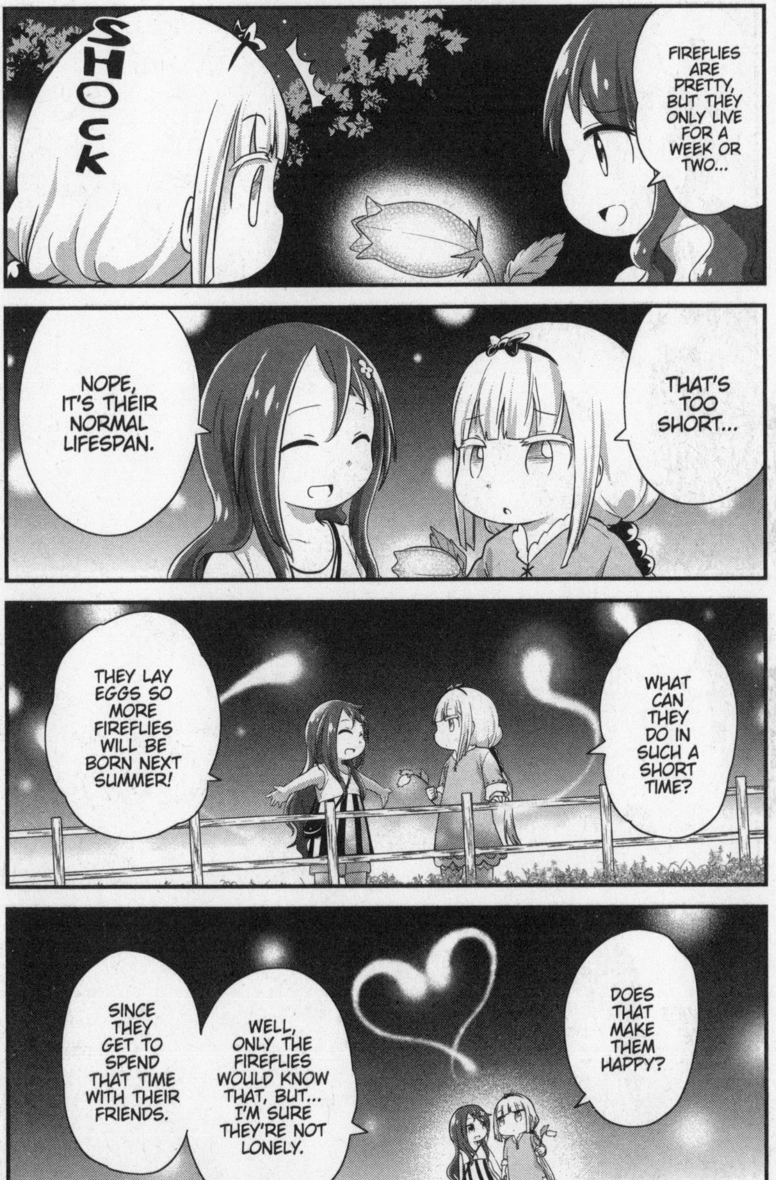
FIREFLIES ARE PRETTY, BUT THEY ONLY LIVE FOR A WEEK OR TWO...
SHOCK
THAT'S TOO SHORT...
NOPE, IT'S THEIR NORMAL LIFESPAN.
WHAT CAN THEY DO IN SUCH A SHORT TIME?
THEY LAY EGGS SO MORE FIREFLIES WILL BE BORN NEXT SUMMER!
DOES THAT MAKE THEM HAPPY?
WELL, ONLY THE FIREFLIES WOULD KNOW THAT, BUT... I'M SURE THEY'RE NOT LONELY.
SINCE THEY GET TO SPEND THAT TIME WITH THEIR FRIENDS.

PRECIOUS PAL

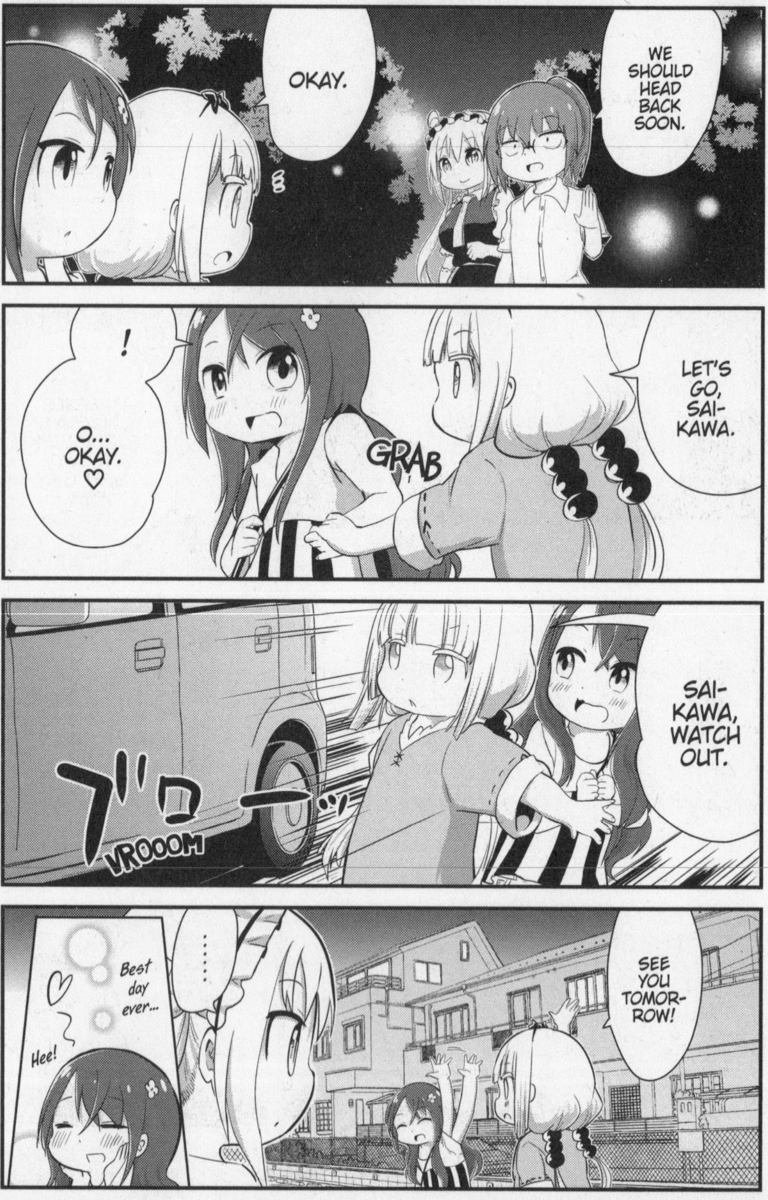
WE SHOULD HEAD BACK SOON.
OKAY.
LET'S GO, SAI-KAWA.
GRAB
!
O... OKAY. ♡
SAI-KAWA, WATCH OUT.
ブローッ
VROOOM
SEE YOU TOMOR-ROW!
......
Best day ever...
Hee!

BIG SISTER TOHRU

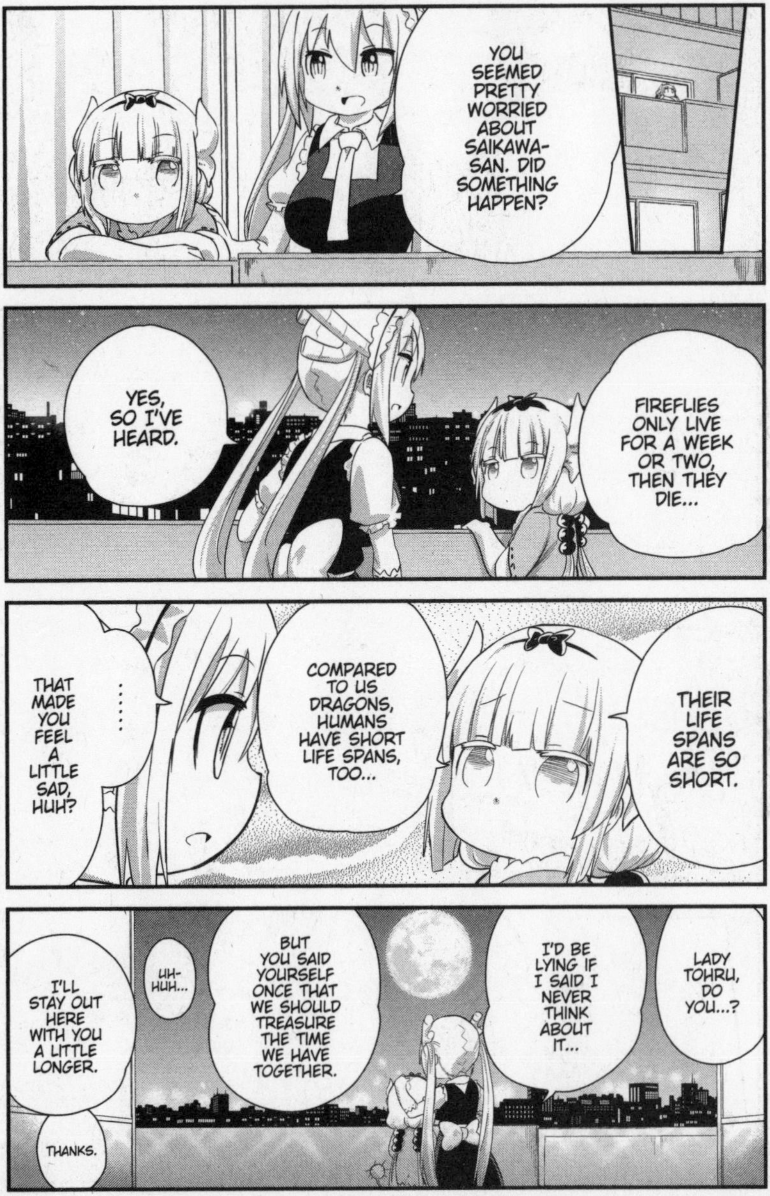
YOU SEEMED PRETTY WORRIED ABOUT SAIKAWA-SAN. DID SOMETHING HAPPEN?
FIREFLIES ONLY LIVE FOR A WEEK OR TWO, THEN THEY DIE...
YES, SO I'VE HEARD.
THEIR LIFE SPANS ARE SO SHORT.
COMPARED TO US DRAGONS, HUMANS HAVE SHORT LIFE SPANS, TOO...
......
THAT MADE YOU FEEL A LITTLE SAD, HUH?
LADY TOHRU, DO YOU...?
I'D BE LYING IF I SAID I NEVER THINK ABOUT IT...
BUT YOU SAID YOURSELF ONCE THAT WE SHOULD TREASURE THE TIME WE HAVE TOGETHER.
UH-HUH...
I'LL STAY OUT HERE WITH YOU A LITTLE LONGER.
THANKS.

SUMMER MEMORIES

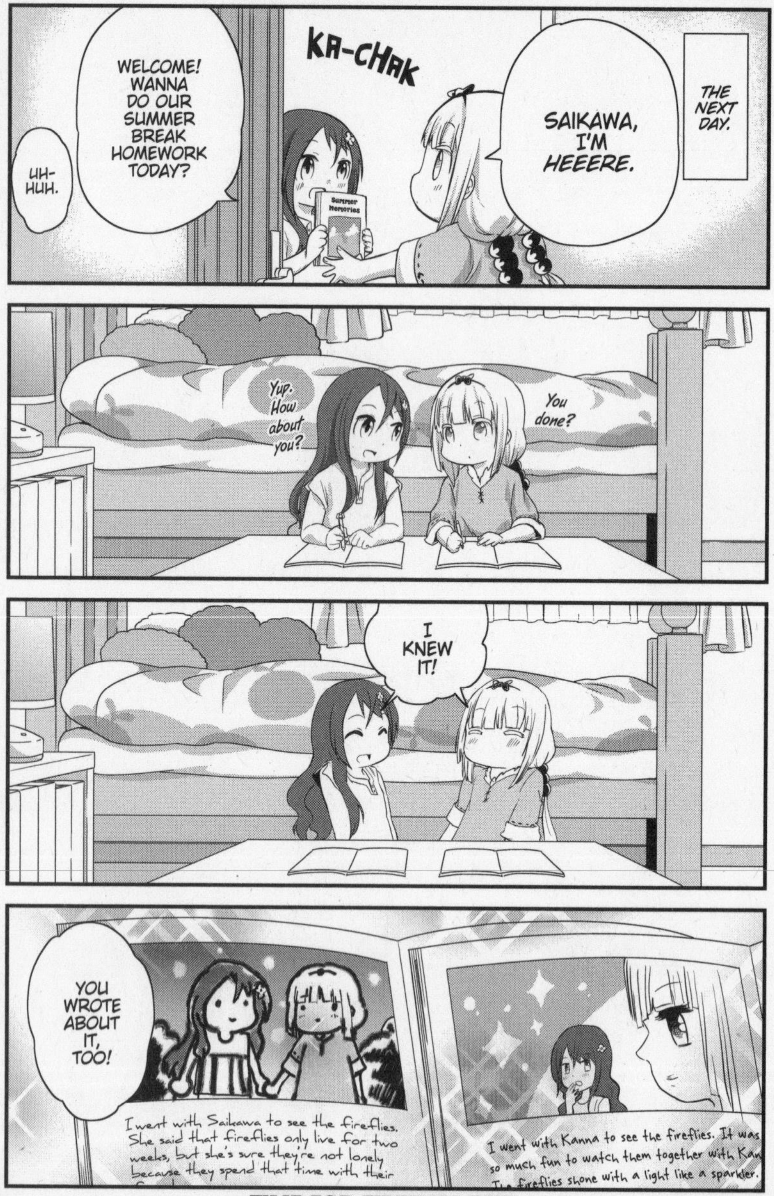

THE NEXT DAY.
SAIKAWA, I'M HEEERE.
KA-CHAK
WELCOME! WANNA DO OUR SUMMER BREAK HOMEWORK TODAY?
UH-HUH.
Summer Memories
You done?
Yup. How about you?
I KNEW IT!
I went with Kanna to see the fireflies. It was so much fun to watch them together with Kan
The fireflies shone with a light like a sparkler.
YOU WROTE ABOUT IT, TOO!
I went with Saikawa to see the fireflies. She said that fireflies only live for two weeks, but she's sure they're not lonely because they spend that time with their

TIME FOR FIREFLIES/END

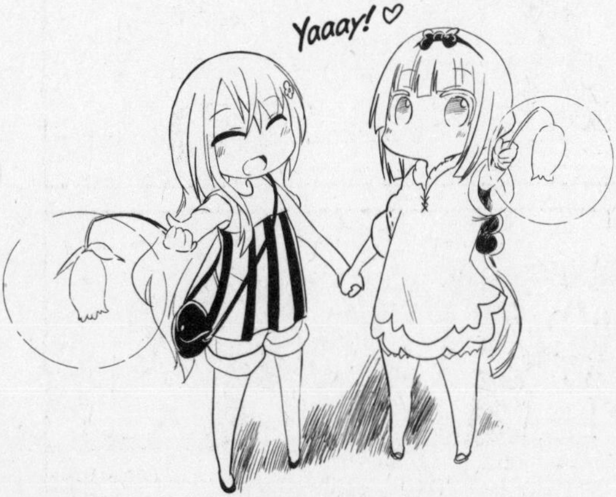
Yaaay! ♡

Miss Kobayashi's Dragon Maid
Kanna's Daily Life

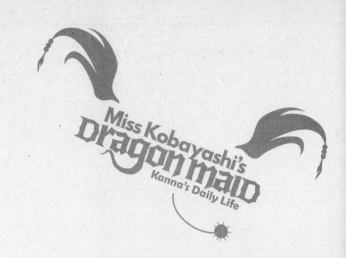

SUMMER IS FOR GHOST STORIES!

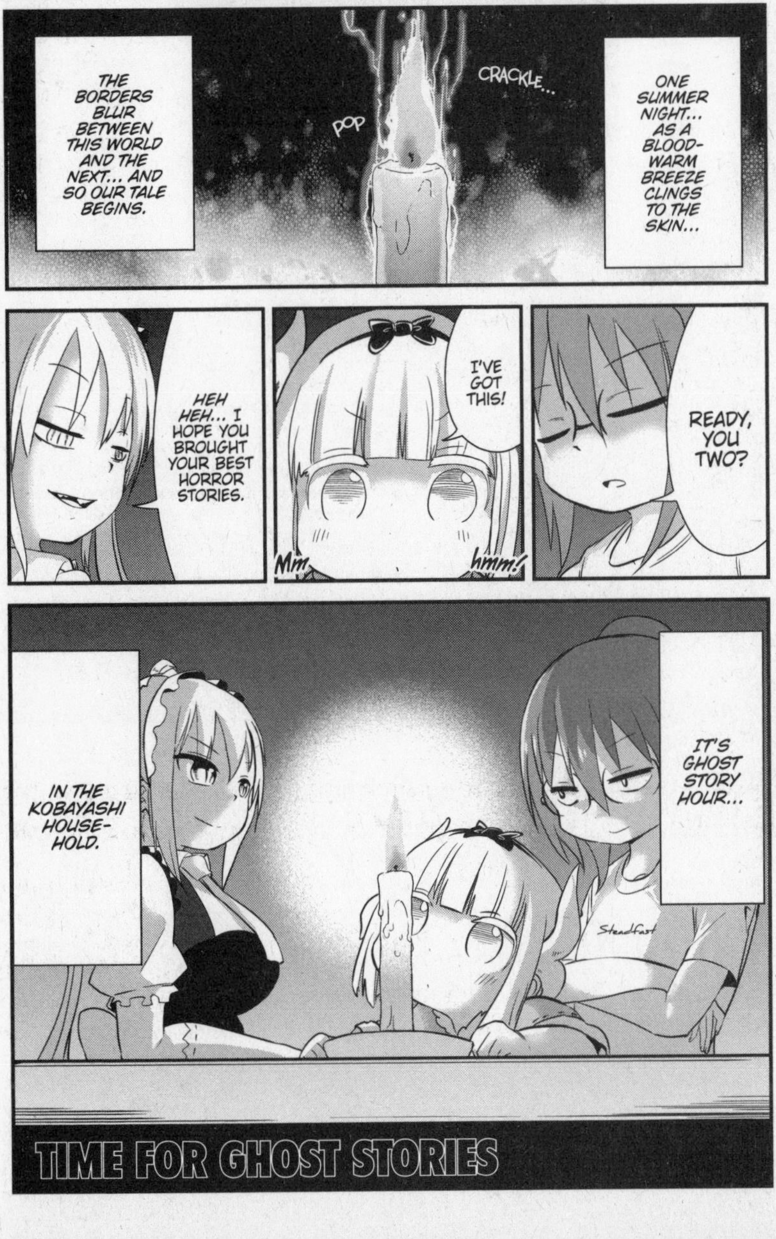
ONE SUMMER NIGHT... AS A BLOOD-WARM BREEZE CLINGS TO THE SKIN...
CRACKLE...
POP
THE BORDERS BLUR BETWEEN THIS WORLD AND THE NEXT... AND SO OUR TALE BEGINS.
READY, YOU TWO?
I'VE GOT THIS!
Mm hmm!
HEH HEH... I HOPE YOU BROUGHT YOUR BEST HORROR STORIES.
IT'S GHOST STORY HOUR...
Steadfast
IN THE KOBAYASHI HOUSE-HOLD.
TIME FOR GHOST STORIES

GHOST STORIES, DRAGON-STYLE

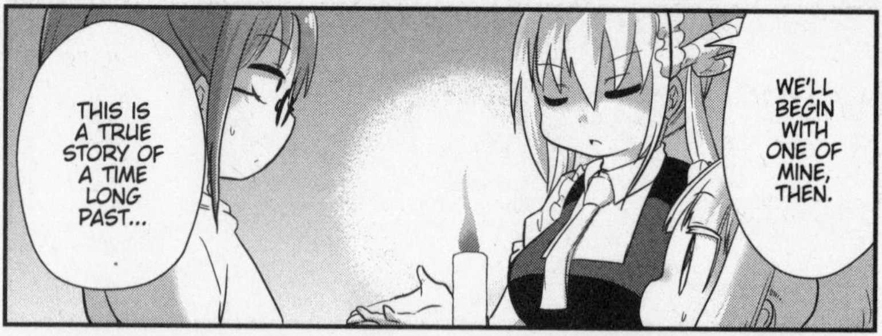
WE'LL BEGIN WITH ONE OF MINE, THEN.
THIS IS A TRUE STORY OF A TIME LONG PAST...

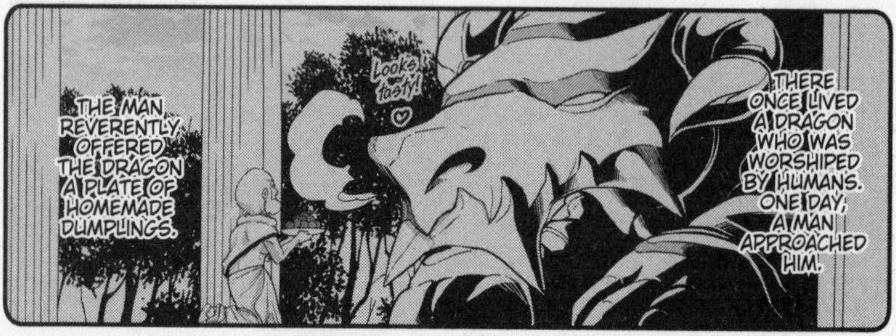
THERE ONCE LIVED A DRAGON WHO WAS WORSHIPED BY HUMANS. ONE DAY, A MAN APPROACHED HIM.
Looks tasty!
THE MAN REVERENTLY OFFERED THE DRAGON A PLATE OF HOMEMADE DUMPLINGS.

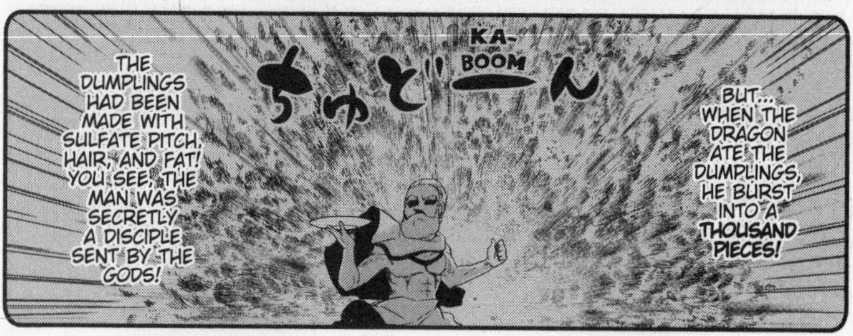
ちゅどーーん
KA-BOOM
BUT... WHEN THE DRAGON ATE THE DUMPLINGS, HE BURST INTO A **THOUSAND PIECES!**
THE DUMPLINGS HAD BEEN MADE WITH SULFATE PITCH, HAIR, AND FAT! YOU SEE, THE MAN WAS SECRETLY A DISCIPLE SENT BY THE GODS!

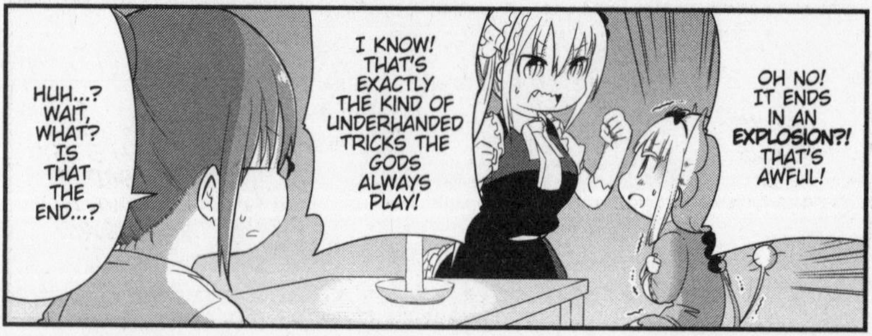
OH NO! IT ENDS IN AN **EXPLOSION?!** THAT'S AWFUL!
I KNOW! THAT'S EXACTLY THE KIND OF UNDERHANDED TRICKS THE GODS ALWAYS PLAY!
HUH...? WAIT, WHAT? IS THAT THE END...?

CULTURE SHOCK

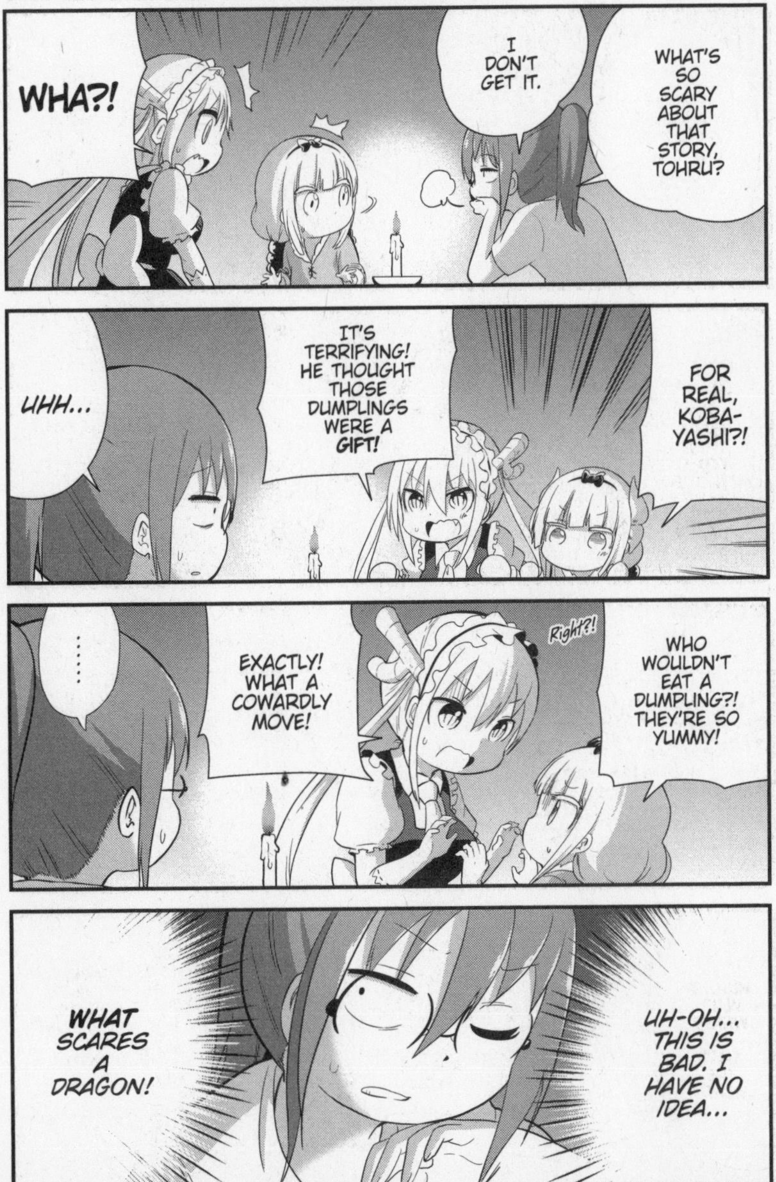
WHAT'S SO SCARY ABOUT THAT STORY, TOHRU?
I DON'T GET IT.
WHA?!
FOR REAL, KOBA-YASHI?!
IT'S TERRIFYING! HE THOUGHT THOSE DUMPLINGS WERE A GIFT!
UHH...
Right?!
WHO WOULDN'T EAT A DUMPLING?! THEY'RE SO YUMMY!
EXACTLY! WHAT A COWARDLY MOVE!
......
UH-OH... THIS IS BAD. I HAVE NO IDEA...
WHAT SCARES A DRAGON!

THAT'S WHAT THEY SAY

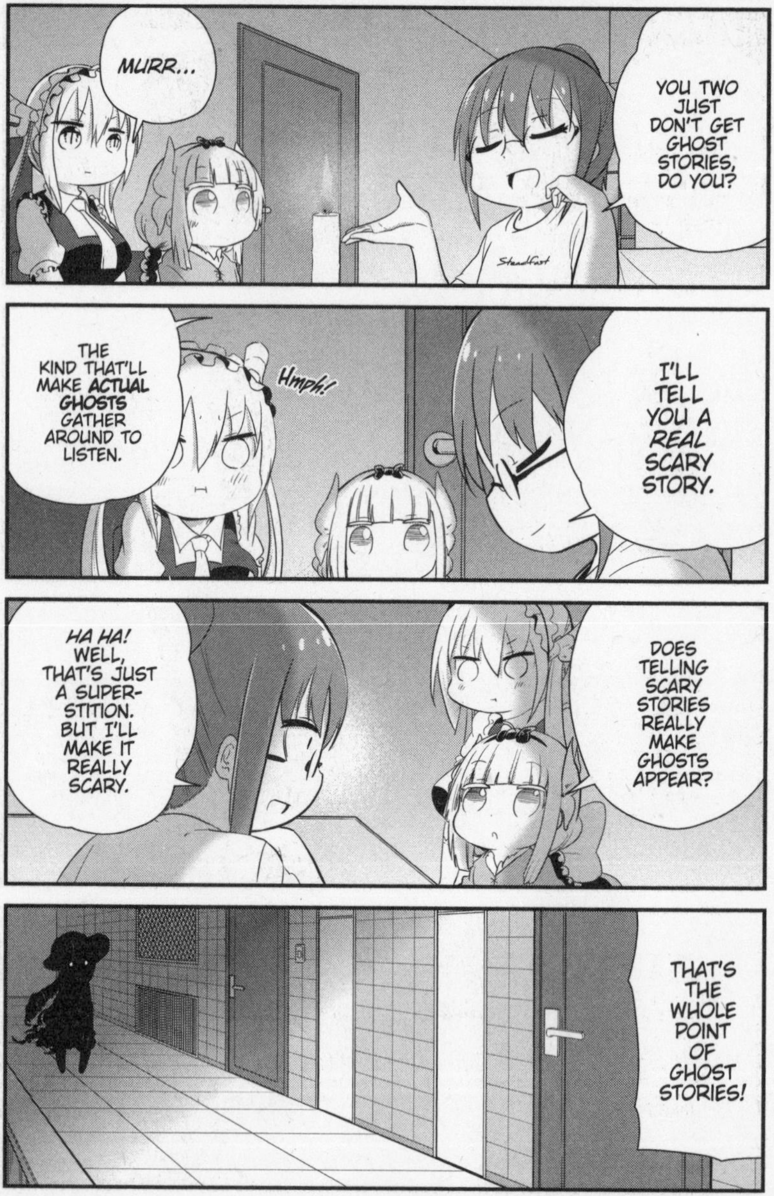
YOU TWO JUST DON'T GET GHOST STORIES, DO YOU?
MURR...
Steadfast
I'LL TELL YOU A *REAL* SCARY STORY.
THE KIND THAT'LL MAKE **ACTUAL GHOSTS** GATHER AROUND TO LISTEN.
Hmph!
DOES TELLING SCARY STORIES REALLY MAKE GHOSTS APPEAR?
HA HA! WELL, THAT'S JUST A SUPER-STITION. BUT I'LL MAKE IT REALLY SCARY.
THAT'S THE WHOLE POINT OF GHOST STORIES!

THE NIGHTMARE

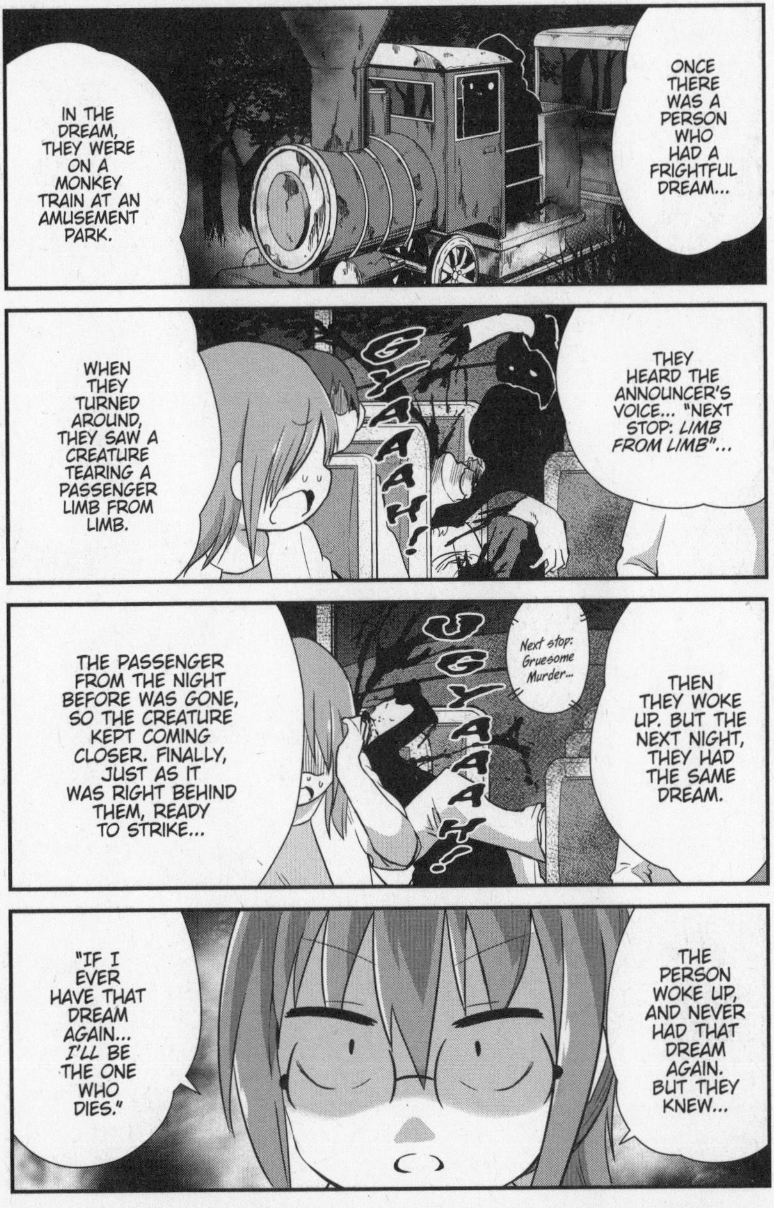
ONCE THERE WAS A PERSON WHO HAD A FRIGHTFUL DREAM...
IN THE DREAM, THEY WERE ON A MONKEY TRAIN AT AN AMUSEMENT PARK.
THEY HEARD THE ANNOUNCER'S VOICE... "NEXT STOP: *LIMB FROM LIMB*"...
GYAAAAH!
WHEN THEY TURNED AROUND, THEY SAW A CREATURE TEARING A PASSENGER LIMB FROM LIMB.
THEN THEY WOKE UP. BUT THE NEXT NIGHT, THEY HAD THE SAME DREAM.
Next stop: Gruesome Murder...
UGYAAAAAH!
THE PASSENGER FROM THE NIGHT BEFORE WAS GONE, SO THE CREATURE KEPT COMING CLOSER. FINALLY, JUST AS IT WAS RIGHT BEHIND THEM, READY TO STRIKE...
THE PERSON WOKE UP, AND NEVER HAD THAT DREAM AGAIN. BUT THEY KNEW...
"IF I EVER HAVE THAT DREAM AGAIN... *I'LL* BE THE ONE WHO DIES."

MISSED THE POINT

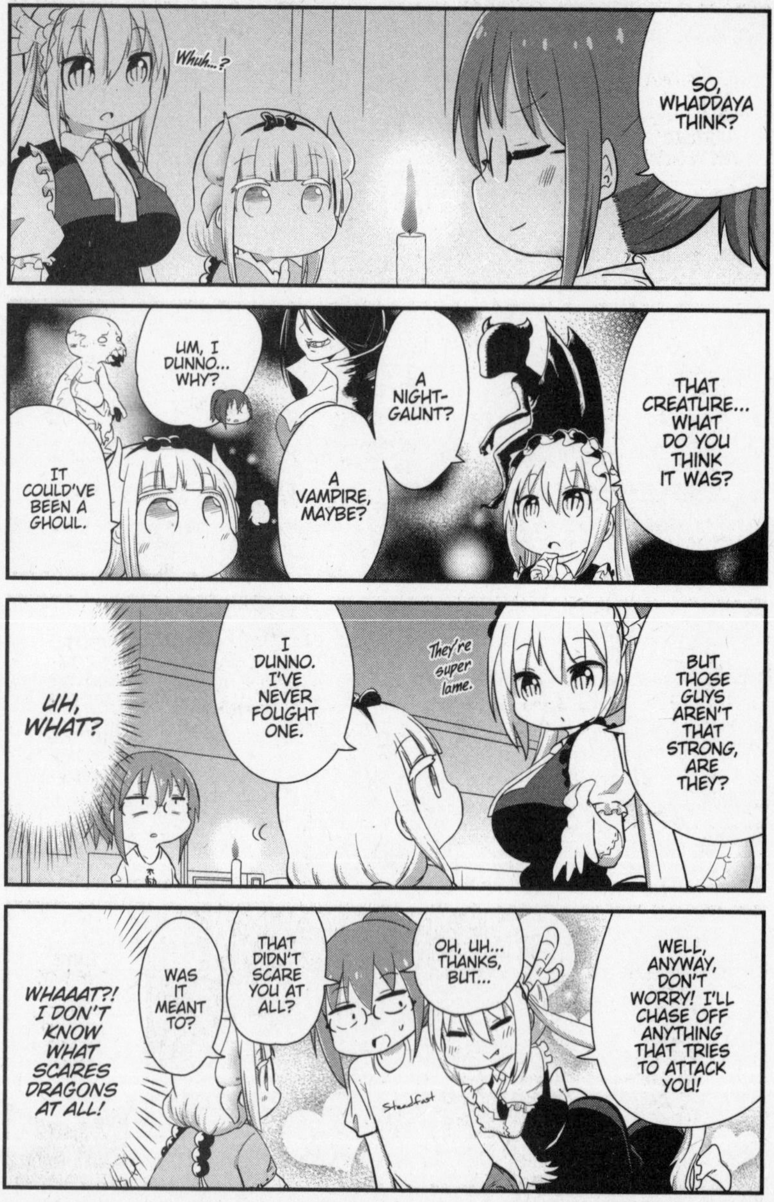
SO, WHADDAYA THINK?
Whuh...?
THAT CREATURE... WHAT DO YOU THINK IT WAS?
A NIGHT-GAUNT?
A VAMPIRE, MAYBE?
UM, I DUNNO... WHY?
IT COULD'VE BEEN A GHOUL.
BUT THOSE GUYS AREN'T THAT STRONG, ARE THEY?
They're super lame.
I DUNNO. I'VE NEVER FOUGHT ONE.
UH, WHAT?
WELL, ANYWAY, DON'T WORRY! I'LL CHASE OFF ANYTHING THAT TRIES TO ATTACK YOU!
OH, UH... THANKS, BUT...
THAT DIDN'T SCARE YOU AT ALL?
WAS IT MEANT TO?
Steadfast
WHAAAT?! I DON'T KNOW WHAT SCARES DRAGONS AT ALL!

WHERE AM I?

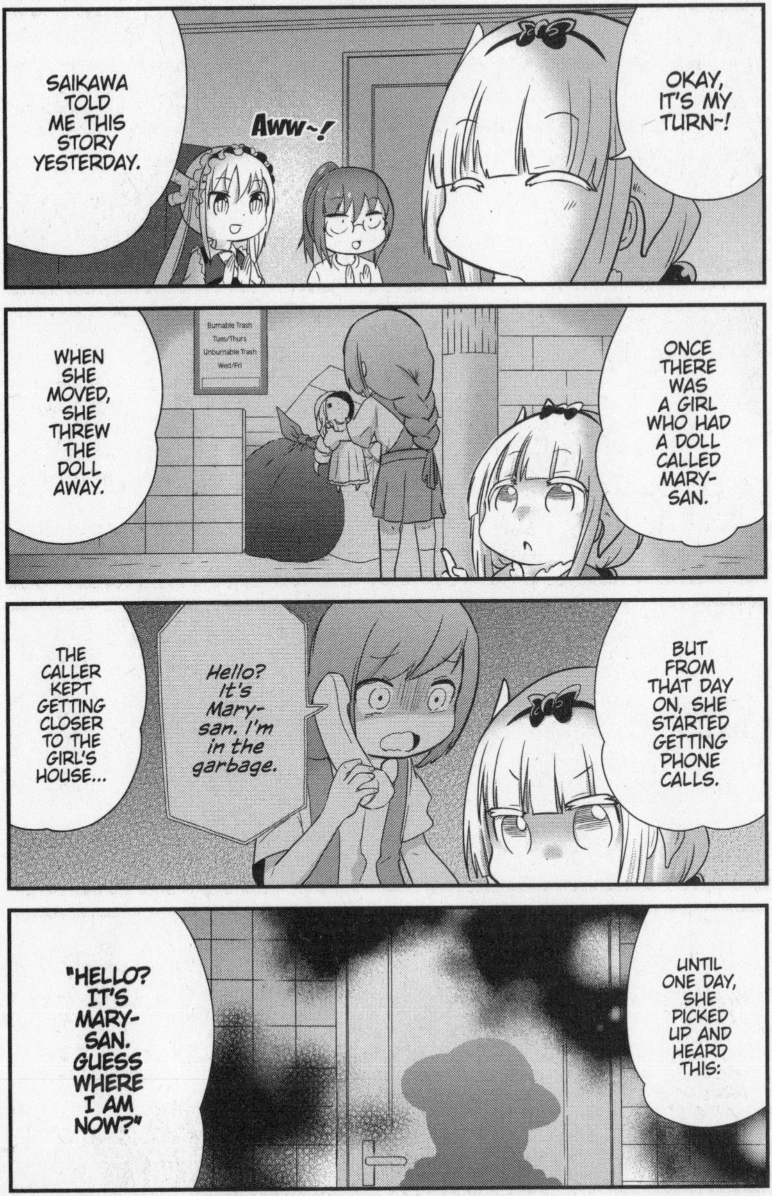
OKAY, IT'S MY TURN~!
Aww~!
SAIKAWA TOLD ME THIS STORY YESTERDAY.
ONCE THERE WAS A GIRL WHO HAD A DOLL CALLED MARY-SAN.
Burnable Trash Tues/Thurs Unburnable Trash Wed/Fri
WHEN SHE MOVED, SHE THREW THE DOLL AWAY.
BUT FROM THAT DAY ON, SHE STARTED GETTING PHONE CALLS.
Hello? It's Mary-san. I'm in the garbage.
THE CALLER KEPT GETTING CLOSER TO THE GIRL'S HOUSE...
UNTIL ONE DAY, SHE PICKED UP AND HEARD THIS:
"HELLO? IT'S MARY-SAN. GUESS WHERE I AM NOW?"

STRANGE REACTIONS

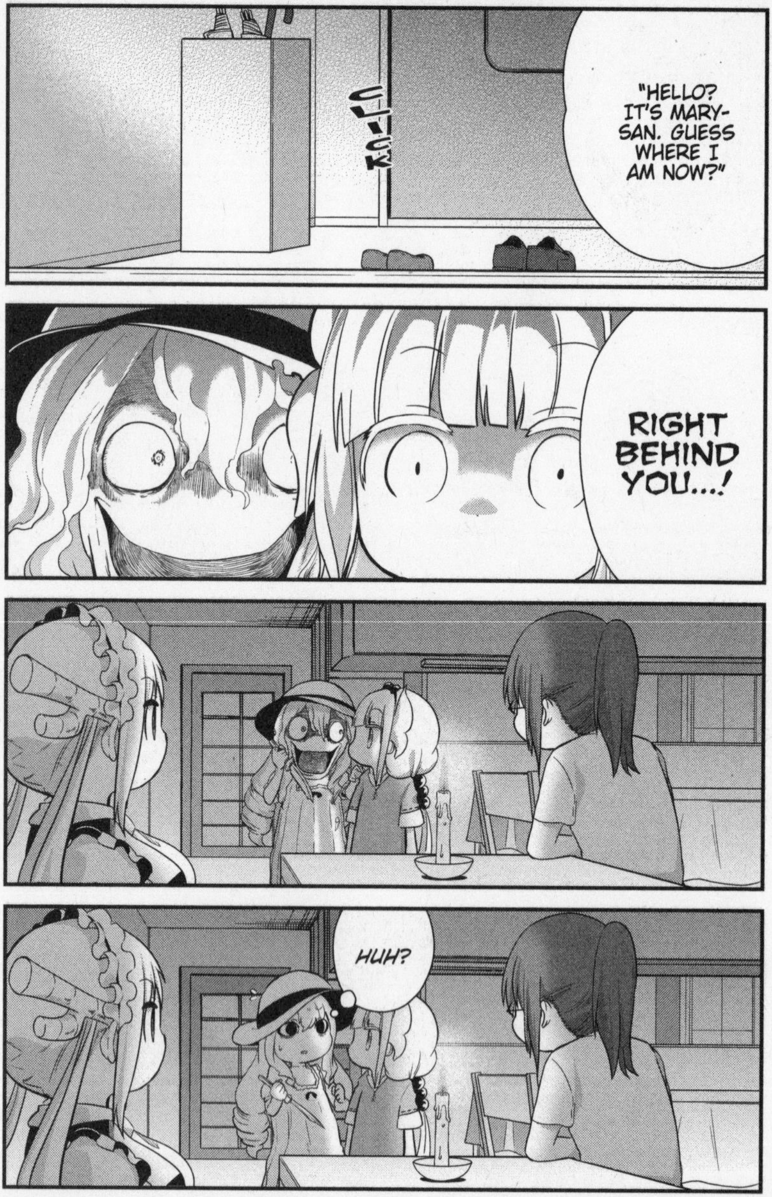
"HELLO? IT'S MARY-SAN. GUESS WHERE I AM NOW?"
CLICK
RIGHT BEHIND YOU...!
HUH?

NICE TO MEET YOU

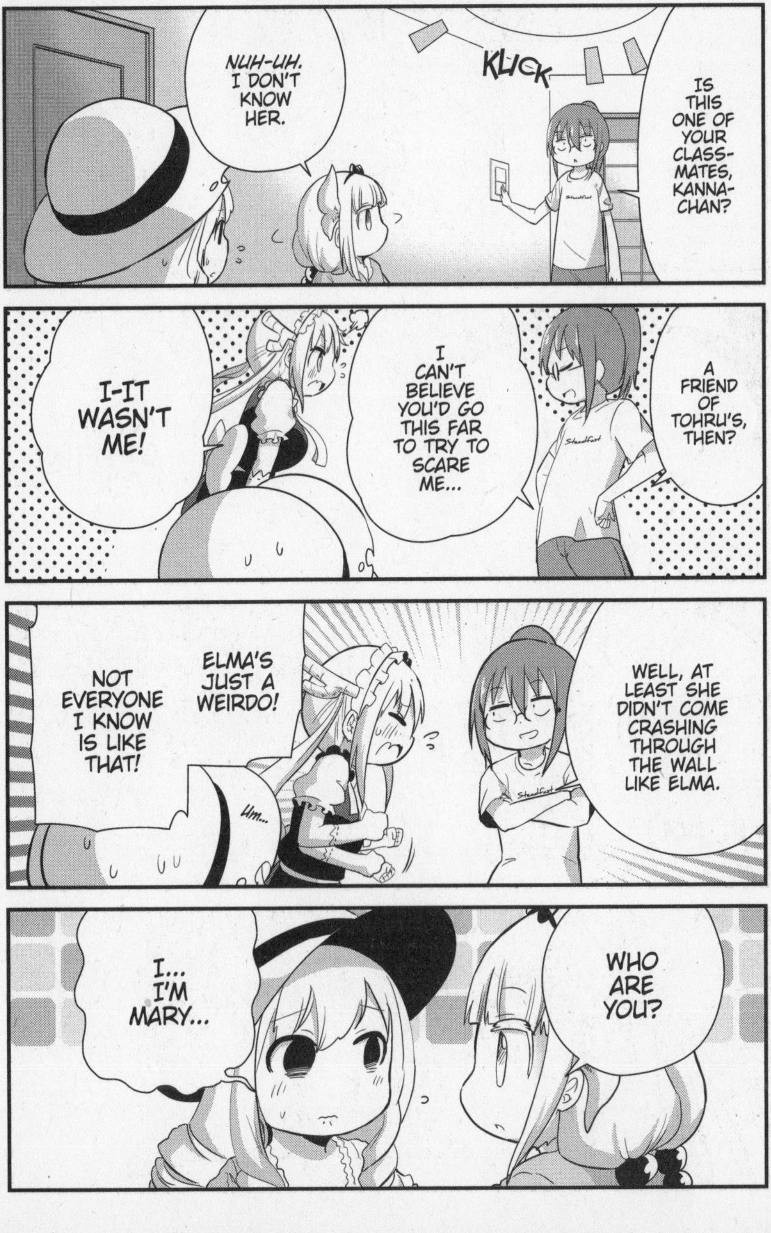
IS THIS ONE OF YOUR CLASSMATES, KANNA-CHAN?
KLICK
NUH-UH. I DON'T KNOW HER.
A FRIEND OF TOHRU'S, THEN?
I CAN'T BELIEVE YOU'D GO THIS FAR TO TRY TO SCARE ME...
I-IT WASN'T ME!
WELL, AT LEAST SHE DIDN'T COME CRASHING THROUGH THE WALL LIKE ELMA.
ELMA'S JUST A WEIRDO!
NOT EVERYONE I KNOW IS LIKE THAT!
Um...
WHO ARE YOU?
I... I'M MARY...

DON'T GIVE UP

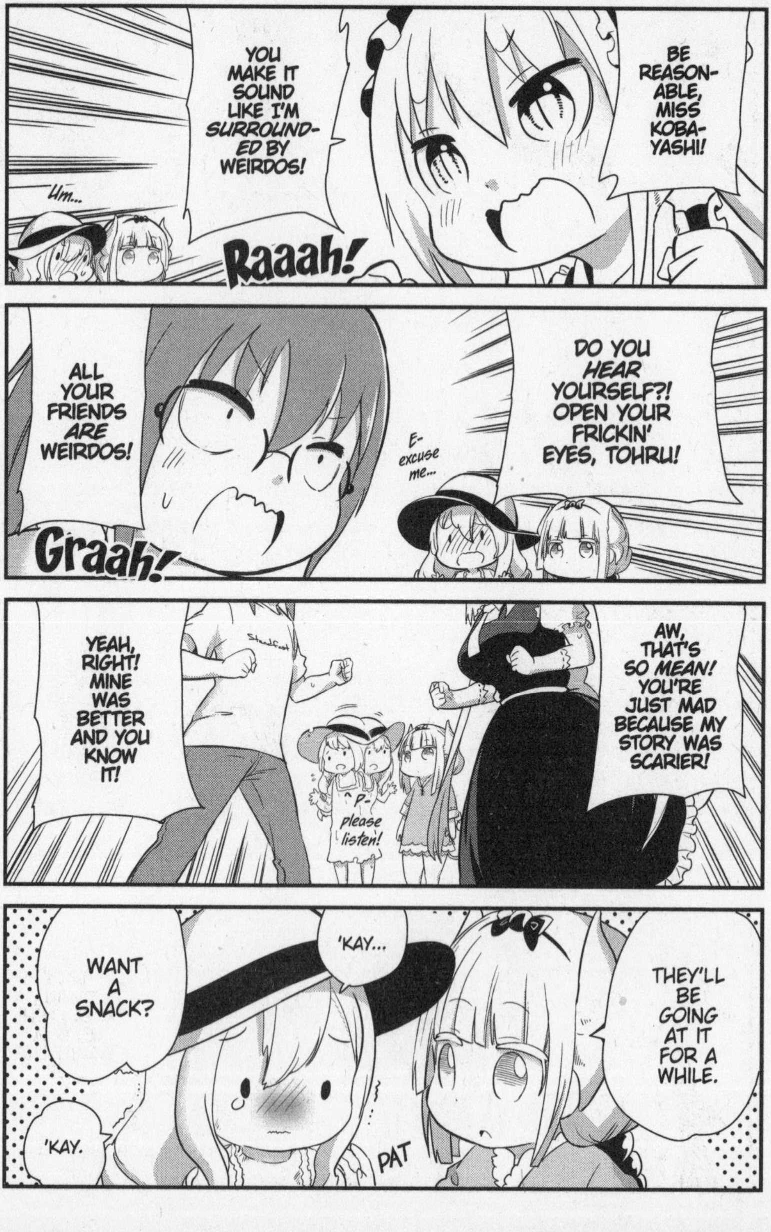
BE REASONABLE, MISS KOBAYASHI!
YOU MAKE IT SOUND LIKE I'M SURROUNDED BY WEIRDOS!
Raaah!
Um...
DO YOU HEAR YOURSELF?! OPEN YOUR FRICKIN' EYES, TOHRU!
E-excuse me...
ALL YOUR FRIENDS ARE WEIRDOS!
Graah!
AW, THAT'S SO MEAN! YOU'RE JUST MAD BECAUSE MY STORY WAS SCARIER!
P-please listen!
YEAH, RIGHT! MINE WAS BETTER AND YOU KNOW IT!
THEY'LL BE GOING AT IT FOR A WHILE.
'KAY...
WANT A SNACK?
'KAY.
PAT

FAREWELL

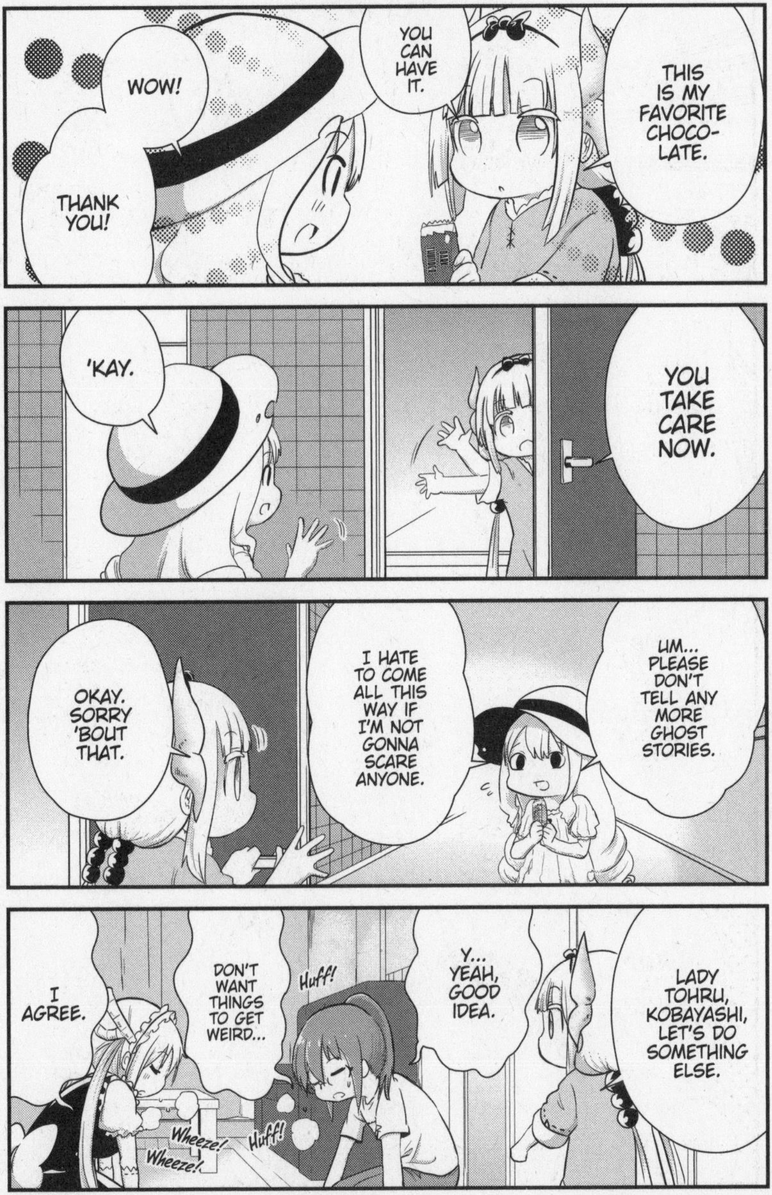
THIS IS MY FAVORITE CHOCOLATE.
YOU CAN HAVE IT.
WOW!
THANK YOU!
YOU TAKE CARE NOW.
'KAY.
UM... PLEASE DON'T TELL ANY MORE GHOST STORIES.
I HATE TO COME ALL THIS WAY IF I'M NOT GONNA SCARE ANYONE.
OKAY. SORRY 'BOUT THAT.
LADY TOHRU, KOBAYASHI, LET'S DO SOMETHING ELSE.
Y... YEAH, GOOD IDEA.
Huff!
Huff!
DON'T WANT THINGS TO GET WEIRD...
I AGREE.
Wheeze!
Wheeze!

STRANGE WORLD

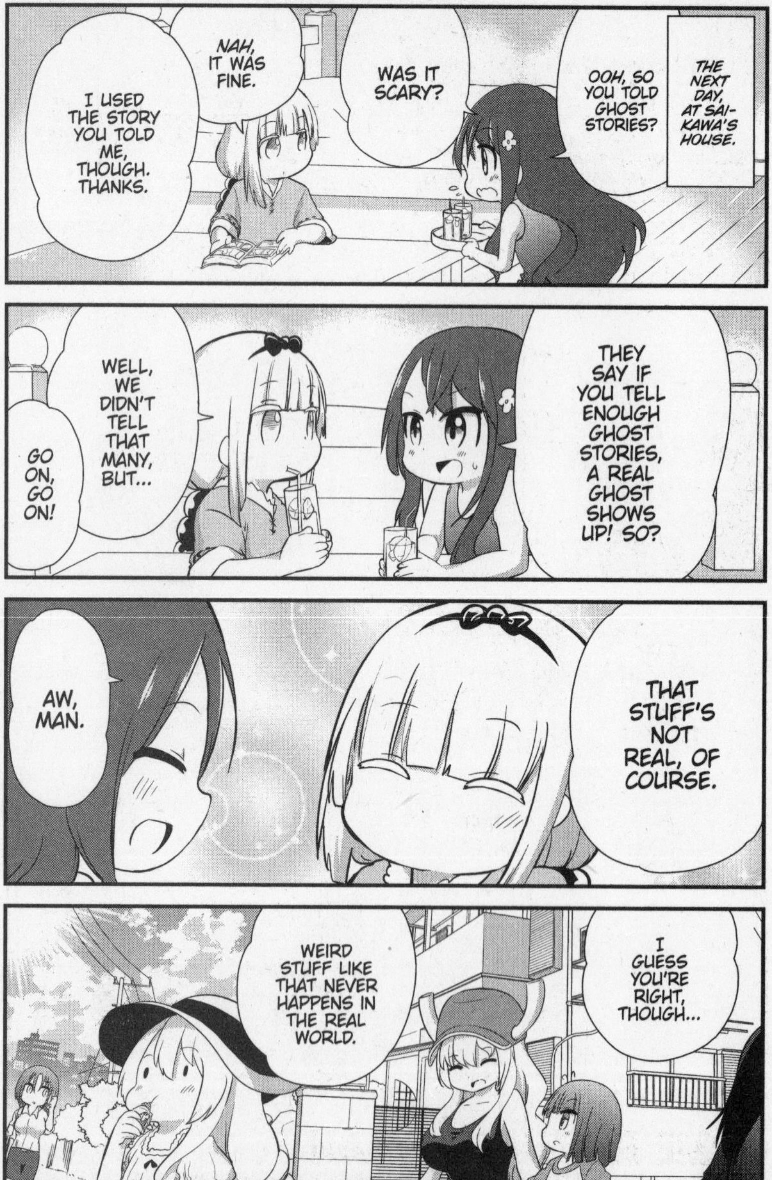
THE NEXT DAY, AT SAI-KAWA'S HOUSE.
OOH, SO YOU TOLD GHOST STORIES?
WAS IT SCARY?
NAH, IT WAS FINE.
I USED THE STORY YOU TOLD ME, THOUGH. THANKS.
THEY SAY IF YOU TELL ENOUGH GHOST STORIES, A REAL GHOST SHOWS UP! SO?
WELL, WE DIDN'T TELL THAT MANY, BUT...
GO ON, GO ON!
THAT STUFF'S NOT REAL, OF COURSE.
AW, MAN.
I GUESS YOU'RE RIGHT, THOUGH...
WEIRD STUFF LIKE THAT NEVER HAPPENS IN THE REAL WORLD.

TIME FOR GHOST STORIES/END

SPOTTED

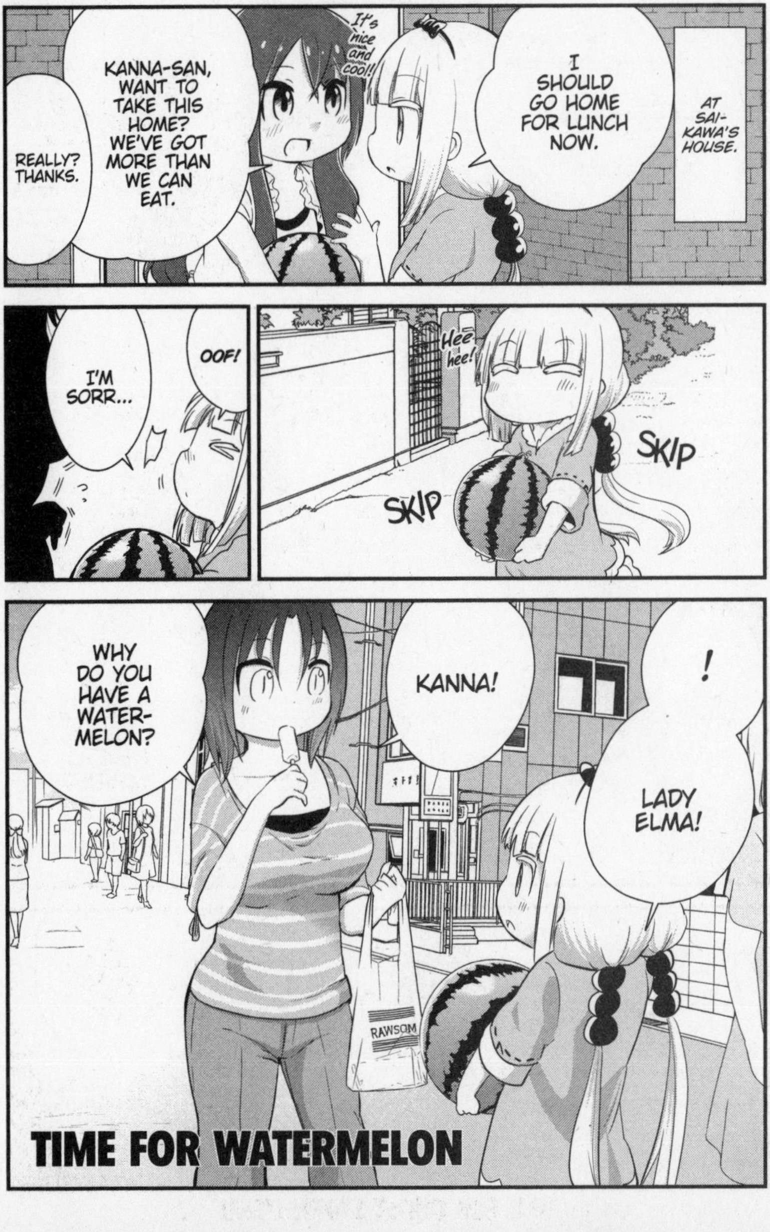
AT SAI-KAWA'S HOUSE.
I SHOULD GO HOME FOR LUNCH NOW.
It's nice and cool!!
KANNA-SAN, WANT TO TAKE THIS HOME? WE'VE GOT MORE THAN WE CAN EAT.
REALLY? THANKS.
Hee hee!
SKIP
SKIP
OOF!
I'M SORR...
!
LADY ELMA!
KANNA!
WHY DO YOU HAVE A WATER-MELON?
RAWSOM
TIME FOR WATERMELON

WARM WELCOME

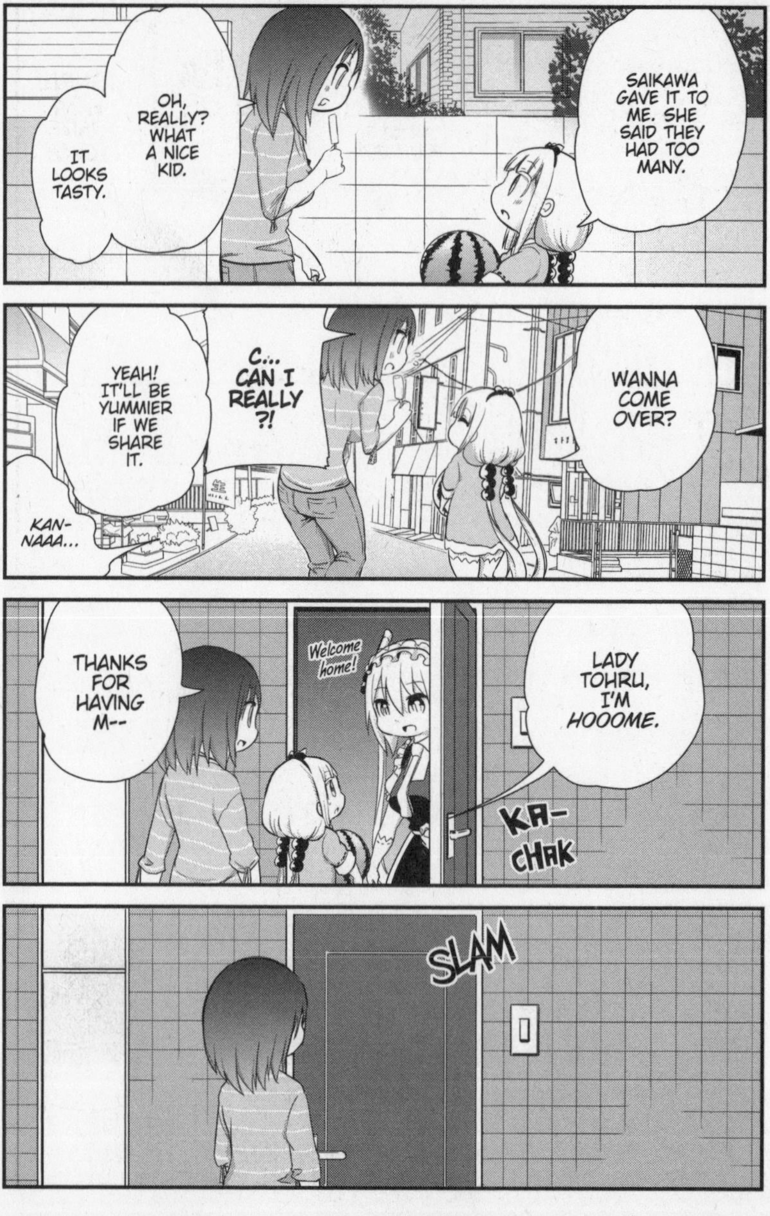
SAIKAWA GAVE IT TO ME. SHE SAID THEY HAD TOO MANY.
OH, REALLY? WHAT A NICE KID.
IT LOOKS TASTY.
WANNA COME OVER?
C... CAN I REALLY?!
YEAH! IT'LL BE YUMMIER IF WE SHARE IT.
KAN-NAAA...
LADY TOHRU, I'M HOOOME.
Welcome home!
KA-CHAK
THANKS FOR HAVING M--
SLAM

HOW IS THAT "NICE"?

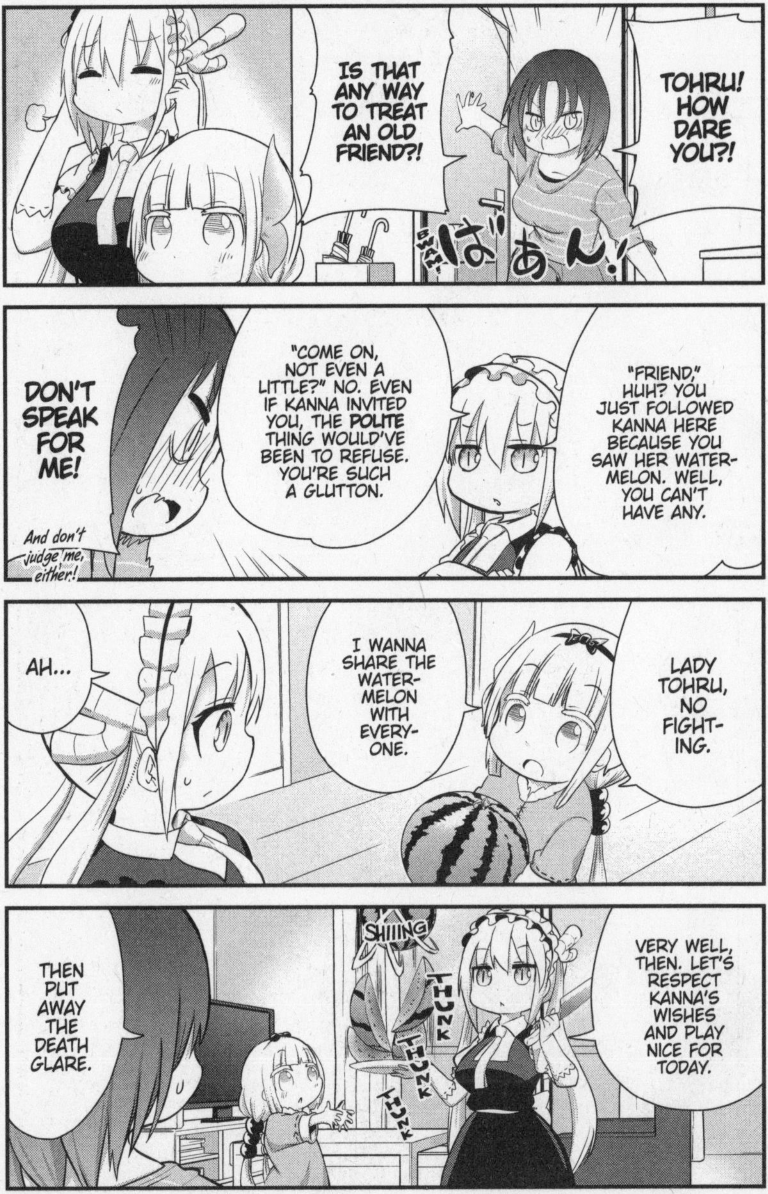
TOHRU! HOW DARE YOU?!
IS THAT ANY WAY TO TREAT AN OLD FRIEND?!
BWAM!
ばあん!
"FRIEND," HUH? YOU JUST FOLLOWED KANNA HERE BECAUSE YOU SAW HER WATER-MELON. WELL, YOU CAN'T HAVE ANY.
"COME ON, NOT EVEN A LITTLE?" NO. EVEN IF KANNA INVITED YOU, THE **POLITE** THING WOULD'VE BEEN TO REFUSE. YOU'RE SUCH A GLUTTON.
DON'T SPEAK FOR ME!
And don't judge me, either!
LADY TOHRU, NO FIGHT-ING.
I WANNA SHARE THE WATER-MELON WITH EVERY-ONE.
AH...
VERY WELL, THEN. LET'S RESPECT KANNA'S WISHES AND PLAY NICE FOR TODAY.
SHIIING
THUNK
THUNK
THUNK
THEN PUT AWAY THE DEATH GLARE.

THE TASTE OF SUMMER

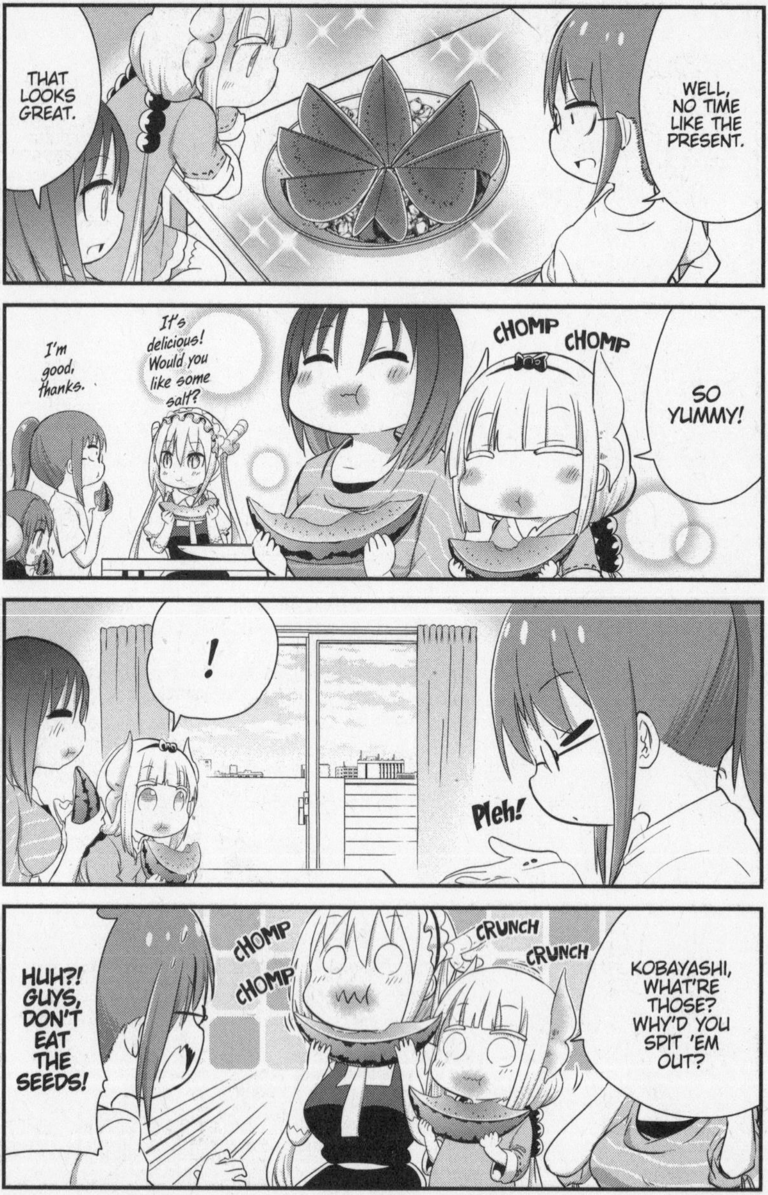
WELL, NO TIME LIKE THE PRESENT.
THAT LOOKS GREAT.
SO YUMMY!
CHOMP CHOMP
It's delicious! Would you like some salt?
I'm good, thanks.
Pleh!
!
KOBAYASHI, WHAT'RE THOSE? WHY'D YOU SPIT 'EM OUT?
CRUNCH CRUNCH
CHOMP CHOMP
HUH?! GUYS, DON'T EAT THE SEEDS!

THE RIND WAS GOOD, TOO

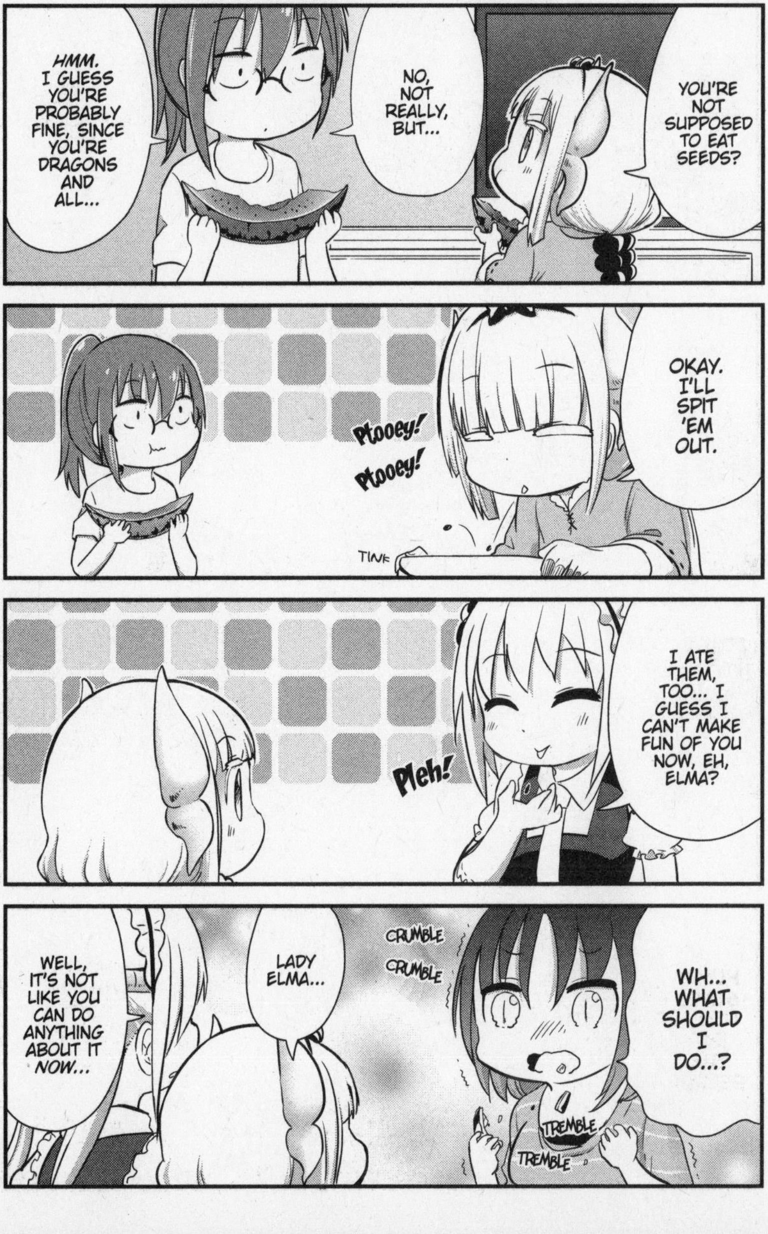
YOU'RE NOT SUPPOSED TO EAT SEEDS?
NO, NOT REALLY, BUT...
HMM. I GUESS YOU'RE PROBABLY FINE, SINCE YOU'RE DRAGONS AND ALL...
OKAY. I'LL SPIT 'EM OUT.
Ptooey!
Ptooey!
TINK
I ATE THEM, TOO... I GUESS I CAN'T MAKE FUN OF YOU NOW, EH, ELMA?
Pleh!
WH... WHAT SHOULD I DO...?
CRUMBLE
CRUMBLE
TREMBLE
TREMBLE
LADY ELMA...
WELL, IT'S NOT LIKE YOU CAN DO ANYTHING ABOUT IT NOW...

A PERFECT CYCLE

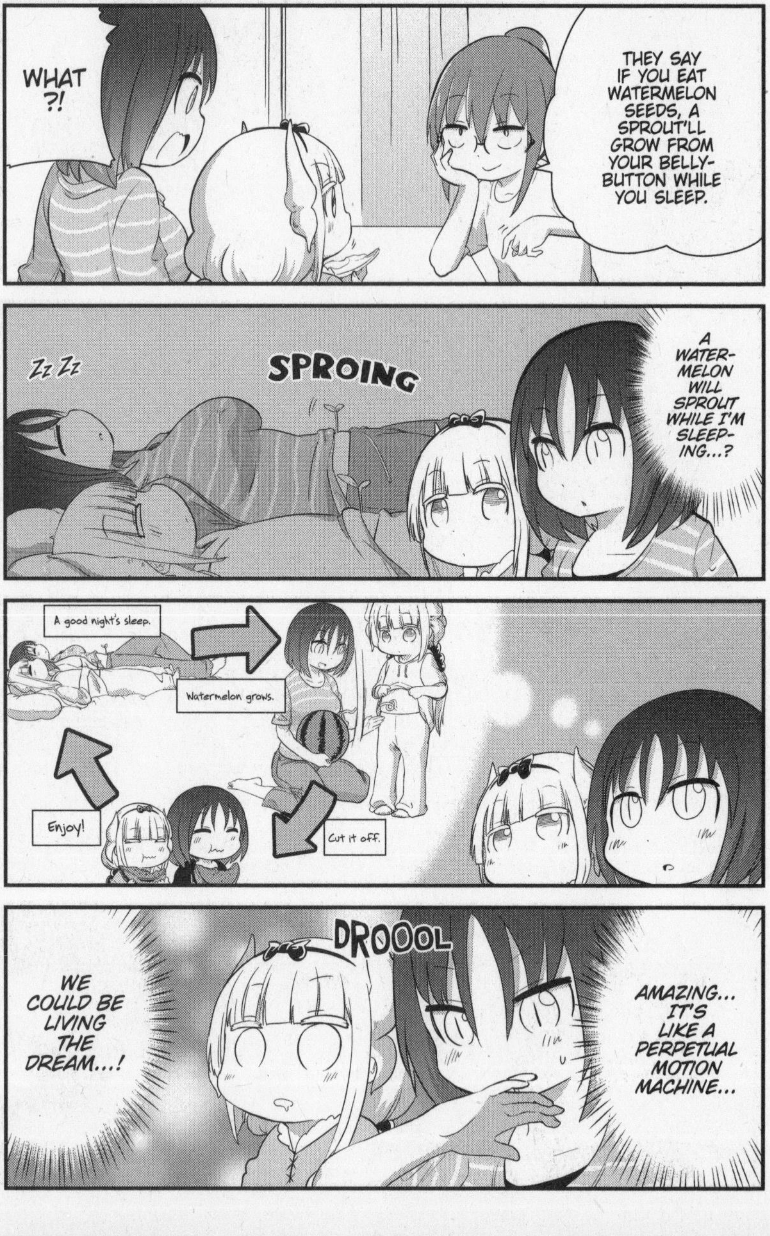
THEY SAY IF YOU EAT WATERMELON SEEDS, A SPROUT'LL GROW FROM YOUR BELLY-BUTTON WHILE YOU SLEEP.
WHAT ?!
A WATER-MELON WILL SPROUT WHILE I'M SLEEP-ING...?
SPROING
Zz Zz
A good night's sleep.
Watermelon grows.
Cut it off.
Enjoy!
AMAZING... IT'S LIKE A PERPETUAL MOTION MACHINE...
DROOOL
WE COULD BE LIVING THE DREAM...!

MADNESS DESCENDS

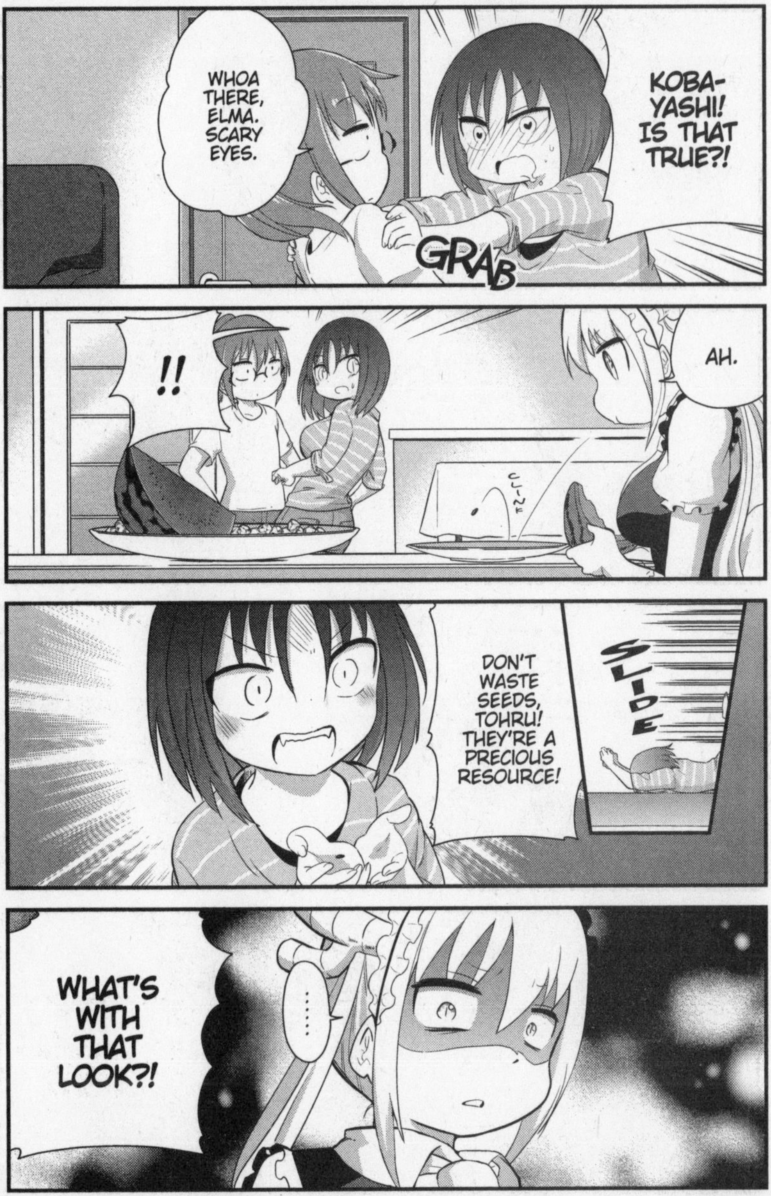
KOBA-YASHI! IS THAT TRUE?!
GRAB
WHOA THERE, ELMA. SCARY EYES.
AH.
CLINK
!!
SLIDE
DON'T WASTE SEEDS, TOHRU! THEY'RE A PRECIOUS RESOURCE!
......
WHAT'S WITH THAT LOOK?!

RAPID FIRE!

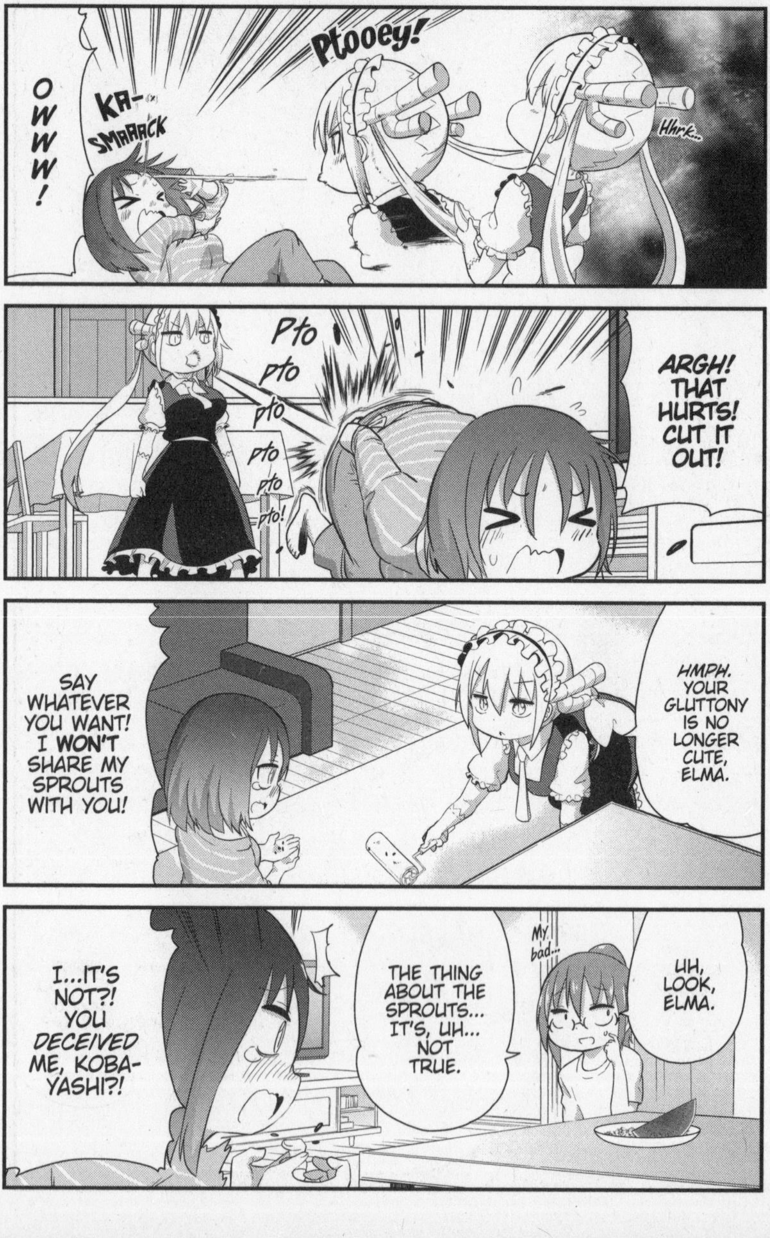
Hhrk...
Ptooey!
KA-SMAAACK
OWWWW!
ARGH! THAT HURTS! CUT IT OUT!
Pto
pto
pto
pto
pto
pto!
HMPH. YOUR GLUTTONY IS NO LONGER CUTE, ELMA.
SAY WHATEVER YOU WANT! I WON'T SHARE MY SPROUTS WITH YOU!
UH, LOOK, ELMA.
My bad...
THE THING ABOUT THE SPROUTS... IT'S, UH... NOT TRUE.
I...IT'S NOT?! YOU DECEIVED ME, KOBAYASHI?!

KANNA GETS A BRAINSTORM

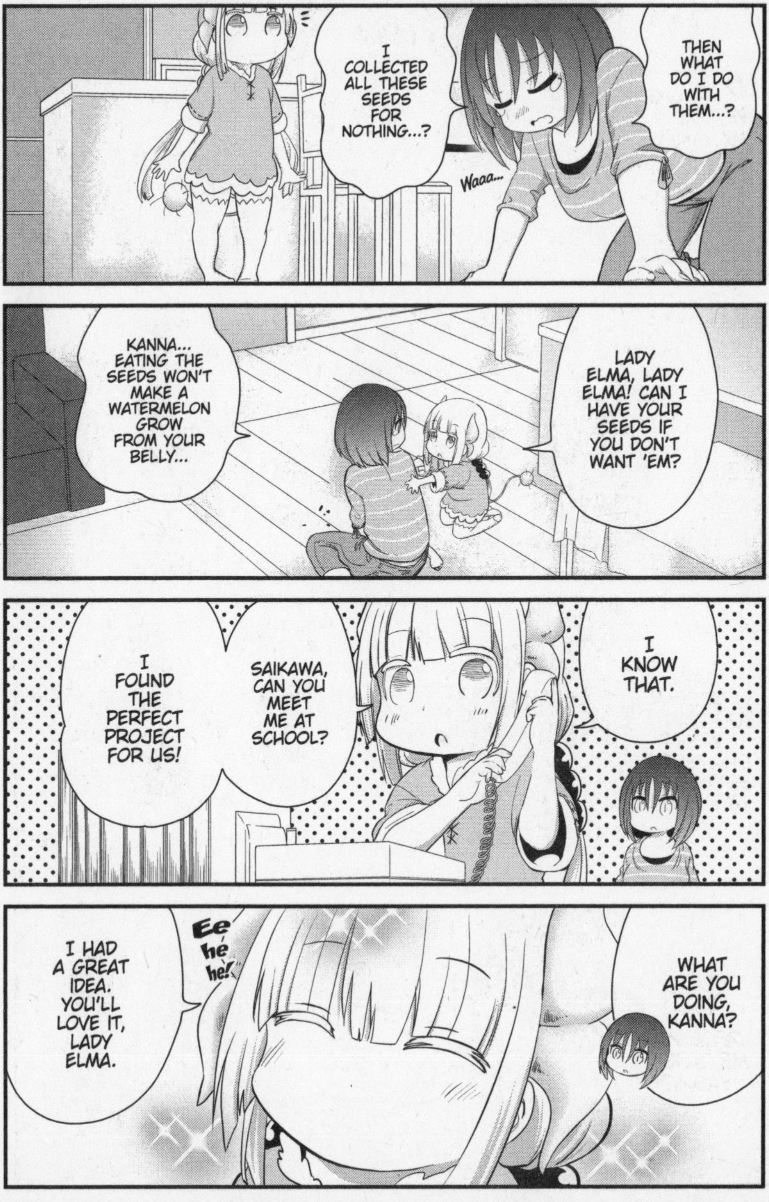
THEN WHAT DO I DO WITH THEM...?
I COLLECTED ALL THESE SEEDS FOR NOTHING...?
Waaa...
LADY ELMA, LADY ELMA! CAN I HAVE YOUR SEEDS IF YOU DON'T WANT 'EM?
KANNA... EATING THE SEEDS WON'T MAKE A WATERMELON GROW FROM YOUR BELLY...
I KNOW THAT.
SAIKAWA, CAN YOU MEET ME AT SCHOOL?
I FOUND THE PERFECT PROJECT FOR US!
WHAT ARE YOU DOING, KANNA?
Ee hé hé!
I HAD A GREAT IDEA. YOU'LL LOVE IT, LADY ELMA.

SHARED GOALS!

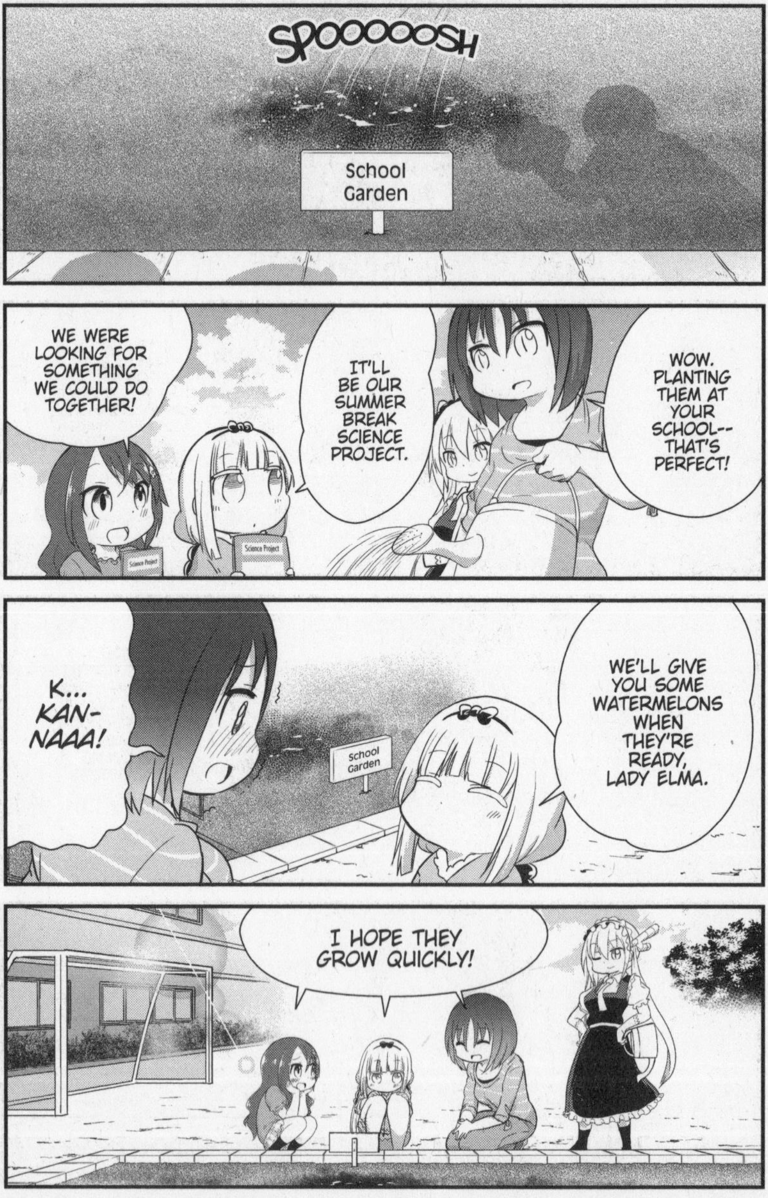
SPOOOOOSH
School Garden
WOW. PLANTING THEM AT YOUR SCHOOL--THAT'S PERFECT!
IT'LL BE OUR SUMMER BREAK SCIENCE PROJECT.
WE WERE LOOKING FOR SOMETHING WE COULD DO TOGETHER!
Science Project
Science Project
WE'LL GIVE YOU SOME WATERMELONS WHEN THEY'RE READY, LADY ELMA.
School Garden
K... KAN-NAAA!
I HOPE THEY GROW QUICKLY!

HUMANS AND DRAGONS

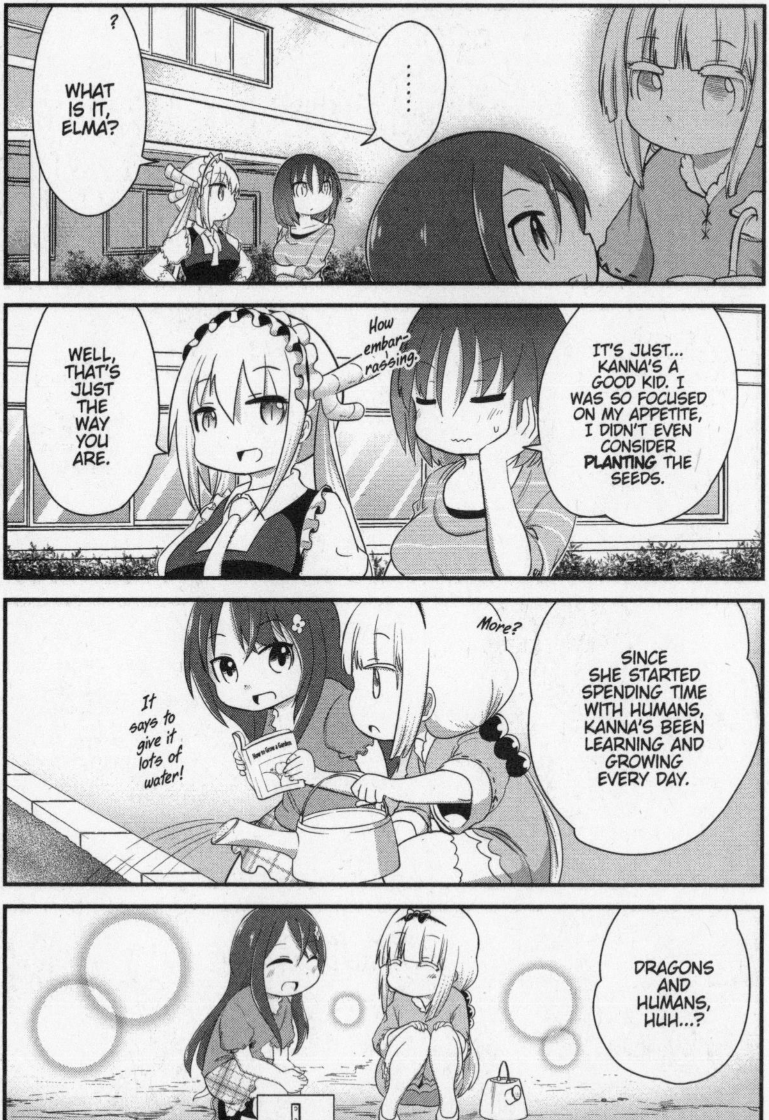
......
?
WHAT IS IT, ELMA?
IT'S JUST... KANNA'S A GOOD KID. I WAS SO FOCUSED ON MY APPETITE, I DIDN'T EVEN CONSIDER **PLANTING** THE SEEDS.
How embar-rassing.
WELL, THAT'S JUST THE WAY YOU ARE.
SINCE SHE STARTED SPENDING TIME WITH HUMANS, KANNA'S BEEN LEARNING AND GROWING EVERY DAY.
More?
It says to give it lots of water!
How to Grow a Garden
DRAGONS AND HUMANS, HUH...?

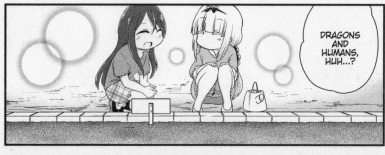

BEWARE OF OVEREATING, FOLKS!

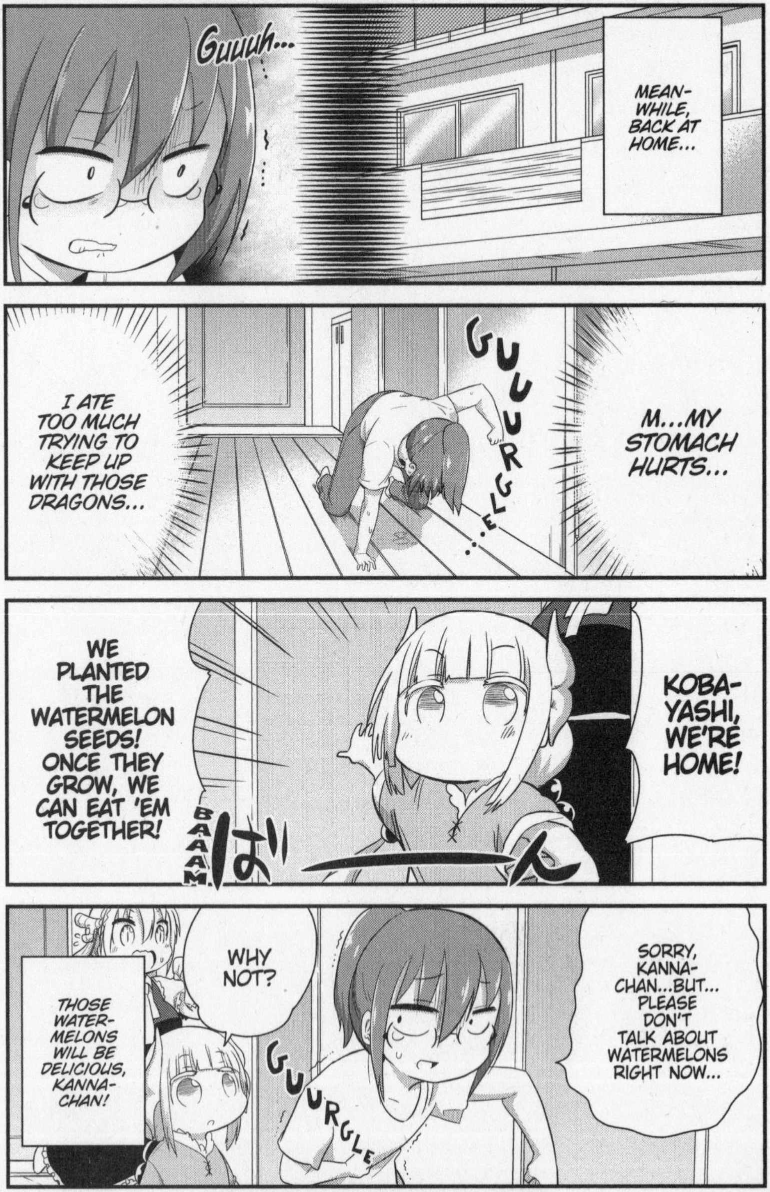
MEAN-WHILE, BACK AT HOME...
Guuuh...
M...MY STOMACH HURTS...
GUUURGLE...
I ATE TOO MUCH TRYING TO KEEP UP WITH THOSE DRAGONS...
KOBA-YASHI, WE'RE HOME!
WE PLANTED THE WATERMELON SEEDS! ONCE THEY GROW, WE CAN EAT 'EM TOGETHER!
BAAAAM
ばーん
SORRY, KANNA-CHAN...BUT...PLEASE DON'T TALK ABOUT WATERMELONS RIGHT NOW...
GUUURGLE
WHY NOT?
THOSE WATER-MELONS WILL BE DELICIOUS, KANNA-CHAN!

TIME FOR WATERMELON/END

FLOP
FLOP

I
wonder
if the
watermelons
sprouted
yet?

Miss Kobayashi's Dragon Maid

Kanna's Daily Life

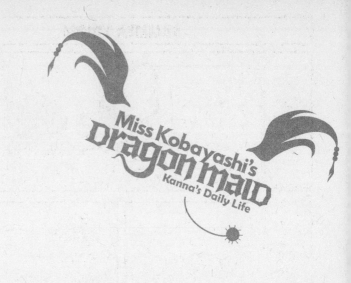

SUMMER STORM

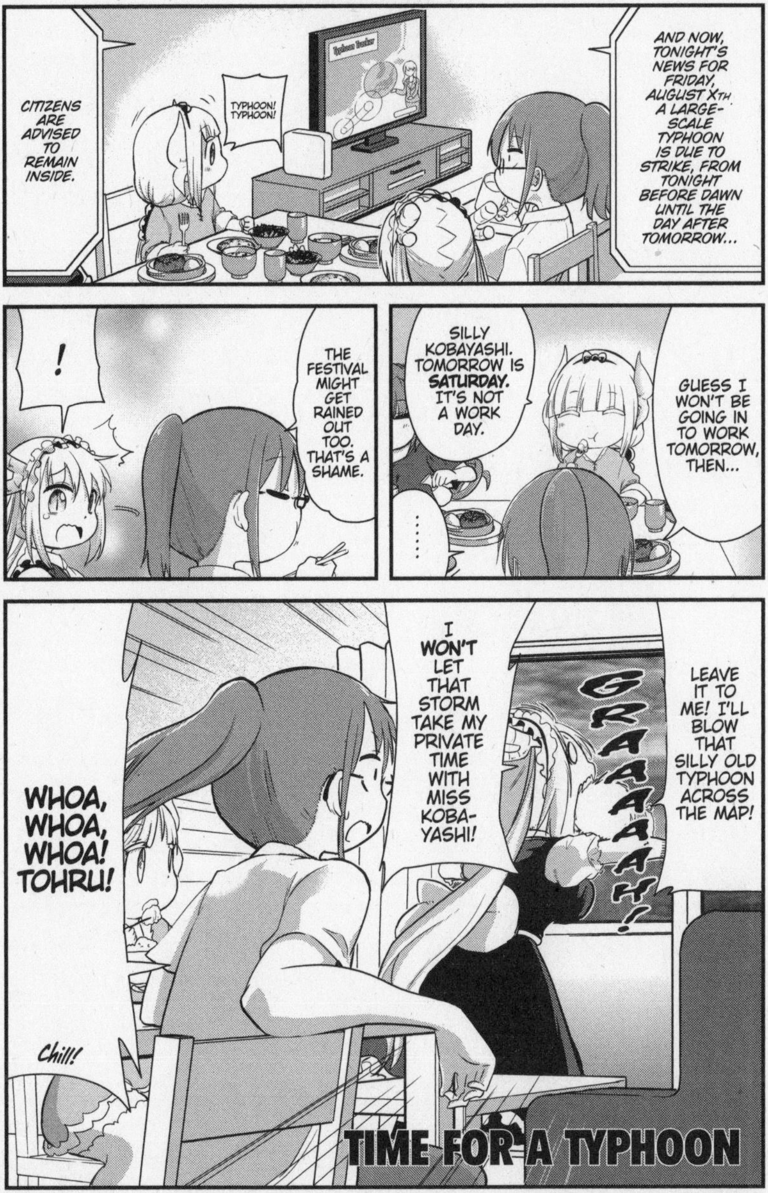
AND NOW, TONIGHT'S NEWS FOR FRIDAY, AUGUST XTH A LARGE-SCALE TYPHOON IS DUE TO STRIKE, FROM TONIGHT BEFORE DAWN UNTIL THE DAY AFTER TOMORROW...
Typhoon Tracker
TYPHOON! TYPHOON!
CITIZENS ARE ADVISED TO REMAIN INSIDE.
GUESS I WON'T BE GOING IN TO WORK TOMORROW, THEN...
SILLY KOBAYASHI. TOMORROW IS SATURDAY. IT'S NOT A WORK DAY.
......
THE FESTIVAL MIGHT GET RAINED OUT TOO. THAT'S A SHAME.
!
LEAVE IT TO ME! I'LL BLOW THAT SILLY OLD TYPHOON ACROSS THE MAP!
GRAAAAAH!
I WON'T LET THAT STORM TAKE MY PRIVATE TIME WITH MISS KOBAYASHI!
WHOA, WHOA, WHOA! TOHRU!
Chill!
TIME FOR A TYPHOON

SO GREEDY

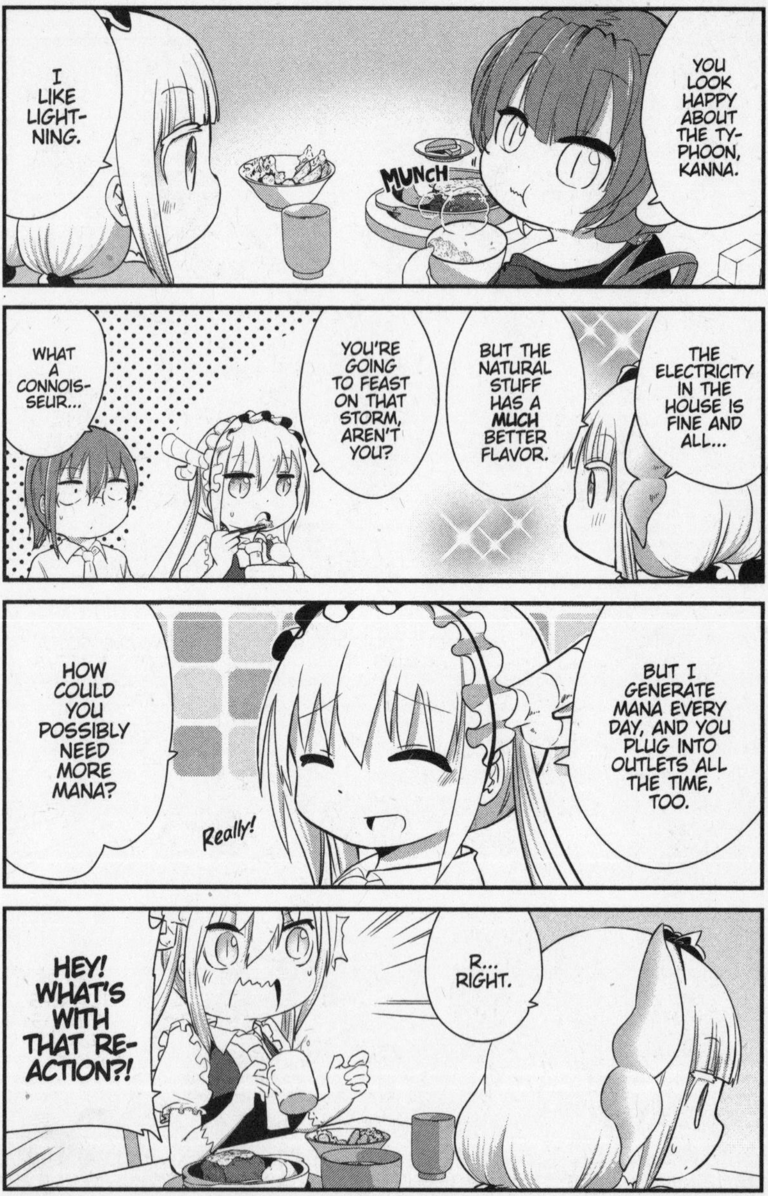
YOU LOOK HAPPY ABOUT THE TY-PHOON, KANNA.
MUNCH
I LIKE LIGHT-NING.
THE ELECTRICITY IN THE HOUSE IS FINE AND ALL...
BUT THE NATURAL STUFF HAS A MUCH BETTER FLAVOR.
YOU'RE GOING TO FEAST ON THAT STORM, AREN'T YOU?
WHAT A CONNOIS-SEUR...
BUT I GENERATE MANA EVERY DAY, AND YOU PLUG INTO OUTLETS ALL THE TIME, TOO.
Really!
HOW COULD YOU POSSIBLY NEED MORE MANA?
R... RIGHT.
HEY! WHAT'S WITH THAT RE-ACTION?!

WORDS CAN CUT

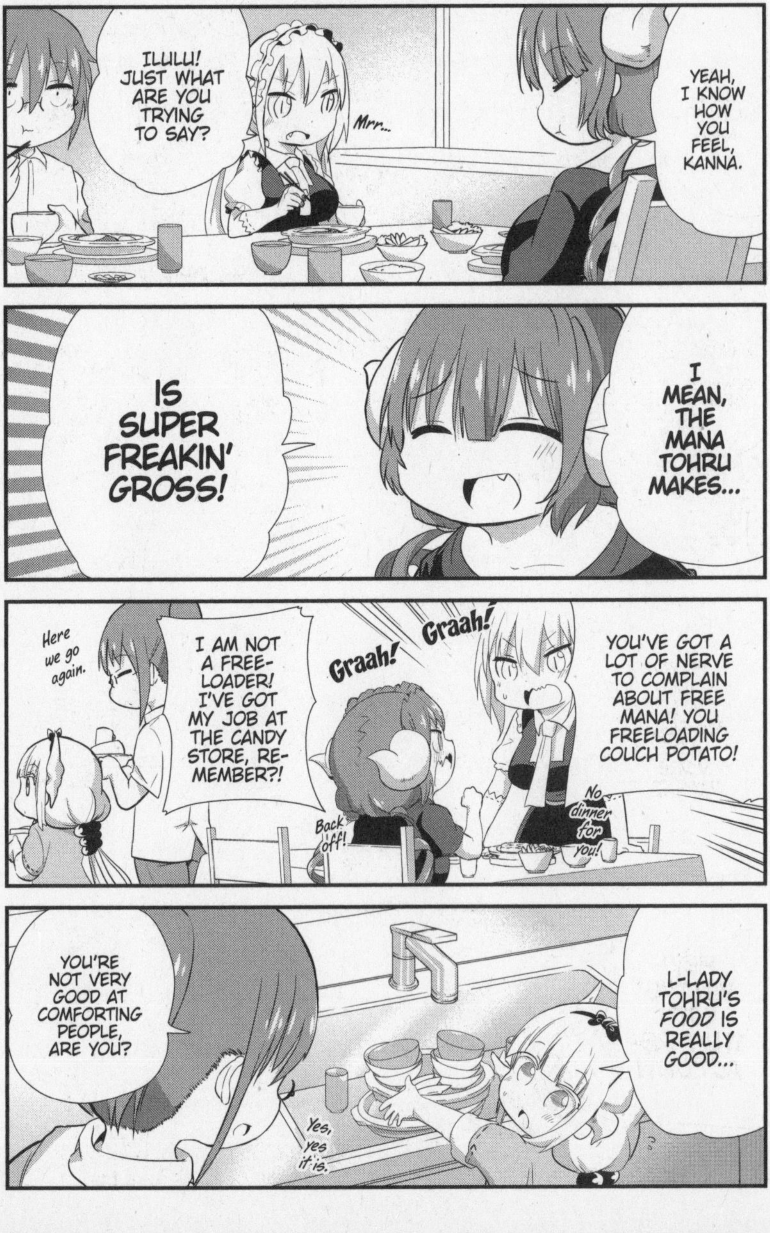
YEAH, I KNOW HOW YOU FEEL, KANNA.
Mrr...
ILULU! JUST WHAT ARE YOU TRYING TO SAY?
I MEAN, THE MANA TOHRU MAKES...
IS SUPER FREAKIN' GROSS!
YOU'VE GOT A LOT OF NERVE TO COMPLAIN ABOUT FREE MANA! YOU FREELOADING COUCH POTATO!
No dinner for you!
Graah!
Graah!
Back off!
I AM NOT A FREE-LOADER! I'VE GOT MY JOB AT THE CANDY STORE, RE-MEMBER?!
Here we go again.
L-LADY TOHRU'S FOOD IS REALLY GOOD...
Yes, yes it is.
YOU'RE NOT VERY GOOD AT COMFORTING PEOPLE, ARE YOU?

BUSINESS WARRIOR

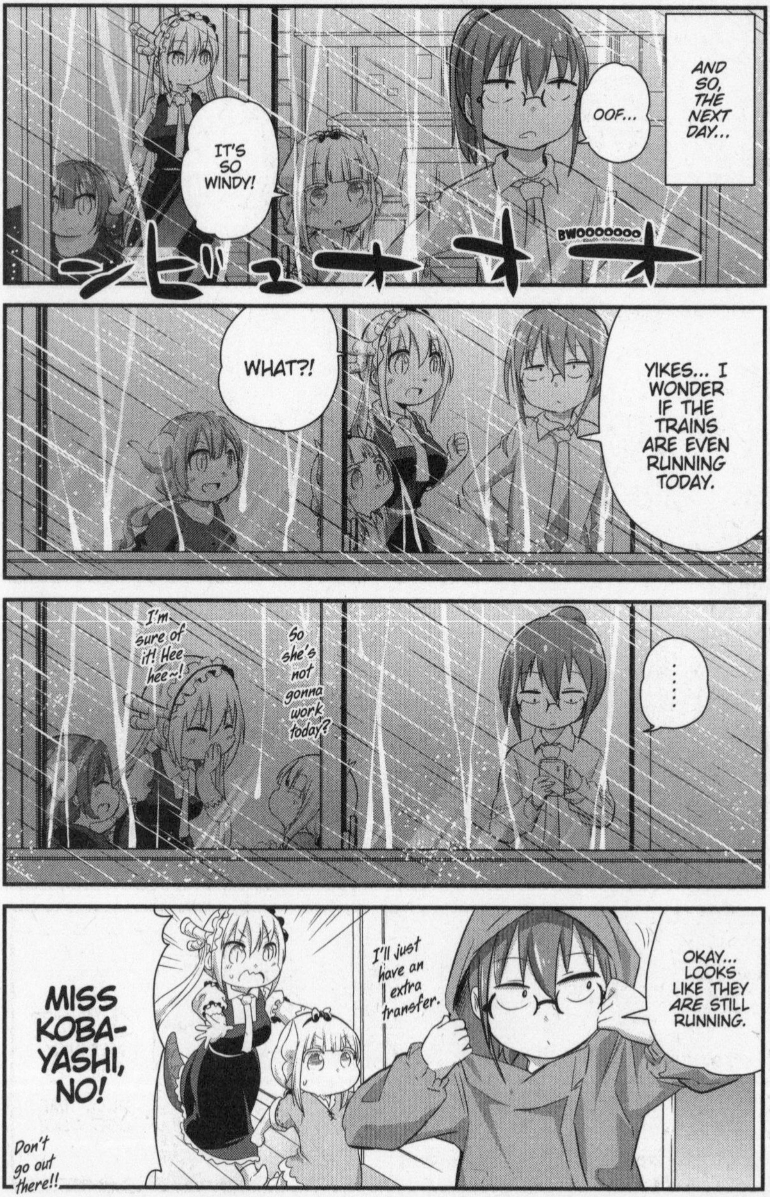
AND SO, THE NEXT DAY...
OOF...
BWOOOOOOO
IT'S SO WINDY!
YIKES... I WONDER IF THE TRAINS ARE EVEN RUNNING TODAY.
WHAT?!
......
So she's not gonna work today?
I'm sure of it! Hee hee~!
OKAY... LOOKS LIKE THEY ARE STILL RUNNING.
I'll just have an extra transfer.
MISS KOBA-YASHI, NO!
Don't go out there!!

KIDS DON'T CARE

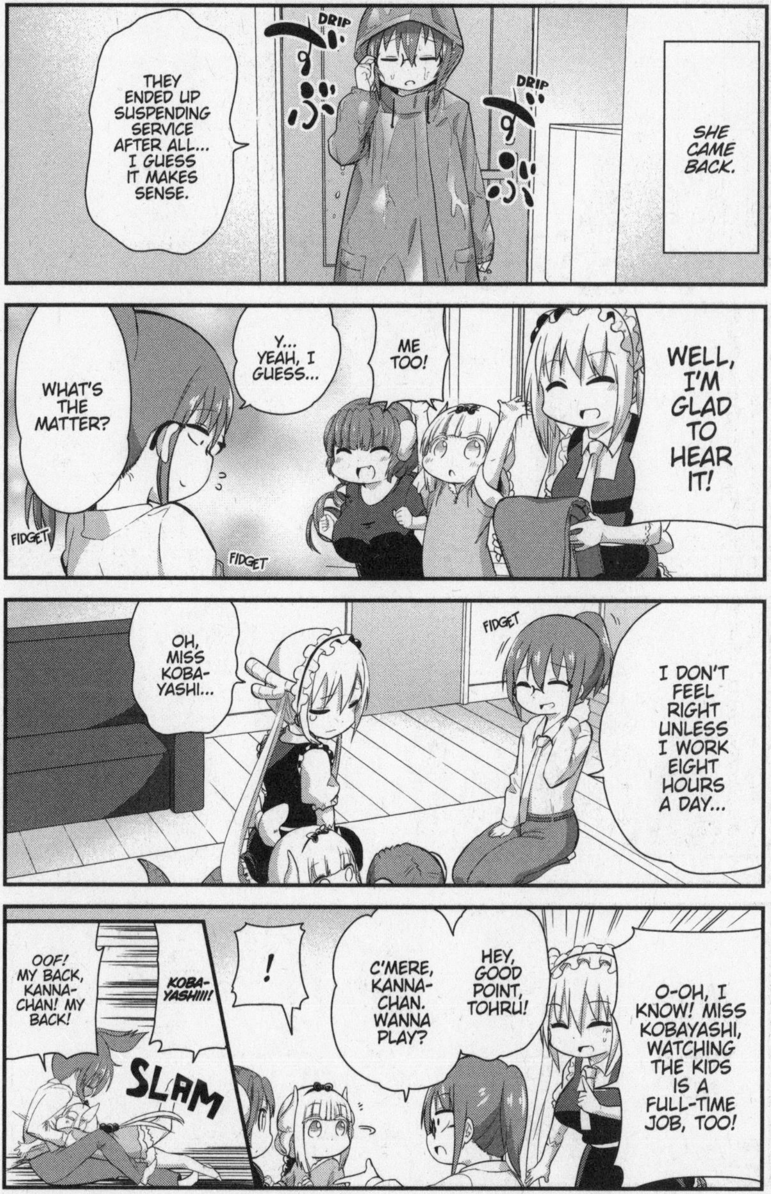
SHE CAME BACK.
DRIP
DRIP
THEY ENDED UP SUSPENDING SERVICE AFTER ALL... I GUESS IT MAKES SENSE.
WELL, I'M GLAD TO HEAR IT!
ME TOO!
Y... YEAH, I GUESS...
WHAT'S THE MATTER?
FIDGET
FIDGET
I DON'T FEEL RIGHT UNLESS I WORK EIGHT HOURS A DAY...
FIDGET
OH, MISS KOBA-YASHI...
O-OH, I KNOW! MISS KOBAYASHI, WATCHING THE KIDS IS A FULL-TIME JOB, TOO!
HEY, GOOD POINT, TOHRU!
C'MERE, KANNA-CHAN. WANNA PLAY?
!
KOBA-YASHIII!
SLAM
OOF! MY BACK, KANNA-CHAN! MY BACK!

CAN'T RESIST IT

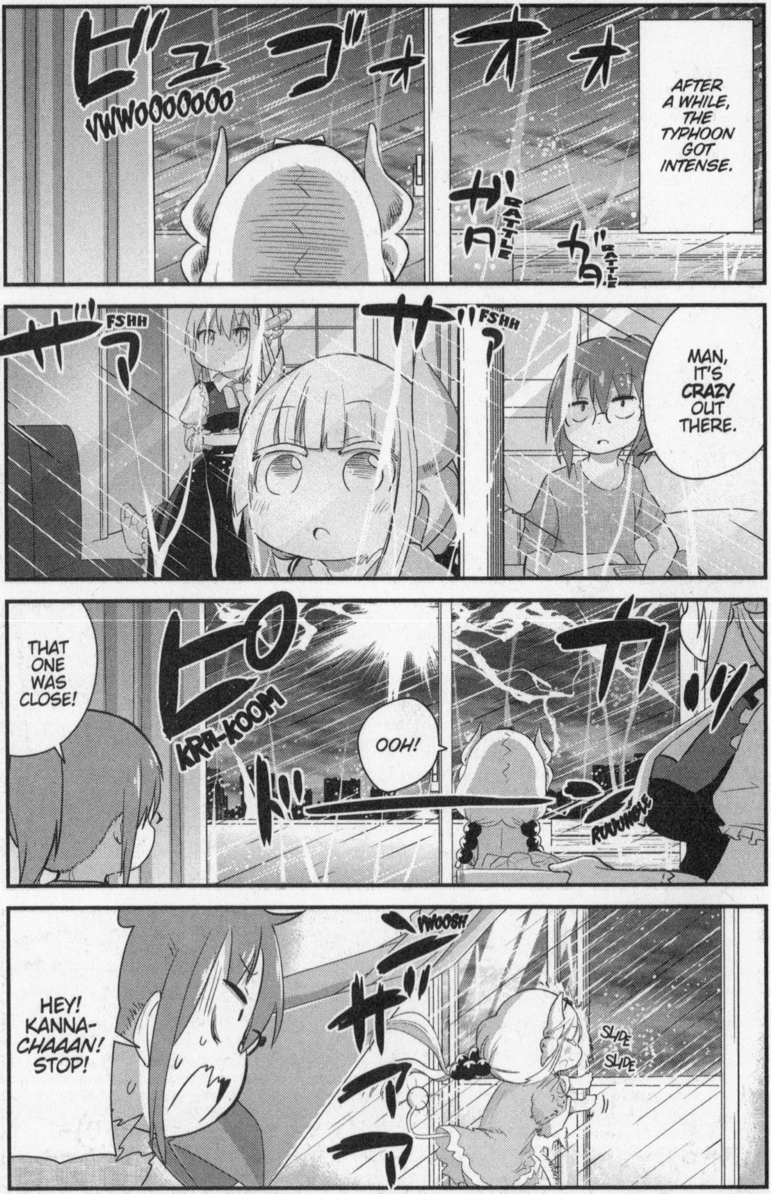
AFTER A WHILE, THE TYPHOON GOT INTENSE.
RATTLE
RATTLE
VWWOOOOOOO
FSHH
MAN, IT'S CRAZY OUT THERE.
FSHH
RUUUMBLE
OOH!
KRA-KOOM
THAT ONE WAS CLOSE!
SLIDE
SLIDE
VWOOSH
HEY! KANNA-CHAAAN! STOP!

I LOVE LIGHTNING!

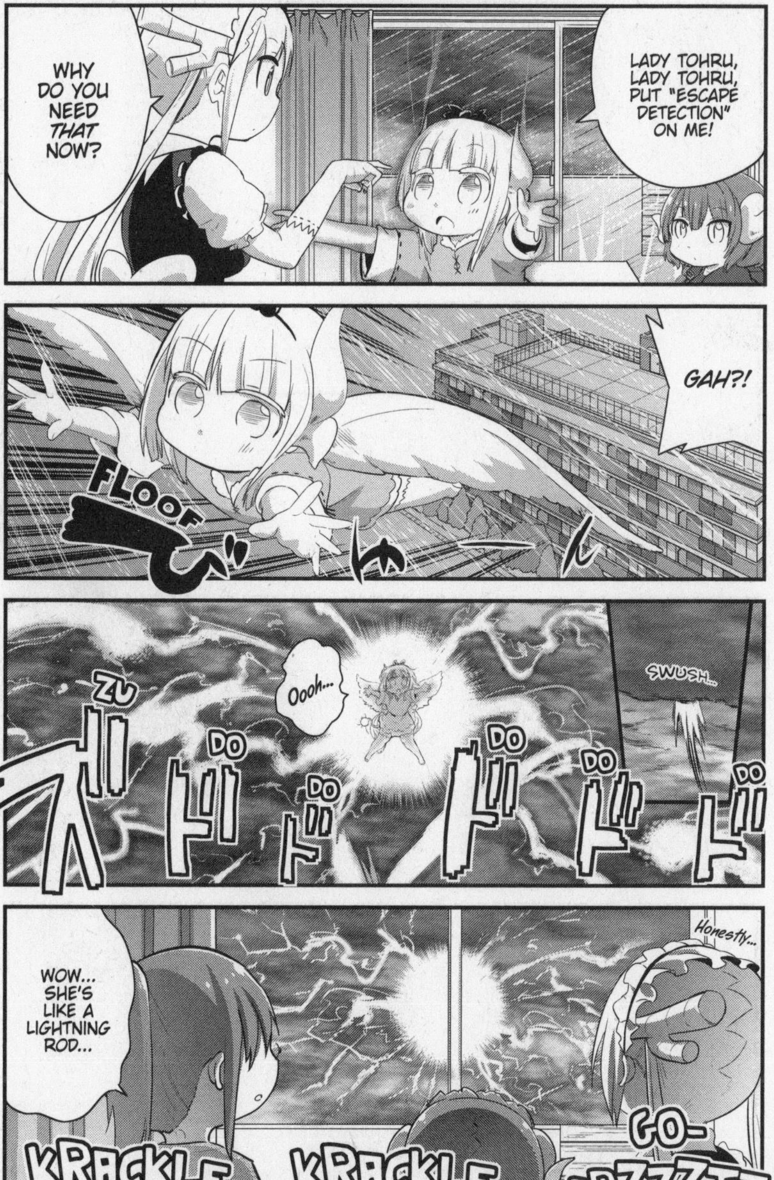
LADY TOHRU, LADY TOHRU, PUT "ESCAPE DETECTION" ON ME!
WHY DO YOU NEED THAT NOW?
GAH?!
FLOOF
SWUSH...
Oooh...
ZU
DO
DO
DO
DO
DO
Honestly...
GO-
BRZZZTT
KRACKLE
KRACKLE
WOW... SHE'S LIKE A LIGHTNING ROD...

GOOD INTENTIONS

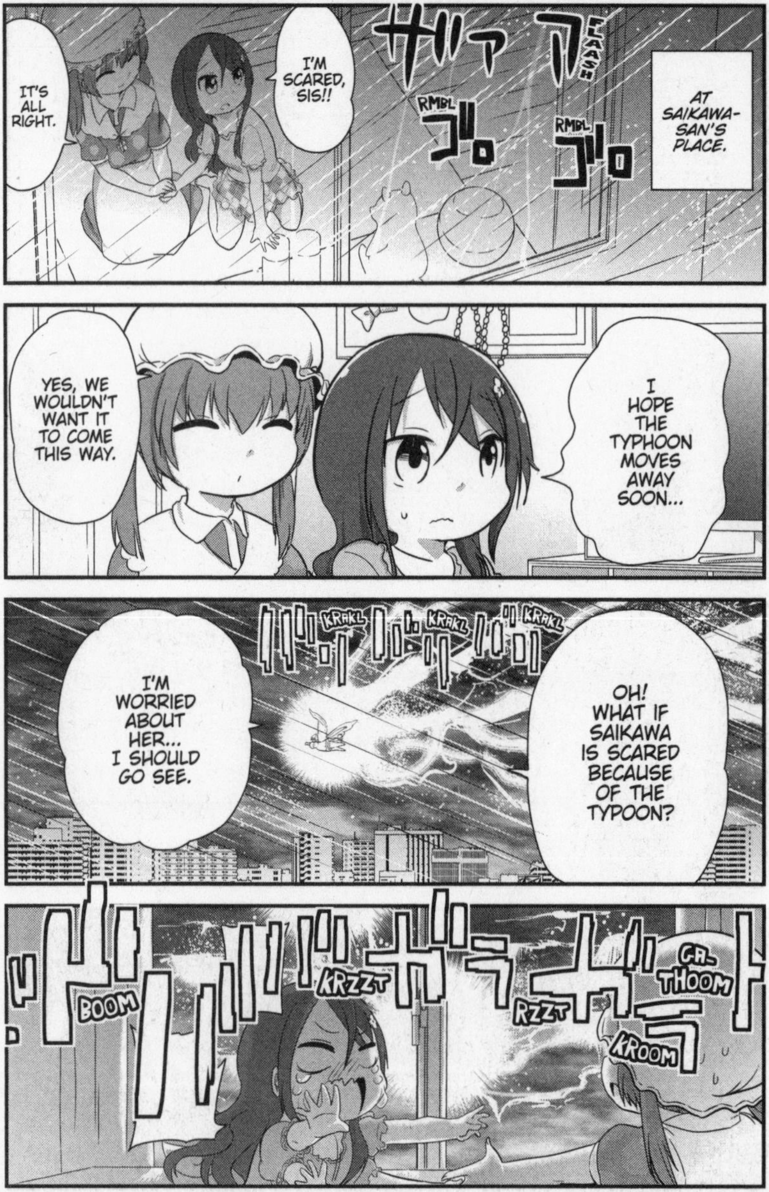
AT SAIKAWA-SAN'S PLACE.
FLAASH
RMBL ゴロ
RMBL ゴロ
I'M SCARED, SIS!!
IT'S ALL RIGHT.
I HOPE THE TYPHOON MOVES AWAY SOON...
YES, WE WOULDN'T WANT IT TO COME THIS WAY.
KRAKL
KRAKL
KRAKL
OH! WHAT IF SAIKAWA IS SCARED BECAUSE OF THE TYPOON?
I'M WORRIED ABOUT HER... I SHOULD GO SEE.
CA-THOOM
KROOM
RZZT
KRZZT
BOOM

MISS KOBAYASHI'S POWER OUTAGE

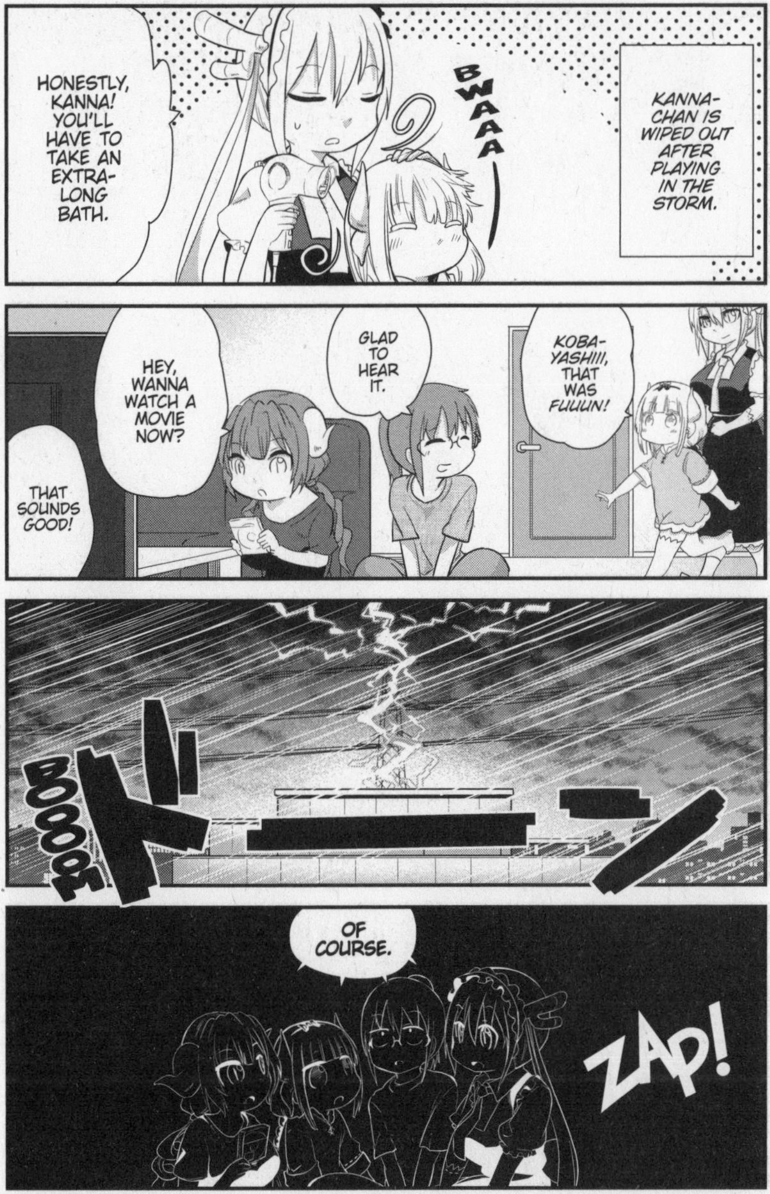
KANNA-CHAN IS WIPED OUT AFTER PLAYING IN THE STORM.
BWAAA
HONESTLY, KANNA! YOU'LL HAVE TO TAKE AN EXTRA-LONG BATH.
KOBA-YASHIII, THAT WAS FUUUN!
GLAD TO HEAR IT.
HEY, WANNA WATCH A MOVIE NOW?
THAT SOUNDS GOOD!
BOOOOOM
ZAP!
OF COURSE.

MY SWEET HOME

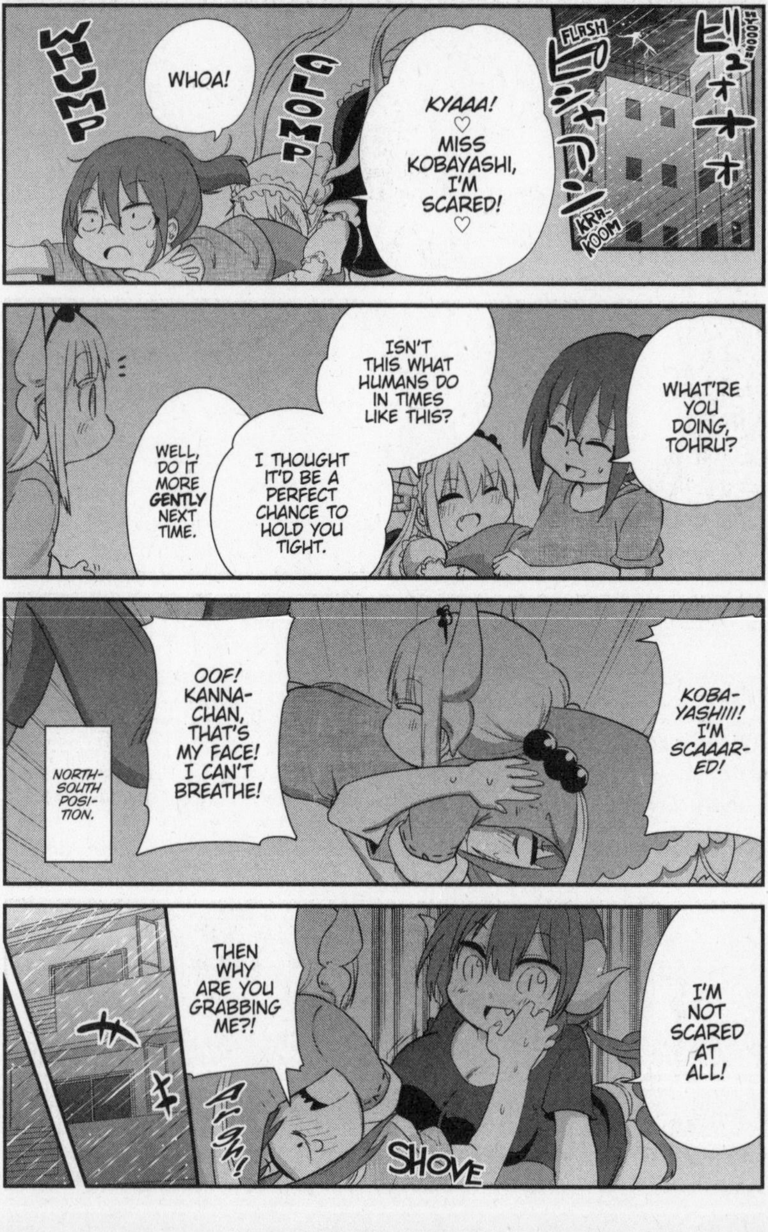
HYOOOSH
FLASH
KRA-KOOM
KYAAA! ♡ MISS KOBAYASHI, I'M SCARED! ♡
GLOMP
WHOA!
WHUMP
WHAT'RE YOU DOING, TOHRU?
ISN'T THIS WHAT HUMANS DO IN TIMES LIKE THIS?
I THOUGHT IT'D BE A PERFECT CHANCE TO HOLD YOU TIGHT.
WELL, DO IT MORE GENTLY NEXT TIME.
KOBAYASHIII! I'M SCAAARED!
OOF! KANNA-CHAN, THAT'S MY FACE! I CAN'T BREATHE!
NORTH-SOUTH POSITION.
I'M NOT SCARED AT ALL!
THEN WHY ARE YOU GRABBING ME?!
SHOVE

IT'S TOUGH BEING AN ADULT

OOOH!

THE NEXT DAY...

IT REALLY CLEARED UP FAST.

OF COURSE WE CAN.

CAN WE GO TO THE FESTIVAL?

SHAKE

SHAKE

KOBAYASHI! SINCE IT'S SUNDAY, YOU DON'T HAVE TO WORK, DO YOU?

!

I'M SO HAPPY WE GET TO SPEND THIS MUCH TIME WITH YOU, KOBAYASHI!

Hey, aren't we gonna get ready?

I'm happy, too. ♥

Sniffle

KANNA-CHAN... I'M SORRY...

SUMMER'S END

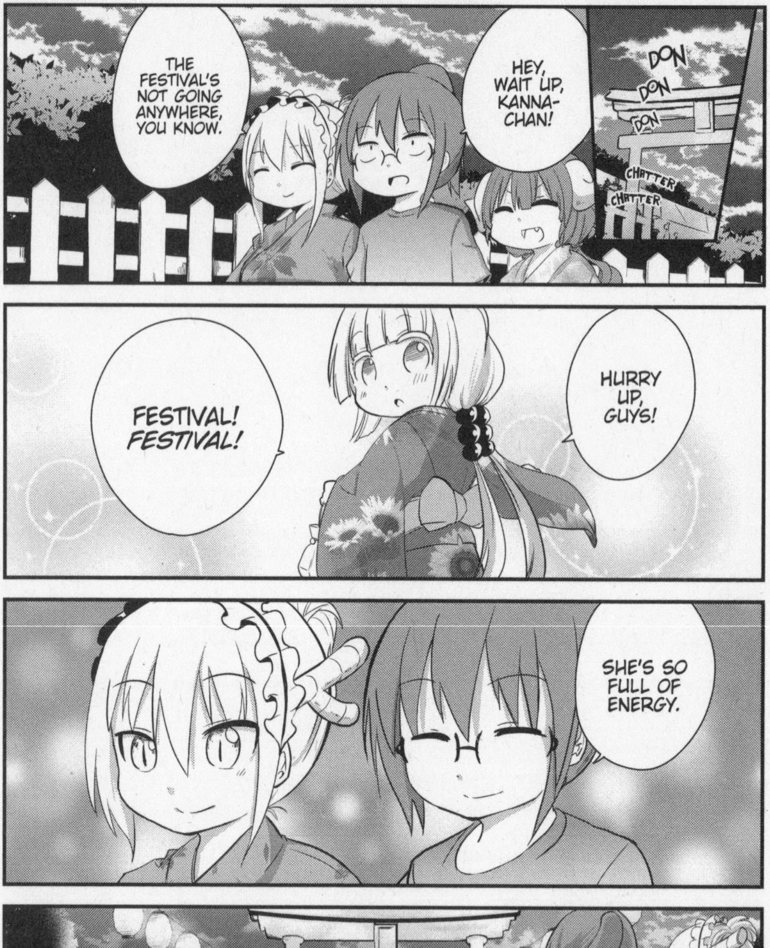
DON
DON
DON
CHATTER
CHATTER
HEY, WAIT UP, KANNA-CHAN!
THE FESTIVAL'S NOT GOING ANYWHERE, YOU KNOW.
HURRY UP, GUYS!
FESTIVAL! FESTIVAL!
SHE'S SO FULL OF ENERGY.

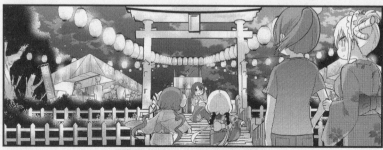

TIME FOR A TYPHOON/END

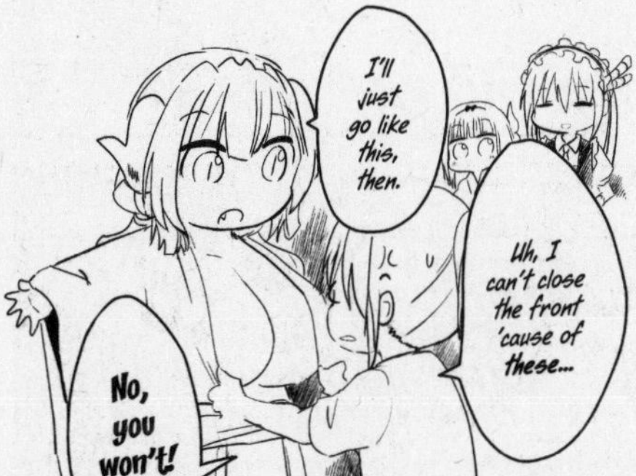
Uh, I can't close the front 'cause of these...
I'll just go like this, then.
No, you won't!

CHARACTER POPULARITY POLL!

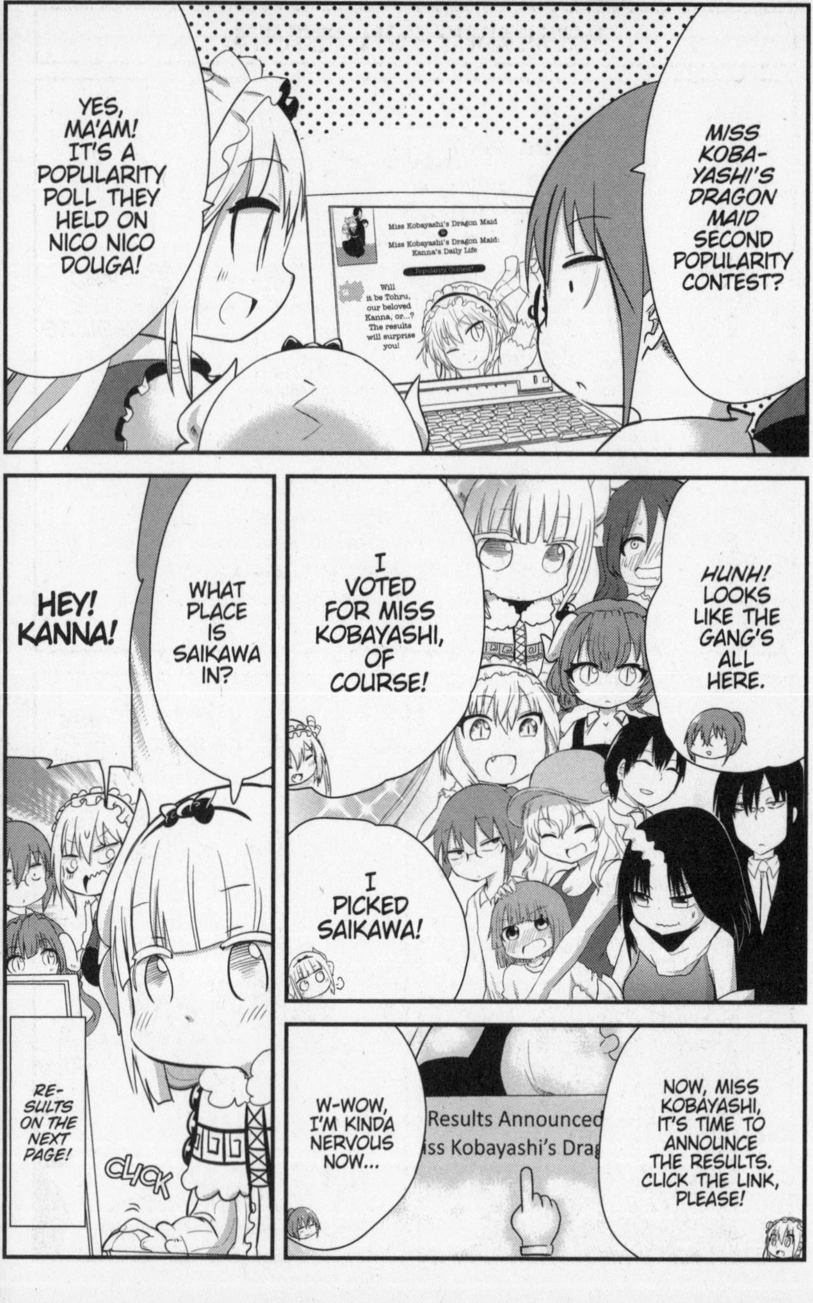
MISS KOBA-YASHI'S DRAGON MAID SECOND POPULARITY CONTEST?
YES, MA'AM! IT'S A POPULARITY POLL THEY HELD ON NICO NICO DOUGA!
Miss Kobayashi's Dragon Maid
Miss Kobayashi's Dragon Maid: Kanna's Daily Life
Popularity Contest!
Will it be Tohru, our beloved Kanna, or...? The results will surprise you!
HUNH! LOOKS LIKE THE GANG'S ALL HERE.
I VOTED FOR MISS KOBAYASHI, OF COURSE!
I PICKED SAIKAWA!
NOW, MISS KOBAYASHI, IT'S TIME TO ANNOUNCE THE RESULTS. CLICK THE LINK, PLEASE!
W-WOW, I'M KINDA NERVOUS NOW...
Results Announced
WHAT PLACE IS SAIKAWA IN?
HEY! KANNA!
CLICK
RE-SULTS ON THE NEXT PAGE!

POPULARITY POLL RESULTS!

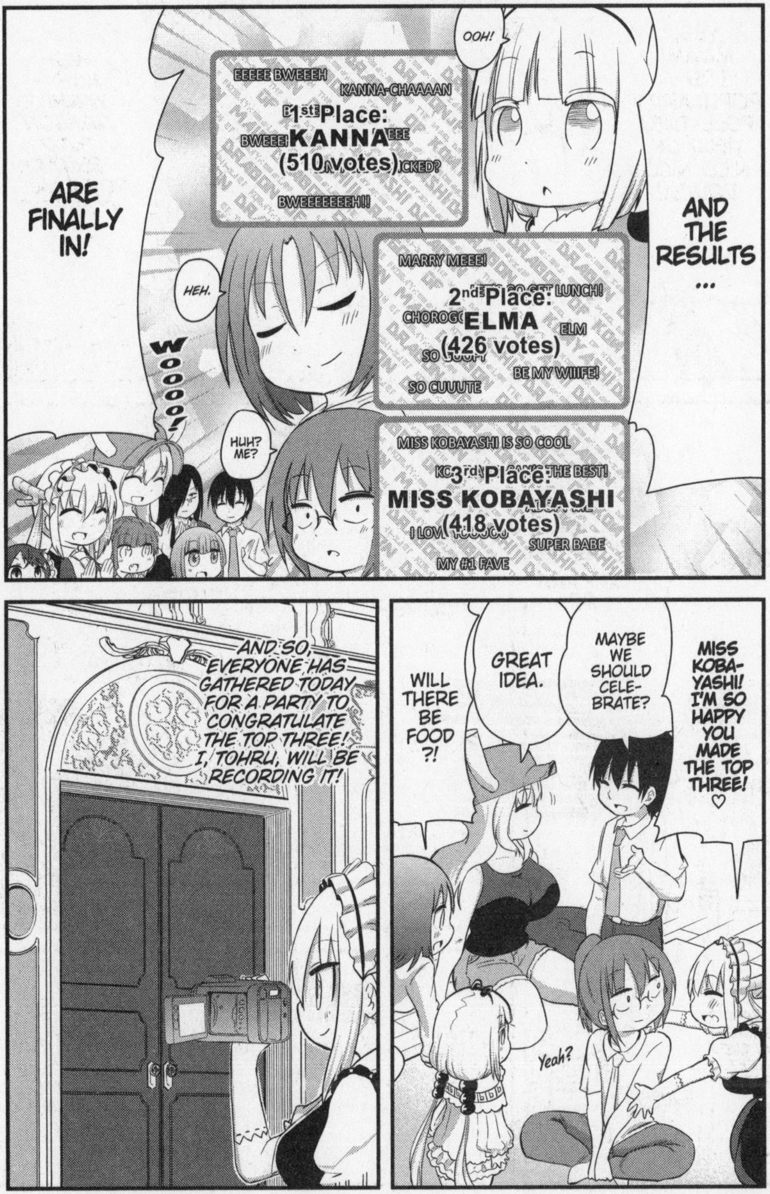

AND THE RESULTS ...
OOH!
EEEEE BWEEEH
KANNA-CHAAAAN
1st Place: KANNA (510 votes)
BWEEEEEEEH!!
ARE FINALLY IN!
MARRY MEEE!
2nd Place: ELMA (426 votes)
BE MY WIIIFE!
SO CUUUTE
HEH.
WOOOOO!
HUH? ME?
MISS KOBAYASHI IS SO COOL
3rd Place: MISS KOBAYASHI (418 votes)
SUPER BABE
MY #1 FAVE
MISS KOBAYASHI! I'M SO HAPPY YOU MADE THE TOP THREE! ♡
MAYBE WE SHOULD CELEBRATE?
GREAT IDEA.
WILL THERE BE FOOD?!
Yeah?
AND SO, EVERYONE HAS GATHERED TODAY FOR A PARTY TO CONGRATULATE THE TOP THREE! I, TOHRU, WILL BE RECORDING IT!

1ST PLACE! KANNA KAMUI!

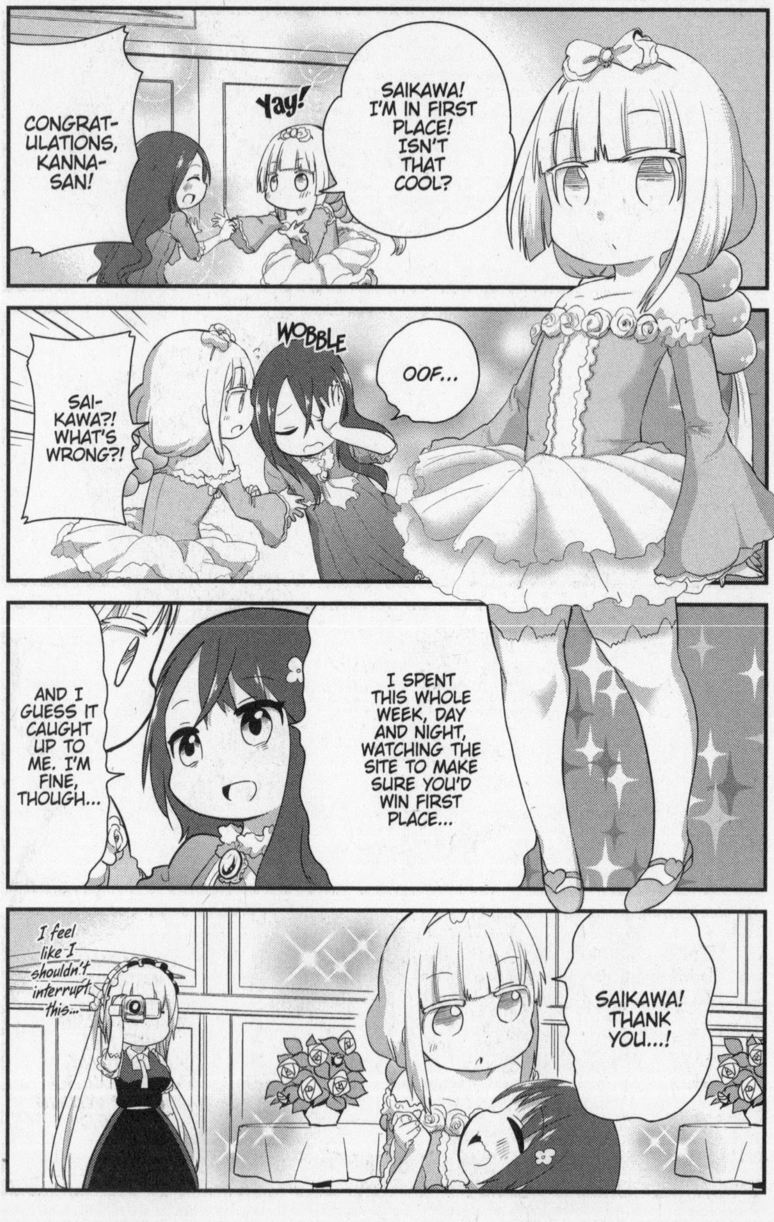
SAIKAWA! I'M IN FIRST PLACE! ISN'T THAT COOL?
Yay!
CONGRAT-ULATIONS, KANNA-SAN!
OOF...
WOBBLE
SAI-KAWA?! WHAT'S WRONG?!
I SPENT THIS WHOLE WEEK, DAY AND NIGHT, WATCHING THE SITE TO MAKE SURE YOU'D WIN FIRST PLACE...
AND I GUESS IT CAUGHT UP TO ME. I'M FINE, THOUGH...
SAIKAWA! THANK YOU...!
I feel like I shouldn't interrupt this...

2ND PLACE! JOUI ELMA!

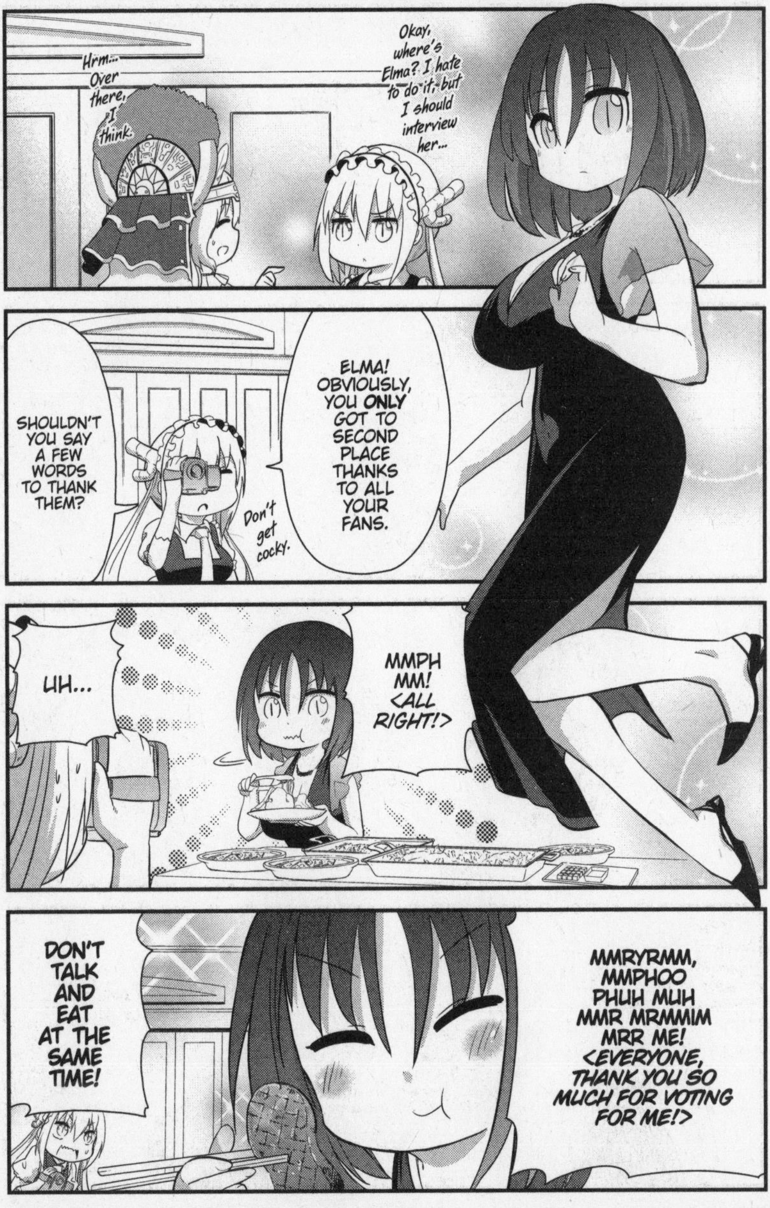
Okay, where's Elma? I hate to do it, but I should interview her...
Hrm... Over there, I think.
ELMA! OBVIOUSLY, YOU ONLY GOT TO SECOND PLACE THANKS TO ALL YOUR FANS.
Don't get cocky.
SHOULDN'T YOU SAY A FEW WORDS TO THANK THEM?
MMPH MM! <ALL RIGHT!>
UH...
MMRYRMM, MMPHOO PHUH MUH MMR MRMMIM MRR ME! <EVERYONE, THANK YOU SO MUCH FOR VOTING FOR ME!>
DON'T TALK AND EAT AT THE SAME TIME!

3RD PLACE! MISS KOBAYASHI!

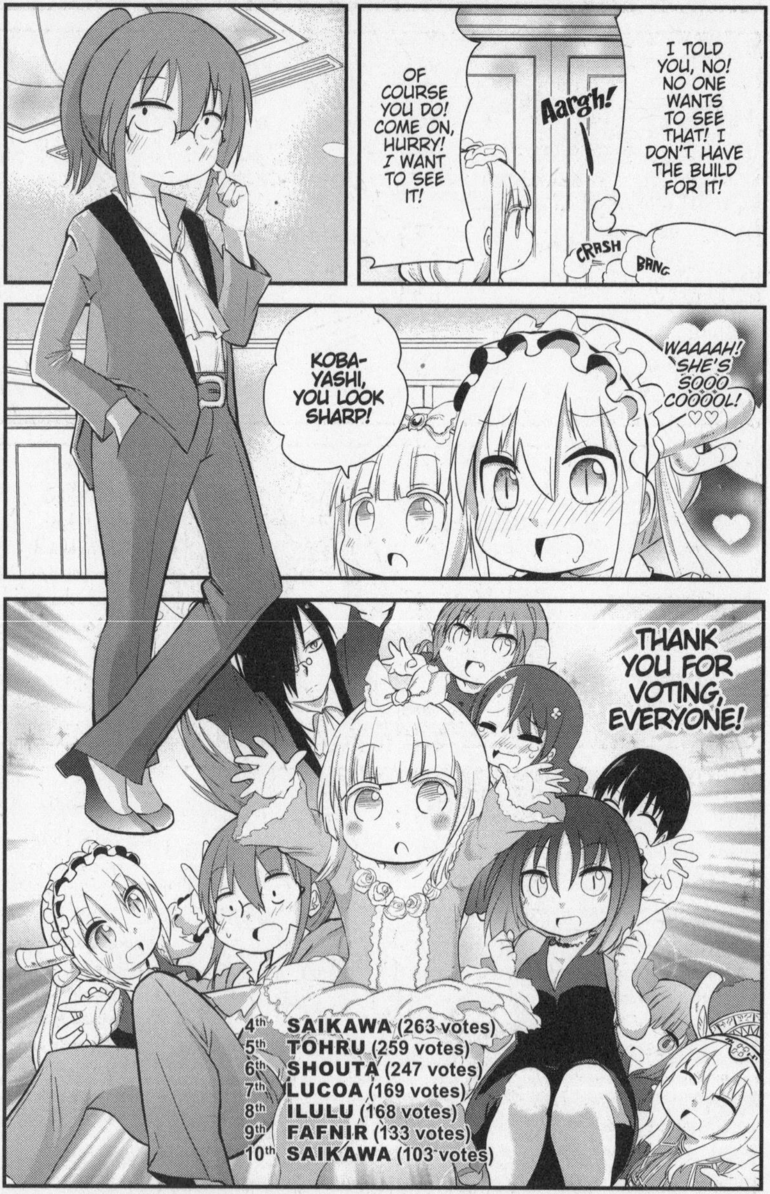
I TOLD YOU, NO! NO ONE WANTS TO SEE THAT! I DON'T HAVE THE BUILD FOR IT!
Aargh!
OF COURSE YOU DO! COME ON, HURRY! I WANT TO SEE IT!
CRASH
BANG
WAAAAH! SHE'S SOOO COOOOL! ♡♡
KOBA-YASHI, YOU LOOK SHARP!
THANK YOU FOR VOTING, EVERYONE!
4th SAIKAWA (263 votes)
5th TOHRU (259 votes)
6th SHOUTA (247 votes)
7th LUCOA (169 votes)
8th ILULU (168 votes)
9th FAFNIR (133 votes)
10th SAIKAWA (103 votes)

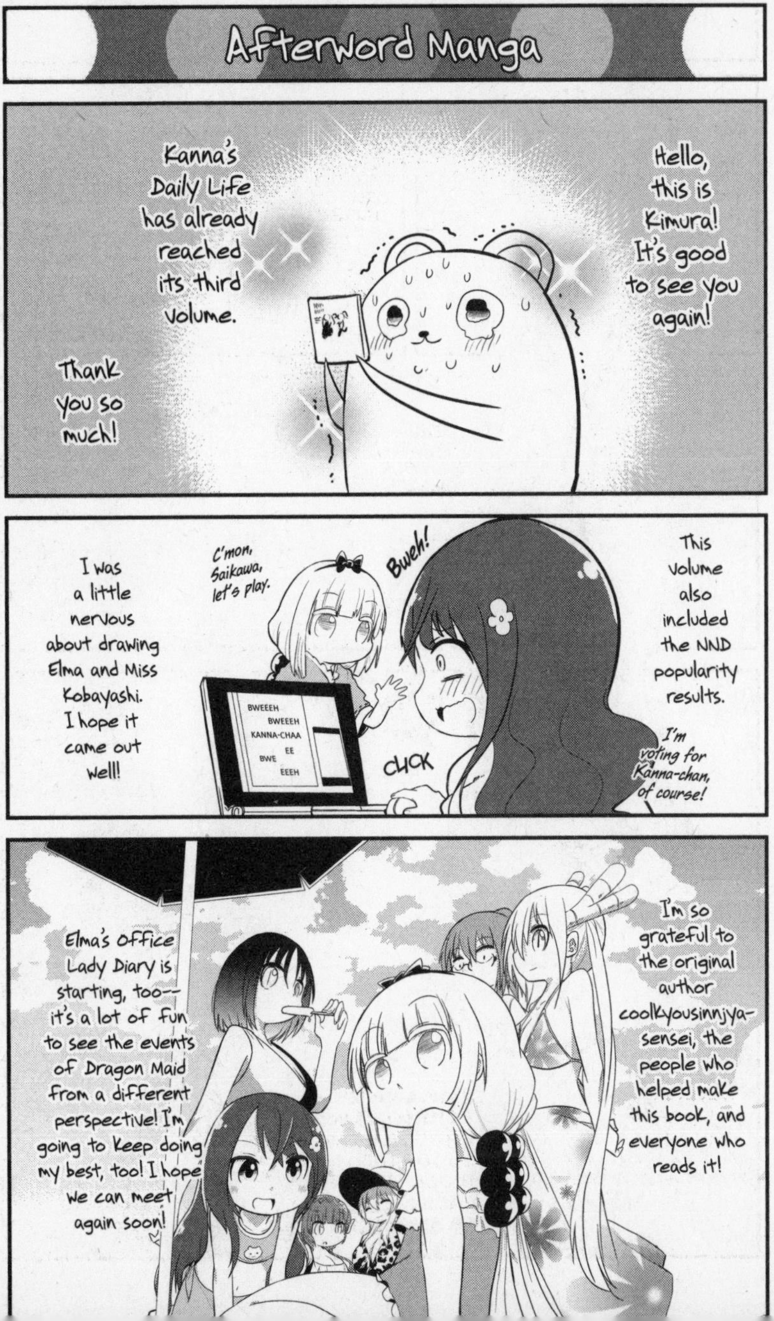
Afterword Manga
Hello, this is Kimura! It's good to see you again!
Kanna's Daily Life has already reached its third volume.
Thank you so much!
This volume also included the NND popularity results.
I'm voting for Kanna-chan, of course!
Bweh!
C'mon, Saikawa, let's play.
BWEEEH BWEEEH KANNA-CHAA EE BWE EEEH
CLICK
I was a little nervous about drawing Elma and Miss Kobayashi. I hope it came out well!
I'm so grateful to the original author coolkyousinnjya-sensei, the people who helped make this book, and everyone who reads it!
Elma's Office Lady Diary is starting, too-- it's a lot of fun to see the events of Dragon Maid from a different perspective! I'm going to keep doing my best, too! I hope we can meet again soon!

AFTERWORD
COOLKYOUSINNJYA

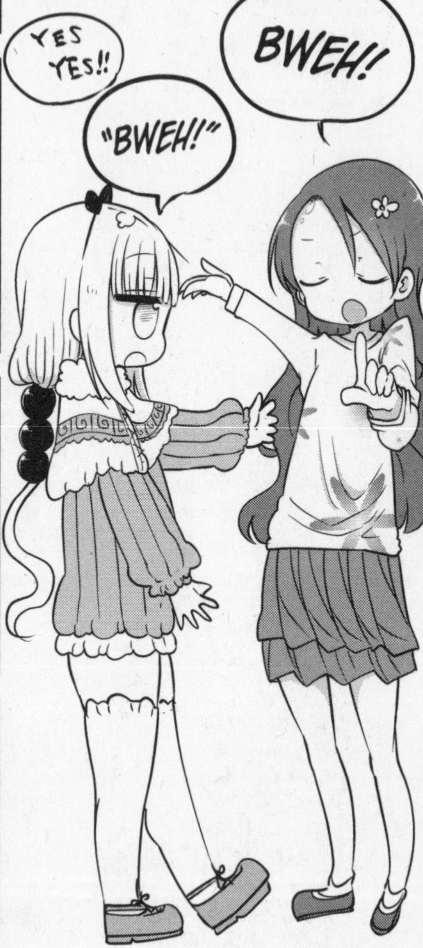
BWEH!
YES YES!!
"BWEH!"

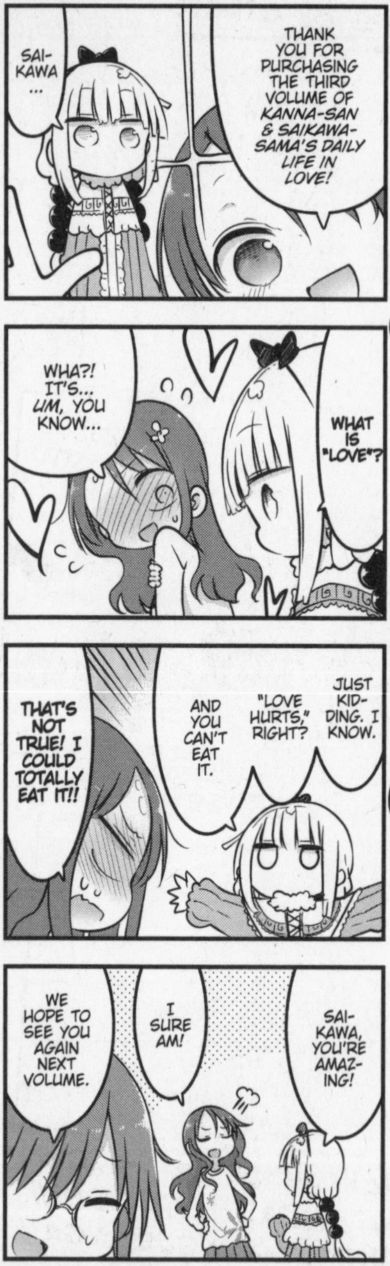
THANK YOU FOR PURCHASING THE THIRD VOLUME OF KANNA-SAN & SAIKAWA-SAMA'S DAILY LIFE IN LOVE!
SAI-KAWA ...
WHAT IS "LOVE"?
WHA?! IT'S... UM, YOU KNOW...
JUST KID-DING. I KNOW.
"LOVE HURTS," RIGHT?
AND YOU CAN'T EAT IT.
THAT'S NOT TRUE! I COULD TOTALLY EAT IT!!
SAI-KAWA, YOU'RE AMAZ-ING!
I SURE AM!
WE HOPE TO SEE YOU AGAIN NEXT VOLUME.

SEVEN SEAS ENTERTAINMENT PRESENTS

FORTY SEVEN Miss Kobayashi's
Dragon maid
Kanna's Daily Life VOL.3

original story by **coolkyousinnjya**   story and art by **#47**

TRANSLATION
Jenny McKeon

ADAPTATION
Shanti Whitesides

LETTERING
Jennifer Skarupa

LOGO DESIGN
KC Fabellon

COVER DESIGN
Nicky Lim

PROOFREADING
Stephanie Cohen
Danielle King

ASSISTANT EDITOR
Jenn Grunigen

PRODUCTION ASSISTANT
CK Russell

PRODUCTION MANAGER
Lissa Pattillo

EDITOR-IN-CHIEF
Adam Arnold

PUBLISHER
Jason DeAngelis

No portion of this book may be reproduced or transmitted in any form without written permission from the copyright holders. This is a work of fiction. Names, characters, places, and incidents are the products of the author's imagination or are used fictitiously. Any resemblance to actual events, locales, or persons, living or dead, is entirely coincidental.

Seven Seas books may be purchased in bulk for promotional, educational, or business use. Please contact your local bookseller or the Macmillan Corporate and Premium Sales Department at 1-800-221-7945, extension 5442, or by e-mail at MacmillanSpecialMarkets@macmillan.com.

Seven Seas and the Seven Seas logo are trademarks of Seven Seas Entertainment, LLC. All rights reserved.

ISBN: 978-1-626928-99-2

Printed in Canada

First Printing: October 2018

10 9 8 7 6 5 4 3 2 1

FOLLOW US ONLINE: *www.sevenseasentertainment.com*

READING DIRECTIONS

This book reads from *right to left*, Japanese style. If this is your first time reading manga, you start reading from the top right panel on each page and take it from there. If you get lost, just follow the numbered diagram here. It may seem backwards at first, but you'll get the hang of it! Have fun!!

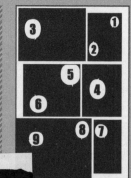